I-MAN
AN OUTLINE OF
PHILOSOPHICAL ANTHROPOLOGY
Abridged Version

I-MAN
AN OUTLINE OF
PHILOSOPHICAL ANTHROPOLOGY

by

Mieczysław A. Krąpiec, O.P., Ph.D., D.D.

ABRIDGED VERSION

by

Francis J. Lescoe, Ph.D., and Roger B. Duncan, Ph.D.

Andrew N. Woznicki, Ph.D., Philosophical Editor

MARIEL PUBLICATIONS
NEW BRITAIN, CONNECTICUT

Library of Congress Catalog No. 85-62103

Krąpiec, Mieczysław A., *I-Man: An Outline of Philosophical Anthropology*, abridged version by Francis J. Lescoe and Roger B. Duncan

ISBN 0-910919-03-8

I-Man: An Outline of Philosophical Anthropology is an abridged version by Francis J. Lescoe and Roger B. Duncan of *Ja-Człowiek: Zarys antropologii filozoficznej* by Mieczysław A. Krąpiec, Lublin: Towarzystwo naukowe Katolickiego Uniwersytetu Lubelskiego, 1979, translated by Marie Lescoe, Andrew Woznicki, Theresa Sandok et al. New Britain: Mariel Publications, 1983.

Acknowledgments

Grateful acknowledgment is made for permission to quote from the following copyrighted material: Paul-Louis Landsberg, *The Experience of Death*, trans. Cynthia Rowland. New York, 1953 © by Philosophical Library Inc.

1 2 3 4 5 6 7 8 9 (Current printing: first digit.)

Distributed by:
MARIEL PUBLICATIONS
196 Eddy Glover Boulevard
New Britain, CT 06053

TO
HIS HOLINESS POPE JOHN PAUL II
WITH ADMIRATION
AND
FILIAL DEVOTION

The International Center for Lublin University Translations
wishes to express its deep gratitude
to the Reverend Leo J. Kinsella
of Our Lady of the Snows, Chicago, Illinois
for financial assistance in the printing of this volume.

FOREWORD

The election of Karol Wojtyła as Pope John Paul II, six years ago, alerted the English speaking world to a completely new philosophy known as *Lublinism*.

As Professor of Ethics for 24 years at the University of Lublin (KUL), Karol Wojtyła helped to develop a philosophy which represents a striking amalgam of St. Thomas Aquinas' realist metaphysics, the insights of contemporary existentialism, and the methodology of phenomenology.

This philosophy has been used with spectacular success in all the seminaries of Poland.

Professors Francis J. Lescoe and Roger B. Duncan are now making available in English, an abridged version of Mieczysław A. Krąpiec's *I-Man: An Outline of Philosophical Anthropology.*

We recommend this book most enthusiastically and we sincerely hope that it will be used extensively in our English speaking Catholic seminaries and universities.

Silvio Cardinal Oddi
Prefect, Sacred Congregation
for the Clergy

Rome, 1985

vii

CONTENTS

CHAPTER I—AT THE ORIGINS OF THE THEORY OF MAN

CHAPTER II—THE HUMAN FACT

CHAPTER III—ATTEMPTS TO INTERPRET THE HUMAN FACT

CHAPTER IV—THE ONTICAL STRUCTURE OF MAN

CHAPTER V—MAN AND KNOWLEDGE

CHAPTER VI—INTENTIONALITY OF KNOWLEDGE AND CULTURE

CHAPTER VII—MAN AND HIS FREE ACTIVITY

CHAPTER VIII—MAN IN THE PRESENCE OF MORAL GOOD AND EVIL

CHAPTER IX—MAN AND SOCIETY

CHAPTER X—MAN AND RELIGION
by Zofia Zdybicka Ph.D.

CHAPTER XI—THE PERSON AN EGO OF A RATIONAL NATURE

CHAPTER XII—THE HUMAN BEING IN THE PERSPECTIVE OF DEATH

PREFACE

This abridged version of Mieczysław A. Krąpiec, I-MAN: AN OUTLINE OF PHILOSOPHICAL ANTHROPOLOGY has been written for two reasons: (a) to make available to the average reader, a shorter and more simplified presentation of the chief insights contained in the original volume and (b) to provide a book which may be used by seminary and college students as a text for a Philosophy of Man course.

CHANGES

The abridged work is approximately half the length of the original volume. For pedagogical reasons, short introductions have been placed at the beginning of each chapter. In addition, a great number of sub-headings have been introduced, which are not found in the original text.

Wherever possible, attempts have been made to simplify the author's abstract philosophical style. Numerous "periodic sentences," 6 or 7 lines in length, have been replaced with shorter sentences. In some instances, certain nuances have been sacrificed as a result of this attempt at simplification. The authors of the abridged edition assume full responsibility for any shortcomings resulting from such adjustments.

Finally, the number of footnotes has been drastically reduced. The student is referred to the corresponding pagination of each chapter in the unabridged volume for more detailed explanations.

GLOSSARY

A student Glossary (Appendix I) containing approximately 100 philosophical terms has been added with a view toward helping a beginner in philosophy. For those seeking further information, paginations in Walter Brugger—Kenneth Baker, *Philosophical Dictionary*. Spokane: Gonzaga University

Press, 1972; and Francis J. Lescoe, *Existentialism: With or Without God.*
New York: Alba House, 1974, have been supplied.

BIBLIOGRAPHY

A special word is in order concerning the bibliography. The authors have
intentionally retained the complete bibliographical listings found in the
unabridged volume.

It is no exaggeration to say that I-MAN: AN OUTLINE OF PHILOSOPH-
ICAL ANTHROPOLOGY contains one of the best current bibliographies in
the area of philosophical anthropology. There are over 1,000 titles in eight
languages.

POLISH TITLES

Included in these listings are over 120 books, monographs and articles in
the Polish language. As far as the authors can ascertain, not one of these
works is available in English.

Obviously, such a large *corpus* of works cannot be ignored by any English
scholar who would claim to do serious work in the field of philosophical
anthropology. The Lublin School of Philosophy, whose best known exponent
and former member is Pope John Paul II, has done highly creative and
innovative work in this area. Familiarity with the contributions of these East
European philosophers is a *sine qua non* for serious scholarship in philosophical anthropology.

INVITATION

The International Center for Lublin University Translations is inviting
scholars and graduate students with an expertise in both philosophy and
philosophical Polish, to contact the Director, indicating the particular article,
monograph or book which they would be interested in translating into
English. The Center will act as a "clearing house" in order to preclude
needless and regrettable duplication.

CHINESE DIVISION

Since the appearance of Andrew Woznicki's *A Christian Humanism: Karol
Wojtyła's Existential Personalism* and M. A. Krąpiec's *I-Man: An Outline of
Philosophical Anthropology,* the International Center for Lublin University
Translations has established a Chinese Division.

In 1983, Professor Audrey Donnithorne of The Australian National University visited the Center in Connecticut to convey an interest on the part of

Chinese scholars to adapt the Lublin philosophical works for use in Catholic seminaries in China. Since few Chinese scholars are familiar with philosophical Polish and few Polish philosophers have an expertise in philosophical Chinese, the English translations will act as a "bridge" between the East and West.

At present, the Chinese Division includes: Dr. Audrey Donnithorne, Coordinating Director; Rev. Matthias Lu, Ph.D. of St. Mary's College, Moraga, California, Director of Translations; Rev. Thomas Tou, Ph.D., Mission Chinoise, Montreal, P.Q., Assistant Director, and Louis Y. Chow, of Mt. St. Mary's Seminary, Emmitsburg, Maryland. We invite interested Chinese scholars who wish to join the Project to contact the Director of the International Center.

ACKNOWLEDGEMENTS

The authors of the abridged edition of I-MAN wish to acknowledge their debt of gratitude to the Reverend Andrew N. Woznicki, Ph.D., Professor of Philosophy at the University of San Francisco. As Assistant Director and Philosophical Editor, Dr. Woznicki has personally read and checked the entire text for philosophical accuracy. He has constantly sought to convey to the authors, insights and philosophical precisions contained in the Polish text for which there are no English equivalents.

It is no exaggeration to say that Professor Woznicki is almost singly responsible for making Lublin Existential Personalism known to the English speaking world. Without his masterful monograph, *A Christian Humanism: Karol WojtyÍa's Existential Personalism* and his study, *Dialogistic Thomism and Dialectical Marxism,* the seminal contributions of the Lublin School of Philosophy would be still unknown to English scholars. The authors as well as the Editorial Board of the Center have been deeply inspired by the genuine (and contagious) enthusiasm, vigor, and total dedication of this remarkable priest-philosopher, and most representative alumnus of the Lublin School of Philosophy.

To the Editor of MARIEL PUBLICATIONS, Dr. Marie E. Lescoe, the authors express their deepest gratitude and appreciation. Her singleness of purpose and unswerving devotion to the Lublin Project have made the English translations a reality. She has given immeasurably of her time, intellectual talents and financial resources to make Lublin Existentialism available to our American seminaries and colleges.

The authors also express their indebtedness to the Literary Editor, Reverend Dr. David Q. Liptak, Chairman of the Theology Department of Holy Apostles College and Seminary, Co-Director of The Pope John Paul II

Bioethics Center and Consulting Editor of *The Catholic Transcript*. An internationally acclaimed homilist, whose publications have been translated into German, Polish, and Chinese, Father Liptak has sought to give correct literary form to the abridged text. His efforts are deeply appreciated.

To the Reverend Leo J. Kinsella, founder of Our Lady of the Snows, Chicago Illinois, the authors and Editorial Board acknowledge with deep gratitude, the encouragement, support and financial assistance which they have received from the very inception of the Lublin Project.

Finally, the authors express their incalculable debt to the translators of the original text of I-MAN. Their names appear on page xx of this volume.

Rev. Francis J. Lescoe, Ph.D.
Roger B. Duncan, Ph.D.

Reverend Francis J. Lescoe, Ph.D., S.T.L. is a former student of Etienne Gilson and Anton Pegis at the Pontifical Institute of Mediaeval Studies in Toronto. He is the author of the following works: *Sancti Thomae Aquinatis Tractatus de Substantiis Separatis; St. Thomas, Treatise on Separate Substances; Existentialism: With or Without God; God as First Principle in Ulrich of Strasbourg; Philosophy Serving Contemporary Needs of the Church*. He is editor of *The Existentialist Drama of Gabriel Marcel; The McAuley Lecture Series*, 15 vols. and co-editor of *The Pope John Paul II Lecture Series in Bioethics*.

In 1973, he received exclusive rights from Gabriel Marcel to translate all of the latter's 31 existentialist plays into English. Currently, he is Chairman of the Philosophy Department of Holy Apostles College and Seminary in Cromwell, Connecticut, Co-Director of The Pope John Paul II Bioethics Center, Director of the recently established Etienne Gilson Center of Christian Philosophy, Director of the International Center for Lublin University Translations and President of the American Catholic Philosophical Association.

Roger B. Duncan received the Ph.D. from Yale University in 1969, where he studied Existentialism and Phenomenology under John Wild and continued his interest in classical philosophy, writing his dissertation on *The Role of the Concept of Philia in Plato's Dialogues*. Articles by Roger Duncan on classical and Thomistic philosophy and a variety of other subjects have appeared in such journals as Phronesis, The New Scholasticism, The New Oxford Review, The Southern Journal of Philosophy, and the Homiletic and Pastoral Review. At present he is Associate Professor of Philosophy at the University of Connecticut, Hartford Branch.

The Religious Perspectives of Human Existence: An Introduction to the Philosophy of Religion (Człowiek i religia) by Zofia Zdybicka, translated by Theresa Sandok, Ph.D. will be available in Spring 1986.

M. A. KRĄPIEC

Mieczysław Albert KRĄPIEC, (Crump-yes) O.P., Ph.D., D.D., was born May 25, 1921 in Berezòwice Mała near Zbaraz and Tarnopol (Podole—now in the Soviet Union). After receiving a classical education in Tarnopol, he entered the Dominican Order in 1939. In 1946, he became Professor of Philosophy at the Philosophical Institute of the Dominican Province in Kraków. Five years later (1951), he was appointed Professor of Philosophy at the Catholic University of Lublin. He served three terms as Dean of the School of Philosophy and in 1970, he was elected President Rector of the University of Lublin, the only Catholic university in the entire Soviet bloc.

Fr. Krąpiec's area of specialization is in metaphysics and philosophical anthropology. For nearly forty years, he has lectured and written widely on the entire range of the theory of real and analogical being.

He has explained the human phenomenon with deep acumen, by drawing on the rich anthropological material contained in the general theory of being. Pivotal to this analysis is the experience of the "I" as subject of one's actions and in which the "I" is simultaneously immanent and transcendent. Such a position, to which Thomas Aquinas had already alluded in his *Summa Theologiae* I, q. 75, a. 1–2), enables us to go beyond a one-sided conception of man. In this way, Fr. Krąpiec has succeeded in constructing a theory of being which is thoroughly classical in content, yet modern in its formulation.

The author has been acclaimed as the organizer and undisputed head of the so-called Lublin School of Philosophy. Together with Jerzy Kalinowski, Stefan Świeżawski, Stanisław Kamiński and Cardinal Karol Wojtyła (Pope John Paul II), he has published a series of studies in philosophy which view contemporary problems in their historical perspective. Chief among these is a genuine Christian humanism which recognizes man's proper place in reality and insures his basic human rights.

Fr. Krąpiec's work has provided an impetus to studies in classical philosophy which are, at once, new and attractive in content and formulation. As such, they provide a most effective antidote to the numerous scientisms and ecclecticisms which pose as genuine philosophical systems of thought.

Dr. Krąpiec is the author of 13 volumes in philosophy and of more than 150 articles and monographs in various Polish and foreign journals.

MAJOR PUBLICATIONS

Realizm ludzkiego poznania (The Realism of Human Knowledge). Poznań, 1959, Pp. 652.

Teoria analogii bytu (Theory of the Analogy of Being). Lublin, Pp. 415.

Dlaczego zło? (Why Evil? Philosophical Reflections), Kraków, 1962. Pp. 190; French translation, *Pourqui le mal?*, Paris, 1967. Pp. 227.

Co-author: *Z teorii i metodologii metafizyki (Selected Problems in the Theory and Methodology of Metaphysics*. Lublin, 1962. Pp. 412.

Struktura bytu. Charakterystyczne elementy systemu Arystotelesa i Tomasza z Akwinu (The Structure of Being. Characteristic Elements of the Systems of Aristotle and Thomas Aquinas). Lublin, 1963. Pp. 361.

Co-author: *Arsitotelesowska koncepcja substancji (The Aristotelian Conception of Substance)*. Lublin, 1966. Pp. 214.

Metafizyka. Wybór podstawowych zagadnień (Metaphysics. A Selection of Fundamental Problems). Poznań, 1966. Pp. 558.

Tomasz z Akwinu. De ente et essentia. Przekład-komentarz-studia (Thomas Aquinas. De ente et essentia. Translation-Commentary-Study), Lublin, 1981. Pp. 164.

Człowiek—kultura—uniwersytet (Man-Culture-University). Lublin, 1982. Pp. 450.

Język i rzeczywistość (Language and Reality). In preparation.

Człowiek i prawo naturalne (Man and Natural Law), Lublin, 1975. Pp. 259.

Metafizyka. Zarys teorii bytu (Metaphysics. An Outline of the Theory of Being. Lublin, 1978. Pp. 549.

THE TRANSLATORS

Marie E. Lescoe, Ph.D. (Fordham University). Professor Emerita, Central Connecticut State University, New Britain, Connecticut.

Rev. Andrew N. Woznicki, Ph.D. (University of Toronto). Professor of Philosophy, University of San Francisco, California.

Theresa H. Sandok, O.S.M., Ph.D. (University of Notre Dame). Professor of Philosophy, Bellarmine College, Louisville, Kentucky.

Rev. Stephen Minkiel, C.M., Ph.D. (Angelicum). Chairman, Philosophy Department, Gannon University, Erie, Pennsylvania.

Frances Tuszynska, Ph.D. (University of Toronto). Los Angeles, California.

Richard J. Fafara, Ph.D. (University of Toronto). Washington, D.C.

Joseph Koterski, Ph.D. (St. Louis University). Professor of Philosophy, University of St. Thomas, Houston, Texas.

Rev. Janusz Ihnatowicz, S.T.L., Th.M. (University of Ottawa). Professor of Theology, University of St. Thomas, Houston, Texas.

Sr. M. Consolata, C.S.S.F., M.A. (Jagellonian University) Enfield, Connecticut.

Rev. Stephen Ptaszynski, M. Div. Terryville, Connecticut.

Stella Kornacki, M.A. Terryville, Connecticut.

Rev. Francis J. Lescoe, Ph.D. (University of Toronto). Chairman, Philosophy Department, Holy Apostles Seminary for Adult Vocations, Cromwell, Connecticut. Director of Lublin Project.

LIST OF ABBREVIATIONS

CWJ—*Collected Works of C. G. Jung*. London: Routledge and Kegan Paul, 1953.

KUL—Katolicki Uniwersytet Lubelski

NECW—Karl Marx/Friedrich Engels, *Collected Works*. New York: International Publishers, 1975.

PG—*Patrologiae Cursus Completus*. Accurante J. P. Migne; *Series Graeca*. Parisiis apud Garnier et Migne, 1886. 162 volumes.

PL—*Patrologiae Cursus Completus*. Accurante J. P. Migne; *Series Latina*. Parisiis apud Garnier et Migne, 1878. 221 volumes.

SCG—*Sancti Thomae de Aquino Doctoris Angelici Summa Contra Gentiles*. Editio Leonina Manualis. Romae, 1934.

ST—*Sancti Thomae de Aquino Summa Theologiae*. Textus editionis Leoninae cum adnotationibus fontium . . . ex editione altera Canadiensi Ottawa 1953. Romae: Albe, Editiones Paulinae, 1962.

SECPWSF—*The Standard Edition of the Complete Psychological Works of Sigmund Freud*. London: Hogarth Press, 1955.

* * * *

BB—Walter Brugger—Kenneth Baker, *Philosophical Dictionary*. Spokane: Gonzaga University Press, 1972.

L—Francis J. Lescoe, *Existentialism: With or Without God*. New York: Alba House, 1974.

CHAPTER I

AT THE ORIGINS OF THE
THEORY OF MAN*

This first chapter consists of seven divisions which are: I. Religious Origins of the Theory of Man, II. The Platonic Concept of Man, III. Aristotle's Theory of Man, IV. Patristic Modifications of the Concept of Man, V. Anthropological Opinions of Avicenna, VI. The Cartesian Concept of Man, VII. Formation of the Philosophical Notion of the Subject.

Different intellectual interests have dominated different periods of history. Antiquity and the Middle Ages were periods of development in philosophical and theological concepts. The Renaissance favored the development of *belles-lettres*. The present age prefers technological studies. The conditions of contemporary life force man to apply his study toward the organization of the most complicated demands of human life in an urban civilization.

The preference for studies that have an immediate practical application cannot, however, negate the value of other areas of knowledge. For man works and thinks, not merely so that his life might become more useful and comfortable, but also to pursue never-aging values whose object is man himself. Further, the highest expressions of the human person, the contemplation of truth and beauty, along with the attainment of the good, have always been recognized as the most eminent goals of man's life.

Humanistic studies, whose subject is man himself and his cultural creations, cannot become outmoded. Man in himself is an interesting and significant subject matter. We do not know ourselves directly, but an indirect way of

---

*Translator's note: "man" is the English equivalent of the Polish *człowiek*, which is synonymous with ἄνθρωπος, *homo, der Mensch*. As such, it includes all human beings, both masculine and feminine genders.

1

getting to know man through his activities and creativity can show us who man is, reveal the meaning of his life, examine his essential functions and the conditions for their attainment and determine his destiny. This will be the chief subject of our considerations in this book. First, we must review the sources of the various concepts of man which have arisen in Western European cultural circles.

I. RELIGIOUS ORIGINS OF THE THEORY OF MAN

The first articulations of a concept of man in Western European culture appeared against the background of religious beliefs and experiences.

THE BIBLICAL CONCEPTION OF MAN

According to the Biblical conception, as expressed in both the Old and New Testaments, man is a special product of God's creativity. It is around man that the world-drama is enacted, a drama in which God takes part and ultimately becomes incarnate, in order to give the crowning meaning to human life.

From the very beginning of the Bible, we learn that man was created "to the image and likeness of God," and that man's lot was completely linked to God in all its essentially human aspects. The foundation for this bond between man's lot and God is man's "soul," which God himself breathed directly into the body. Man's soul is understood as that abode where the inner communion with God takes place.

First, from a general understanding of the term *Ruah* as a spirit, which is a supersubjective reality (almost a divine soul), develops a concept of *Nephesz* as an individual, immortal soul which is joined to the body in an ontic unity. Later, in the Wisdom literature, this concept undergoes a more dualistic interpretation under the influence of Hellenic thought.

The question of man and his soul is further developed in the New Testament where the emphasis is transferred to *Ruah (Pneuma)* understood as a spiritual element directing man from within to supernatural ends. Here the *pneuma* is the object of divine intervention and, thus understood, completely bound up with the life and works of Christ.

GREEK RELIGION AND PHILOSOPHY

Orphic beliefs enter as a second source of Western European anthropology. As early as the period of Homer we find these beliefs rivaling older views. According to Homer, man who lives only on this earth, possesses a soul (ψυχή) which is the element of life. After death, his "shade" enters the netherworld, where it loses consciousness. According to Orphic tradition, however, the soul enters man's body by breaking away from the divine cosmos, and dwells in man for a short period, after which it returns to its cosmic source. In Orphic language, the soul comes from Zeus and it returns to Zeus. The body is understood as a prison of the soul—its temporary tomb—from which it wants to free itself; this liberation is accomplished by means of ascetic, ethical and ritual observances.[1]

Thus the Orphic religion became the first representative of a strict body-soul dualism. If the soul is part of the cosmic god it possesses a life which does not belong to the body; if it only passes through the body, it is not an entity which is bound to the body.

In the Ionic school, Orphic religious thought is combined with philosophical reasoning. Orphic religion had linked man with God, i.e., with Zeus. The philosophers now argued that Zeus is the entire universe, and that the human soul is only part of this cosmic, pantheistic god. While the whole universe appeared to Anaximander to be emerging from the Unlimited *(apeiron)* as its limited though divine manifestation, Anaximenes added that life is the divine element of the *apeiron*. Just as the soul animates man (a fact which is evident in breathing), so the *apeiron* is animated by life, symbolized by air.

The philosophical concept of the soul was further developed among the Pythagoreans, who understood the soul as *arythmos*—number, a perfect proportion which was the source of motion from within. It was developed further by Heraclitus, who joined the *Logos*—the self-conscious cosmic law—of the microcosm with the *logos* of the macrocosm. The concept of the soul was also developed, finally, with Anaxagoras, who identified the *Nous,* which is one and the same for all, with the human ψυχή.

II. THE PLATONIC CONCEPT OF MAN

Along with the development of Orphism and Pythagoreanism there appears the Platonic concept of man. Here man is the one who exemplifies the structure of the entire cosmos. We observe in the cosmos a changeless reality in itself—the Ideas—and, at the same time, a changeable, material world. Man, as a union of body and soul, is a reflection of this cosmic dualism.

According to Plato, the human soul is tripartite: intellectual, spirited, and vegetative. Animals possess a sensible-spirited soul and plants possess a vegetative soul. The essential element differentiating man from all living things is his intellectual soul (though the intellectual soul is not the exclusive possession of man, since the gods also possess intellectual souls). The essential function of the soul is to animate the body. Besides the function of life, which is the immanent ability to put oneself into motion, Plato designated a strictly immaterial function of the soul, namely knowing the world of Ideas. He writes that the soul does not have a distinct organ of knowledge but, through and by itself, it sees the common properties of all things. It is not the body that knows but the soul. Neither the body nor any other organ is capable of understanding the immaterial, necessary, universal and immutable Ideas. Plato thus united the concept of the soul with the realm of the Idea, thus taking a new and essential step in the understanding of man.

In addition, Plato accepted Orphic religious conceptions of the person, e.g., the soul is a being which existed previously without the body. The soul, he adds, was weighed down by some transgression and was sent to the body to be liberated. When the sin is atoned for, the soul becomes free. Plato describes endless activities of the soul, its various incarnations, judgment after death, change of bodies etc. To make all this understandable, he accepted the immateriality of the soul and its fundamental opposition to the body, its independence of the body and its simplicity. In a word, man is an immortal soul governing the body like a sailor in a ship, or a rider on a horse.[2]

Plato's theory of man must therefore be described as a dualism which found expression in both ontological and epistemological positions.

III. ARISTOTLE'S THEORY OF MAN

According to Cicero, Aristotle was at first under the influence of Plato in his approach to the problems of anthropology. Once he began to direct his own thinking, however, he changed his notion of the soul.

In discussing Platonism, Aristotle had attacked the theory of Ideas, showing it both superfluous and erroneous. But in Platonism there existed a certain symmetry between the eternal and immaterial Ideas and the soul, which is likewise eternal, simple and immaterial, and contemplates the Ideas through itself. Now if the concept of the Ideas is false, so is the Platonic concept of the soul. There are, then, no universal Ideas, nor is there any purely "ideal" soul. Only concrete, sensibly-known entities exist: (*Tode Ti*).

Aristotle found it necessary to oppose, on the one hand, Platonic spiritualism and, on the other, Democritean materialism, which held that the soul was only a composite of well-fitted atoms. Against the Platonic notion of the soul, Aristotle advanced the argument that the human soul needs bodily organs in order to perform its essential functions. On the other hand, he asserted, against Democritus, that these organs are only instruments of psychical being and are not its essence. And just as, on the one hand, a soul cannot exist without the body so, on the other hand, the soul is not just a body. Rather, it is the principle of life and of sensible and intellectual knowledge; in a word, it is the form—*eidos*—which performs its functions by means of bodily organs. But a body without a soul is lifeless, just as a soul without bodily organs does not manifest any of its essential functions. For this reason, the soul may be defined as the first act of the physical, organic body which potentially has life—"*actus primus corporis physici, vitam habentis.*"[3]

Hence the soul, which is joined to the body as its living act, did not exist prior to the body. The soul is one, as there is one human life, but it possesses the three functions for which Plato posited a separate soul. Hence the one intellectual soul performs the functions of the vegetative soul in its relation to the vegetative functions of the body; it fulfills the sensible functions in relation to sensible knowledge, and in addition, performs the intellectual, cognitive, functions.[4]

It is at this point, however, that Aristotle encountered a great difficulty because, by accepting Plato's insight concerning the nature of man's conceptual and intellectual knowledge, he was forced to accept an intellect which could in some way understand intelligible substances. Aristotle held the position that the agent intellect is of divine origin, separate from the body, without sensation, simple and in act from its own being.[5] This intellect participates in the life of God—*Noesis Noeseos*—"thought thinking thought." There must be also another power of the soul, the possible intellect, which belongs to the individual soul, while the agent intellect is something divine and immortal.[6] But man is not immortal and the human soul, which is essentially joined to the body, is not a substance separated from the body (which is why it dies along with the body). For the soul is not a substance: it is only the function and act of the body, and thus shares the destiny of the body.

EPICUREANS AND STOICS

The Epicureans also denied the immortality of the soul, accepting Democritus' theory that it was composed of atoms. Similarly the Stoics recognized only a corporeal soul. They also called the soul and life "Zeus' spark," but Zeus himself they thought of as the universal material cosmos. For this reason the soul loses its individuality upon death and is dispersed throughout the universe.

In summary, the Greek tradition has left us two powerful elements of thought, namely, the Platonic, Orphic-religious current—wherein man is a god-soul who can liberate himself through philosophy—and a second current, according to which the soul is a function of man but man himself is either a higher animal, who participates for a moment in divine life, or only a moment in a pantheistic whole.

IV. PATRISTIC MODIFICATIONS OF THE CONCEPT OF MAN

Patristic thought, interpreting Christian revelation, arrived at the following principles on the question of the soul:

1. The human soul comes directly from God by virtue of the act of creation.

2. Nature: (a) the soul differs essentially from the body; (b) the soul is imparted to the body, which lives through it.

3. Each individual soul is immortal; death is followed by a judgment of man's actions.

4. Man bears original sin, from which Christ frees him through baptism.

The above propositions give a sharply different outlook on man from the one which Greek tradition set forth. As we have seen above, the Greeks transmitted to the Christians three concepts of the soul and, by the same token, three concepts of man:

(a) Aristotelian: biological.

(b) Stoic: according to which man is an element of the cosmos, and the human soul is only a momentary "light" and manifestation of a cosmic divinity.

(c) Orphic-Platonic: according to which the human soul is one of the cosmic gods; the soul clothed itself with a human body as the result of some sin, and for this reason it needs "redemption"; the soul does not need grace or outside help; its redemption can come from itself, to the degree that it testifies to its divine dignity and despises matter—in a word, to the degree that it becomes a philosopher, and learns to make use of its innate, necessary and true knowledge.

To these Greek ways of thinking, the kind of redemption which Christianity proposed appeared degrading to the soul. Accordingly, Christian theologians found it necessary to make fundamental changes in the Greek concepts of man. Augustine was the first to accomplish this comprehensively.

IRENAEUS, TERTULLIAN

In the thought of Irenaeus of Lyons, the image of God appears in man's soul. Man is comprised of body, soul and spirit. There are people who guide themselves only by their body. There are those who are directed by their soul. And there are those who are directed by the Spirit. The Christians obviously profess to belong to the last group. Influenced by the Stoics, Irenaeus understands the soul as something material, which evidently, in his way of thinking, means "created." The soul extends throughout, and animates, the entire body. It is an image of Christians who are in the whole world and who must fulfill a role analogous to the one which the soul performs in the human body. (The tripartite division of the human soul into body, soul, and spirit, need not indicate human ontic status, but can be taken as an expression of the essential levels of human aspiration).

In the opinion of some apologists, Arnobius for example, the soul's immortality is God's gift, bestowed only on those who believe in Christ. Others, such as Lactantius, have a more orthodox understanding of man's destiny, with personal immortality of the soul and a proportionate reward for one's life.

In a famous definition of the soul, Tertullian acknowledged its natural immortality, free will, rationality, and its ability to improve itself.[7] Again, under the Stoic influence, he includes corporeity as one of the soul's properties, although here as elsewhere this notion seems to function as a synonym for "dependency on God."

THE ALEXANDRIAN SCHOOL

In the Alexandrian school, Platonism held complete sway: The soul was understood as a substance, *rationabiliter sensibilis et mobilis*.

According to Origen, man is only a fallen, pure spirit. In his justice, God created all spirits equal. Some of the spirits acknowledged God and remained as angel-spirits. Others, however, turned in upon themselves. They fell, and were deprived of the spiritual state. Man is also a fallen spirit who, in future ages, will return to his original dignity. In connection with this understanding of man's condition Origen accepted—what his contemporaries viewed as blasphemous—that Christ's soul existed before He became man.

For Clement of Alexandria, the body was the tomb of the soul. The soul by itself is a rational spirit. It receives, however, another bodily spirit, an irrational soul, born concomitantly with the body. Immortality, however, is received only through grace.

ST. JEROME

Toward the end of the fourth century, St. Jerome enumerated previous opinions concerning the soul, according to five questions:

"1. Whether it fell from the heavens as the philosopher Pythagoras and all the Platonists and Origen thought.

2. Whether it is a substance emanating from God as the Stoics, Manicheans, and the Spanish Priscillian heresy maintained.

3. Whether the souls are found as formerly created in a divine 'treasury' as some churchmen held in their stupidity.

4. Whether God is constantly creating them and sending them into bodies, according to what we find in the Gospel: 'My father always works and I also work.'

5. Whether they come into existence through inheritance, as Tertullian and the greater part of the West do not hesitate to assert."

As we have already pointed out, Christians found it difficult to reconcile the Gospel with Greek philosophy, especially in the area of understanding the human soul. For if we were to admit the human soul's ability to know eternal truth, then, as a consequence, we would be forced to agree that man is a god, since he participates in the eternal by knowing necessary, permanent and changeless truths. Such a condition, according to Greek tradition, is a divine prerogative. According to this position, which was that of Platonism, the human soul as god would need no other redemption except that which it could attain through philosophy.

ST. AUGUSTINE

Because St. Augustine was aware of this dilemma, he preferred to deny the possibility of authentic intellectual knowledge; he held that by itself the human soul was incapable of knowing truth. Rather than diminish Christ's redemptive role, he accepted the concept of illumination; it is Christ who teaches, wherever human knowing is accomplished.

According to St. Augustine, man is composed of both body and soul; he *is* both body and soul. The soul, however, is the more important element of the two, and is designated to rule the body. For Augustine, the problem is to establish the spirituality of the soul.[8]

As a former Manichean materialist, St. Augustine is careful to say that the soul is not a body, nor does it have spatial dimensions or any corporeal attributes. He sees in this fact a negative proof for the spirituality of the soul. Positively, he argues for its spirituality by appealing to the soul's consciousness of itself as a spirit who understands, recalls, and possesses a will.

Augustine has no clear opinion concerning the origin of the soul. He knows that it does not come from God's substance because it is a creature and, hence distinct from God. It did not evolve from matter, or from an animal soul. No soul existed as man before the body; neither was it imprisoned in a body as punishment. It was not formed from some kind of immaterial substance which was to have been created at the beginning of the world. He recognizes that if we say that souls are derived from the souls of parents there remains the difficulty of preserving the reality of man's person; while if we say that souls are created directly by God at the moment they are joined with the body, there is the difficulty of accounting for the inheritance of original sin. On the other hand, if we say souls were created by God at the beginning of creation, and God unites them later with bodies, or if we say souls unite themselves with bodies, it is difficult to understand the reason for the union of body and soul. In the end, he cannot decide between traducianism and creationism.

Augustine declares that the soul is a mirror reflecting the eternal truth of God; this guarantees its immortality. In a manner recalling Plato's *Phaedo*, Augustine argues that the soul imparts life to the body; it is completely in the body and complete and whole in every part of the body, but not subordinate to the body. Finally, the union of body and soul, that is, man himself, is a mystery.

The reason for the union of body and soul is to be found in the soul's role as mediator between the divine ideas and the body. The soul contemplates the ideas and shows them to the body. The soul must govern the body and ultimately submit the body and itself to God through interior acts, especially through love.

NEMESIUS

An additional source of anthropology for later scholasticism was Nemesius of Emesa, who concentrated on the following points:

1. Considerations about man are, at the same time, a study of the entire universe, since man is a microcosm.

2. Man is composed in a completely unique way—the Greek thinkers were wrong here.

3. The foundation for human dignity is man's soul, which is incorporeal, substantial, and not reincarnated.

4. The soul's presence in the body is a unique reality, comparable to a radiation in the atmosphere.

5. The soul could have begun its existence on the first day of creation.

6. The soul is immortal.

7. The soul is endowed with knowledge, free will and freedom of choice.

8. The body is destined for resurrection.

BOETHIUS

The "Last Roman", Boethius, had a profound influence on the Middle Ages. He had a fundamentally Platonic notion of man, replete with preexistence of the soul and reincarnation. Specifically, if man is evil, he slowly bestializes himself, literally.

SCOTUS ERIUGENA

In the West, the last witness to the tradition of Origen and Dionysius was John Scotus Eriugena (born c. 800 in Ireland). According to Eriugena man, including his body, is an Idea of God. The body, however, becomes material through its union with the principles of substance and accident, but it is capable of "respiritualizing" itself.

Man was created to the image and likeness of God but he sinned and fell into difficulties. As a result:

(a) A separation from the ideas and a division of bodily nature into ideal and real. Because God foresaw man's fall, He created earth beforehand as a place of punishment and exile for fallen human nature.

(b) A second effect of sin is a division into sex. Originally, man was sexless and was to multiply in a sexless manner. After man's sin, God had to add reproduction in the manner of animals to his nature.

(c) Differentiation of mankind according to place, hierarchy and time.

All these things are not acts of revenge on God's part but only a necessary effect of sin. There is a possibility of returning to the original status by way of death, resurrection of the body, return of the body to the soul, return of the spirit to a divine nature by means of contemplation, and the return of all nature to God.

Thus neither the Western Fathers nor the Greek Eastern Fathers limited themselves, in their study of man, to a mere repetition of the content of revelation, or to an explanation of Greek philosophy. The notion of man which was developed in the first centuries of Christianity was a unique and original notion. This concept takes into account Christian revelation as rendered in Greek philosophical terminology by the Fathers, who usually were not aware of the systematic meaning of the terminology which they used. The result is that the thought of the Fathers concerning the question of man and the soul is more Greek in its expression than specifically Christian.

V. THE ANTHROPOLOGICAL OPINIONS OF AVICENNA

From the middle of the twelfth century on, the Aristotelianism of Avicenna exerted a powerful influence on the philosophical thought of western Europe. In the manner of certain contemporary formulations, the great Arabian philosopher begins his treatise on man in the style of a phenomenological work. He emphasizes the uniqueness of human reality and its distinct reality in the world, especially in comparison with animals. While in the classical current of philosophy discussions about man formed an integral part of the philosophy of nature, Avicenna inquires about the characteristic traits of man's transcendence in relation to nature. He records the following:

(a) Man is a *social being.* Isolated from society, he is not able to develop and to fulfill his human task. An animal is self-sufficient and, by nature, possesses all the equipment which enables it to lead a normal life. Man's existence, on the other hand, is existence in society.

(b) Man is a being who creates *culture,* since he is both a discoverer and user of fine as well as practical arts. Of course, animals also build "homes" for themselves, e.g., nests, etc., but their activity is instinctive and always the same, while man's activity is the result of reflection and creative invention.

(c) Man uses *language.* It is true that animals also make sounds, but animal "language" cannot be compared with that of men. Animal language is "natural" and non-articulated. Animals invent no new, particular sounds; neither do they impose a significative sense on naturally expressed sounds. By contrast, human language is a collection of sounds which are freely chosen, selected and established by man. The result is, that everything can be expressed. Language reveals itself as a recognized sign of man's transcendence with respect to his surroundings.

(d) Man differs from animals by living in accordance with *morality,* especially by recognizing and living according to what is appropriate and what is inappropriate. From childhood, man is inclined to recognize things which are permitted, and those which are forbidden (the feeling of shame), and to recognize moral values. These feelings are totally alien to animals, since they are directed only by instinct.

(e) Since man *looks to the future,* he plans his life accordingly. On the other hand, the animal is completely absorbed by the here and now.

(f) Since man is an individualized, specific being, he is an entity *separate from the world,* different from everything that can be called the environment. Man's improvement takes place through the soul, which is the inner center of activity.

SPIRITUALITY OF THE SOUL

As a *substantia solitaria,* the soul is the source of activity, the immaterial principle of the organization of the body, expressing itself as through an instrument, by means of the body. Now in Avicenna's understanding, the basic argument for the spirituality of the soul is its "self-cognition," which excludes the possibility of using a bodily organ. For if the soul would know with the help of a corporeal instrument, i.e., an organ, it would not be able to know itself; it could not know its own organ or the fact that it knows intellectually. Avicenna even goes on to claim that the soul would know itself, even if separated from any sensible knowledge. For this reason, the soul is a self-subsisting spiritual substance, and its existence does not depend on the body.

IMMORTALITY OF THE SOUL

Concerning his second question, the immortality and preexistence of the soul, Avicenna's statement is interesting, inasmuch as he rejects the preexistence of the soul, but, at the same time, retains its immortality. He thereby breaks with the position according to which the very beginning of a being is inescapably also bound up with its termination. For Avicenna, the reason for rejecting the soul's preexistence is its probable distinctness and separateness in relation to other souls. For the only reason for the separateness of souls is the union of soul with body as the principle of individuation. Hence, unless there is a union with the body, the very basis for the separateness of different souls is destroyed. If souls preexisted there would be nothing whereby souls could be different from one another. As a result, only one soul would exist which, because it is spiritual or indivisible, could not divide itself and become many. But having once acquired individuality by its relationship to matter, the soul can live on as a separate entity after man's death.

The reason for the immortality of the soul is the fact that it does not originate from the body, which can in no way be considered to be an efficient cause of the soul. The soul was created as a pure and simple form, and thus is immune to death, since it cannot be divided into simpler composing elements.

These views concerning the relation of soul to body are reminiscent of Platonic views, with, however, the following difference; with respect to the origin and creation of the soul and its first period of inhabiting the body, Avicenna emphasizes the role of the body alone. In proportion, however, as the soul develops, the role of the body becomes increasingly weaker, since the soul is increasingly present in itself as a perfect substance.

It will be remembered that Aristotle was seeking an explanation: How is it possible that in the end result of the action of material forms on our sense organs, there appear abstract, immaterial, intellectual essences? For, if all knowing has its beginning in a sensible perception of the material world, then there must arise, at some moment in the knowing process, the intervention of a power which is called the "agent intellect." According to Aristotle's opinion, the agent intellect must act within the soul, but, at the same time, it is separate from the body, since of its nature, it is constantly in act.

In the eyes of many commentators, such an assertion was synonymous with an affirmation of the transcendent character of the agent intellect with respect to a knower. According to Avicenna, however, we must distinguish between two active intellects: one is the soul itself as a substance which receives intellectual forms; and the second is a substance which imparts these forms to the soul.

The elements of anthropological thought which first made their appearance in the ancient period and were expanded in mediaeval times, reached a flowering in the thirteenth century, in the great philosophical synthesis of Thomas Aquinas, who treated these questions in connection with the theory of analogically-conceived being.[9]

René Descartes, however, treated the matter quite differently. He began the great current of the "philosophy of the subject" by making man the focalpoint.

VI. THE CARTESIAN CONCEPT OF MAN

Descartes' concept of man is closely connected with his new philosophical starting-point. Beginning with universal doubt, Descartes found in it a foundation for certitude. If I doubt, I am thinking. Thought exists, even though I am dreaming or led into error by an evil demon. Even though what I think may be a dream or a delusion, the fact that I do think cannot be doubted. Hence, the foundation of knowledge should be sought not in the object but in the subject and in the conscious spirit.

From Descartes' time, there occurs a fundamental division of objects constituting the world. In ancient and mediaeval times, two divisions of being were recognized: living and non-living. Descartes introduces a division of beings into conscious and unconscious. For ancient thinkers, everything which was living possessed a soul as the first principle of life. But from Descartes arose the theory that consciousness is something distinct from matter. Life was now understood as a purely material process and then, because the soul lost its union with life, it also lost its union with the body. The soul became a thinking thing: a *res cogitans*. Hence we have a clear-cut dualism made all the more distinct by the complete subjection of the body as a *res extensa* to mechanistic laws. For the body can have only "passive" properties, i.e., a three-dimensional extension; but dynamic qualities like motion come from God, who, once at the beginning, freed the world from passivity. From that time on, the sum total of motion has remained invariable. As a result, there are two substances in the world, a thinking substance and an extended substance: soul and body. There are two separate worlds, which have no contact with each other. Not only inorganic bodies, but even animals, have no souls, because they lack consciousness.

There is only one exception where the soul and body are in contact; namely man:

> Now there is nothing that this nature teaches me more expressly or more
> obviously than that I have a body which is in poor condition when I feel
> pain, which needs food or drink when I have the feelings of hunger or
> thirst, and so on . . . Nature also teaches me by these feelings of pain,
> hunger, thirst, and so on that I am not only residing in my body, as a pilot in
> his ship, but furthermore, that I am intimately connected with it, and that
> the mixture is so blended, as it were, that something like a single whole is
> produced. For if that were not the case, when my body is wounded I would
> not therefore feel pain . . . And when my body needs food or drink, I
> would simply know the fact itself, instead of receiving notice of it by having
> confused feelings of hunger and thirst.[10]

Descartes did not explain this union of the body and soul, though he
advances the possibility that the soul unites with the body in the brain.

As for the role of the senses, Descartes teaches that sensible impressions
are useful for living, but not for the attainment of truth.

Error is an act of the will and not of the intellect, since judgment belongs
to the will. Descartes has no notion of a soul constituted of powers; the soul
alone, insofar as it performs various functions, bears different names.

There are also intellectual representations. These are of two kinds: those
which the spirit refers to external sources, and those which it derives from
itself (passions). Affections are produced by external powers mediated by
"living powers" in the blood. The direction of these affections for the usefulness of the spirit constitutes the object of ethics.

The soul as a spirit distinct from the body is subject to the laws of the
spirit:

> I first take notice here that there is a great difference between the mind
> and the body, in that the body, from its nature, is always divisible and the
> mind is completely indivisible. For in reality, when I consider the mind,
> that is, when I consider myself insofar as I am only a thinking being, I
> cannot distinguish any parts, but I recognize and conceive very clearly that
> I am a thing which is absolutely unitary and entire. And although the whole
> mind seems to be united to the whole body, nevertheless when a foot or an
> arm or some other part of the body is amputated, I recognize quite well that
> nothing has been lost to my mind on that account. Nor can the faculties of
> willing, perceiving, and so forth be any more properly called parts of the
> mind, for it is one and the same mind which as a complete unit wills,
> perceives, and understands, and so forth. But just the contrary is the case
> with corporeal or extended objects . . .[11]

VII. FORMATION OF THE PHILOSOPHICAL NOTION OF THE SUBJECT

The ensemble of questions concerning man shared the vicissitudes of philosophy itself. For man, his vital structure, his essential character of activity, his origins and destiny, were always of interest to philosophy. Even in the original Pre-Socratic period, when the special object of interest was the discovery of the cosmos, spontaneous religious thinking reacted in creating for itself an image of the cosmos as a living and all-embracing divinity.

In the history of philosophy, we can discern two different approaches to the philosophical analyses relating to man. Descartes' notable significance is partly due to the fact that he can be considered a "boundary figure" between the ancient-mediaeval and the modern-contemporary approach to anthropological questions.

The ancient and mediaeval periods presented philosophical anthropology as interconnected with a general theory of reality. In this reality, man occupied a very important, though not the most important, place. He was the object of revealing analyses in the light of a previously constructed system and in the light of the "first principles." In the eyes of ancient and mediaeval classical thinkers, man was simply a spiritual being who nevertheless had his predetermined place in the total picture of reality. In this picture were combined the general structure of the universe, the hierarchical arrangement of communities, and the hierarchical arrangement of beings, among whom God occupied the highest position, then the angels, and below them, man; then animals, plants and finally, the inanimate world.

Against this background man was shown as occupying a special place, joining together the world of matter with the world of the spirit. Hence, an understanding of man presupposed at least some understanding of beings, both higher and lower in the hierarchy.

The situation was radically changed when an analytical way of thinking about man became the point of departure for a coherent construction, in imitation of mathematics, of a closed philosophical system. In Descartes' thought, the primary "given" is no longer the world and its prephilosophical image, but human thought; and not every thought, but only clear and distinct ones; in a word, a subjective idea. Henceforth, the analysis of a clear and distinct idea became the Archemedian fulcrum and final criterion for judging the truth and accuracy of solutions.

PHILOSOPHY OF THE HUMAN SUBJECT

Henceforth philosophy becomes a philosophy of the human subject. More and more philosophy becomes an anthropology. For if man, his recognition, his psychic reactions and his cognitive situation, become the one "bridge" which unites him with the rest of the world, then, in fact, human cognitions and the mental reactions joined to them become the first objects of analysis. The analysis of man and the disclosure of his cognitive structures become the principal efforts of philosophers like Kant. On the other hand, the objective world is gradually given over to doubt, to such a degree that it appears as a function of the subject. Even in Hegel, whose subjective philosophy takes on an appearance of a strongly objective philosophical system, we are dealing with an extrapolating human thinking about the world, which becomes "obedient" to the dialectic that it has discovered.

The reaction to this fictitious, idealistic objectivism becomes Kierkegaard's philosophy of human "existence." One way or the other, then, all the philosophical currents of the nineteenth century, with the exception of Marxism, are philosophies of the subject; they are precisely philosophical anthropologies. The starting point of all these philosophies is human cognition. This course of events is still continuing in existentialist, Kantian and transcendental directions. In such a state of affairs, philosophy resolves itself, almost totally, into an anthropology, a theory of man.

Once man was able to break away from the objectively real world, and the only data for philosophical analysis were those things which first appear in human knowledge, the "enlightening" aspect of philosophy disappeared. There was nothing to elucidate, if elucidation was to take place by a rejection of a real and objective world.

Within existentialism, philosophical anthropology dismantled all transcendence, contenting itself with piecemeal phenomenological descriptions.

Finally, what was perceived as an overemphasis on the subject's role became a convenient occasion for the construction of an antisubjective picture of reality. This reality resolved itself into *structure*, examined purely objectively through a logical analysis of cultural facts, especially language as the principal structure, and understood as responsible for the pseudo-subjectivity of man. "Structuralist" anthropology, which is a purely objective methodology, destroyed the human subject, explaining him "rationally" as an interiorization of language.

* * * * * *

The course of the history of philosophy, thus, completed a full circle. Philosophical thought emerged in the seventh century B.C. from a prepersonal "unlimited"; now it has arrived at the "disclosure" of a fundamental, infinite structure of a collection of accidents, which is supposed to be the total reality.

The vagaries of human thought which we have sketched above prompt us to present "the human fact" and to propose, in the light of the history of philosophy, an account of the essential structure of man highlighting his characteristic traits, and exhibiting the context of human rationality.

CHAPTER II

THE HUMAN FACT

This chapter deals with: (1) The problem of determining the human fact. Theoretical interpretation and description interweave, yet it is possible to determine the human fact on the basis of prescientific knowledge. (2) The nature of the human fact. Man's nature as rational animal and, consequently, as being-toward-death, is manifested in community, tradition, language, aesthetic experience and creation, and culture.

I. THE PROBLEM OF DETERMINING THE FACT

Two stages in the theoretical procedure of any genuine science must be distinguished: (1) establishment and description of facts, (2) interpretation and explanation of the facts. In philosophical anthropology, we must first indicate the fact which is assigned us for explanation, and then outline the manner in which the explanation of the data will take place. The given fact which is to be explained is man himself, understood in his ontic and essential properties.

The first concern, then, is the philosophical determination of the so-called "human fact." In accomplishing this, however, we encounter some difficulty. First of all, it is not easy to separate a description of the human fact from a theoretical interpretation. The reason is that there are no "bare facts" which are not interconnected with some kind of cognitive experience, determining and directing a recognition of the fact itself. Secondly, it is frequently stipulated that the "human fact" here should be an image of man that is given us by the specialized sciences. Philosophy, it is said, should reflect on man only when science has given its judgment, since only then shall we be dealing with a human fact which has been rationally established.

But the matter is not so simple. The image of man which is given by the specialized sciences is only seemingly uniform. In reality, it is differentiated with respect to the different perspectives taken by particular sciences. For it is evident that the very selection of aspects and the employed method of research already imply a specific position on what is to count as knowledge.

Understood in a classical sense, philosophy arises from a prescientific knowledge, and from data belonging to this knowledge, it elaborates on it in its own manner. Philosophy is an independent cognitive area of knowledge whose conclusions do not belong to the specialized sciences.

Hence, at the very starting point of philosophy, we can utilize a prescientific description of the human "fact." In this description, we emphasize those elements which were already emphasized in universal consciousness. In addition, we can utilize descriptions of the human fact which have exerted a special influence on the history of culture. Statements of this kind have already become a common "good" in the prescientific understanding of man.

In the general consciousness of educated people, man still remains, in his ontic structure, a mystery to himself. It is true that contemporary psychology has been able to explain much about how man responds to various stimuli and what are the laws of his actions. It is also true that the natural sciences have brought to light a whole range of complexities in the area of social life. Nevertheless, man as man still remains, as Alexis Carrell has expressed it, "an unknown being."

Precisely what does "man" mean? Every answer at once becomes involved in some philosophical system. However, this neither threatens knowledge nor makes it impossible, since systems tend to develop on the boundaries of a prescientific knowledge which is available to all.

RATIONAL ANIMAL

In prescientific, so-called "common sense" knowledge, man shows himself to be a highly developed mammalian vertebrate animal who, thanks to his intellect, transcends the whole of nature and the animal world. Such an understanding would agree with the definition of man asserted in some philosophical circles, i.e., "rational animal" (*animal rationale.*)

ZOON LOGIKON

When, however, we look at the "animal" side of ourselves, we immediately perceive our shortcomings. As many have pointed out man, in comparison to other animals, is characterized by inadequacies rather than by a perfection of "natural equipment." He does not possess a hair-covering which would protect him from changing temperatures and inclement weather. Nor does he have any developed organs for struggle, enabling him to capture his prey or resist his many enemies. In comparison with other animals, his senses of smell, sight, and hearing are weak, and he is in constant danger of losing his life. As a species of animal, man should have disappeared long ago from the face of the earth.

Yet it is man alone who has remarkably survived the difficult eras of struggling with nature. He has developed and subdued the earth. He has destroyed animals stronger that himself. He has changed the face of the earth, never completely adjusting to it, but making it suit his own needs. He has fashioned for himself an "artificial" niche in the form of homes, estates, cities, and everything which is associated with urban culture. We can assert somewhat paradoxically that man as animal was forced to treat his deficiency of natural specialization as one of the "raw materials" of his new nature.

HUMAN INTELLIGENCE

Everything which is understood by the term "culture" was achieved by human reason. As a matter of fact, in a certain sense, many animals have "intelligence." This is evident in the purposeful adjustment of the animal species to its environment. The more "intelligent" an animal is, the better it can adapt itself to the changing conditions of its habitat. Considered from this point of view, man is incomparably more intelligent than any kind of animal. This is so because he is able to fashion for himself artificial, i.e., cultural, conditions which are necessary for subsistence and development. At the same time, he is better able to take advantage of the forces of nature and better able to arrange them in accord with his objectives.

But human intelligence is something essentially different from that of animals. For the fundamental property which differentiates man from other creatures of nature is his ability to know *rationally*. In agreement with philosophical tradition extending all the way back to Socrates and Plato, it was customary to point, above all, to concepts as the specifically fundamental elements of man's rationally-knowing structures. In contrast to sensible knowledge, concepts had shown themselves as the universal, necessary and stable elements on which a genuine human knowledge can be built. Later psychological researches showed that imagination alone is not sufficient to explain what we call "thought," which transcends the sensible character of the knowledge peculiar to animals.

This transcendence of man's thought (independently of an interpretation of its ontical character) is something which is not subject to discussion. In other words, the universal understanding of man as *animal rationale* is contained in this definition.

II. RATIONAL ANIMAL— THE CONTENT OF THE HUMAN FACT

The "human fact," as we have seen, is best symbolized by the expression "rational animal." This expression in turn calls attention to those traits which most differentiate man from the whole ensemble of nature. Let us turn our attention to some of those that are easily perceived with respect to their general character.[1]

Human rational activity found its most characteristic expression in the area of *technics* (skills); thus, man is able to use tools which are his own creation. It is true that some animals, e.g., monkeys, can make use of tools to secure food, but they have never created instruments and, in fact, they do not need these tools to assure their life. It is man who, from his first appearance on the earth, uses tools not merely as an extension of some organ but as a kind of embodiment of his thought. Man is constantly improving his tools. Thus by the creations of his own thought, man has dominated the world.

It is certainly a long way from a plain, ordinary stick, or fire, or wheel to contemporary computers directing factory operations and cosmic flights. Yet, thought, taken in its general structure, is the same today as it was yesterday. Paradoxically, ever-changing technology is the way of never-changing human thought.

COMMUNITY

Obviously, such a development of thought connected with technics could never be possible if man were not a *social being*. And we do not mean here the kind of community of which an analogue can be observed among bees or ants—a community operating by instinct and without free will. A human community is an expression of a rational and free human nature. For a human community is a community of persons and, therefore, of people who are striving to develop and improve their knowledge and all that can be achieved through the use of intellect.

TRADITION

Through *tradition*, community makes possible a growth of human culture. Tradition is not something inborn in the human being as, for example, "community" instincts are inborn in ants and bees. Ultimately, man must learn tradition by accepting freely the genuine values which have been achieved by humanity in bygone ages and by rejecting seeming or outmoded values.

LANGUAGE

The assimilation of human tradition which appropriates all the achievements of the labors of former generations is made possible through *language*, which is a system of constantly developing and evolving signs. This system enables man to develop his personal being because it unites him in the streams of tradition with the latter's rational achievements. It enables people to open up to each other and thus to those with whom they can further develop and deepen already acquired cultural values. Man does not have to "start all over again"; thus community progress is possible.

SCIENCE

Man's ability to abstract and to create ideas stands at the basis of *science* as an organized, methodical and fundamental rational knowledge. Scientific knowledge, especially today, has become a highly esteemed sign of the presence and the dignity of man. For in its essence, it is always disinterested knowledge, even though it has impressive practical results. The phenomenon of science, which never occurs in nature, is something undeniably connected with the "human."

ARTISTIC, AESTHETIC AND RELIGIOUS ACTS

Artistic, aesthetic and religious human activities show, perhaps, a type of knowledge even more disinterested than the scientific. The creative activity, as well as the perception and vision connected with works of art, are ends in themselves, in the same way as religious contemplation is its own end. Magnificent temples, religious rites and pilgrimages, are not oriented to the achievement of any concrete advantage or practical interest. In other words, such activities are testimony to the transcendent human spirit not confined to the areas of material gain and natural interest that we notice in the case of animal behavior.

DEATH

Finally, *man alone reflects on the fact of his own death.* In relation to this fact which, with its brutal eloquence breaks out as of prime importance among all the human facts of life, man adopts a reflective stance. Human life becomes a life in the perspective of death: will death totally annihilate us or is there some essential "I" which survives this death? We ask ourselves these questions in a theoretical way, but we all express them more frequently through our actions, our works and creations, through which we hope to endure and to extend our own short biological lives. The very fact of man's religiousness can be recognized as a desire to survive death, a desire for a life under changed conditions, beyond death.[2]

Independently of the way these existential questions are resolved, the very fact of their constant presence is something completely unique in the realm of living creatures. We do not observe, even in the highest animals, either a fear before approaching death, or an attitude of entering into death as any kind of consummation or gateway to a possible afterlife. The animal locates itself totally in transient time and in its own environment. It does not exhibit, in its actions, any transcendence in relation to the "time-space continuum."

CULTURE

Because man is an animal and hence a creature of nature, he constantly expresses his varied transcendence in activities within the world. In this same transcendence, he can likewise make himself, by means of reflection, the object of cognitional, creative, and volitional activity. The result is "culture." Referring to these cultural products, one philosopher has defined man as the "symbolic animal."[3]

* * * * * *

We have given a cursory description of man, insofar as it discloses our prescientific and common sense thinking. But this description explains nothing as yet about the ontological structure of man, his destiny and essential functions. It merely focuses attention on man as a marvelous and unique being, emerging from nature as a part of it, yet transcending that nature and having as the purpose of his activities, not nature but man himself, as he dominates, transforms and organizes nature for a purpose which is beyond space and time.

Attempts to explain "the human fact" have appeared more than once in the history of human thought, in philosophy, religion, scientific studies, etc. Let us examine, however briefly, some of them which have a connection with the subject of the considerations we have presented.

To make this survey more coherent, let us first observe those explanatory attempts which emphasize the biological side of man, trying to reduce the "human fact" to a system of materially biological powers, on the grounds that man is, in a way , a product of nature. To this group, we can add the attempts at the interpretation of man formulated by Julian Huxley, and by Teilhard de Chardin; also the Marxist notion of man, and Freud's depth-psychology, along with the anthropological implications of structuralism.

At the same time, we should point to another source, which emphasizes the spiritual side of man, transcending the biological aspects. The sources of the contemporary understanding of man as a manifestation of the spirit reach all the way back to Descartes. Within this tradition we must give the general outline of the theory of man in Hegel, so that we can present the theories of existentialism.

CHAPTER III

ATTEMPTS TO INTERPRET
THE HUMAN FACT

This chapter is divided into two sections. The first section, *Conceptions of Man as a Creature of Nature*, examines theories which understand the human being as a product of nature. The emphasis is on the biological side of man. The following positions are studied and critiqued: A. The Biologico-Evolutionary Interpretation; which examines Teilhard de Chardin's Directed Naturalistic Evolutionism, B. The Marxist Conception of Man, C. Freud's Psychoanalytical Interpretation of Man; and D. Lévi-Strauss' Structuralism.

The second section of the chapter, entitled *Conceptions of Man as a Subject Manifesting a Spirit*, studies theories which emphasize the spiritual side of man. These are included under/three headings: A. Post-Cartesian Heritage, B. Heidegger's and Jaspers' Existentialism, and C. Scheler's Vision of Man—The Reverse of Power and Value.

I. CONCEPTIONS OF MAN AS A CREATURE OF NATURE*

A. BIOLOGICO-EVOLUTIONARY INTERPRETATION

1. Directed Naturalistic Evolutionism
(The Vision of Teilhard de Chardin)
Among the biologico-evolutionary interpretations of man, a special place is due to the theory elaborated by Teilhard de Chardin.

---

*Cf. *I-MAN*, unabridged edition, pp. 39-87, for primary source quotations.

Teilhard's theory accepts scientific views on evolution as definitively established, and then seeks to find the Divine in matter. Man appears against the background of the cosmos, which always existed and which presented an eternal unification of elements and powers. (Such a position presupposes a henological conception of being. Cf. Greek Presocratics.) Hence, at the beginning of the perceptible world, there already existed "the *Multiple*, which was rising up towards spirit under the magnetic influence of the universal Christ who was being engendered in it."[1]

NOOSPHERE

Reflective thought on the part of man, seems to be the result of an evolutionary process of consciousness. When the spirit in man has freed itself through reflection, the "noosphere" begins to surround the Earth. There are no *spirits* in nature, but there is a *spirit*, "physically defined by a certain tension of consciousness on the surface of the earth." It is a kind of animate covering of our planet, which Teilhard calls "noosphere" or "biosphere."

This spiritual "covering" is nothing foreign to the world; it is only a different state of matter. All opposition between souls and bodies disappears. The phenomenon of the spirit represents, therefore, a certain appearance of a cosmic quantum of consciousness, i.e., a quantum of personality.[2]

CHANGE IN MORALITY AND CONCEPTION OF GOD

With the appearance of a personalistic *centrum*, there follows a change in morality, from a static morality (observance of prohibitions) to a dynamic morality, which is progress in the direction of spiritual good, i.e., God.

Teilhard then advances the postulate that God should be a God of the cosmic synthesis. He will no longer "impose himself on us from without, as master and owner of the estate." While previously all that man needed was a God as "creator of the 'efficient' type, he now has a God of cosmogenesis, i.e., a creator of the 'animating' type that can measure up to our capacity for worship"[3]

Teilhard does hold that God is transcendent, even though he is an *evolutive* god, rising out of the heart of the old maker-God. Yet in this system of convergent cosmogenesis, to create is for God to *unite*, to form one with something. Further, God cannot appear as a prime mover without first becoming incarnate and redeeming, i.e., without becoming "Christified." Christ can no longer "justify" man, except by the same act super-creating the entire universe. Christ must do more than merely "supernaturally sanctify a harvest of souls"; he must also creatively carry the noogenesis of the cosmos to its maturity.

Teilhard insists that we are now witnessing the vision of a universal

"Christic energy, at once super-naturalizing and ultra-humanizing." The Cosmic Christ is the *centrum*, the Omega of the cosmos. His Resurrection has enabled him to become a universal center. The world is "the final and real Host into which Christ gradually descends, until his time is fulfilled."[4]

CRITIQUE

Although Teilhard's vision of reconciling science and religion is a fascinating one, it nevertheless contains very serious deficiencies. First of all, it attempts to explain the "human fact" on the basis of a combination of human science and Christian religion, rather than on prescientific cognition. If man is the result of evolution understood in a wide sense, then Teilhard already implies a philosophical solution that concerns the ontic structure of man. Man appears as the final member of the evolution of the material world. From a philosophical point of view, this position is subject to doubt, because evolution is a theory of nature which is not fully verifiable according to methods applied in natural sciences. Furthermore, the necessary hypothetical conditions of an accepted evolution are either designated or presumed.

Concerning the second element of his synthesis; namely, the "fact of man" seen with the eyes of Revelation, we are dealing not with a cognitive and autonomous position, but rather with a believing one, where the will persuades reason by an act of faith. For faith is not an informing, verifiable cognition that directs itself by a single criterion of truth. Hence, insofar as the "fact of man" (human phenomenon) appears in Revelation, it cannot be taken as some kind of scientific fact that is given further explanation in philosophy. Illumined by faith, man as a human fact is already interpreted in a trans-scientific way. There is no further appeal from such an interpretation because the intellect is unable to verify what is given by faith.[5]

Teilhard's vision of man synthesizes science and religion. However, it is only a vision of a prophet and not a scientific vision, capable of being verified and demonstrated. It can only be accepted as a personal statement but not as an intersubjective, reasonable theory.

EXTRAPOLATION

We can detect many methodological errors in Teilhard's vision; the chief one is a too daring extrapolation of the concept of evolution. For if palaeoanthropological facts allow us to construct a parabola symbolizing man's evolution, this curve was extended by Teilhard into infinity in both directions. As a result, we have been given an impressive, but non-verifiable, vision.

HENOLOGICAL CONCEPT OF BEING

From a purely philosophical point of view, we can charge Teilhard with a henological concept of being, so characteristic of Neoplatonism. For to be a being does not mean to unite, but *to exist*. Teilhard achieves a determination of the spirit in a naturalistic-physical terminology reminiscent of the pronouncements of the Presocratics (Anaxagoras). He does this despite the fact that the description concerns fundamental structural-ontic discussions of man. Further, he completely ignores analyses of the problem made by numerous medieval and contemporary thinkers. Finally, the relationship between the natural and supernatural demands a further critique from another point of view.[6]

B. MARXIST CONCEPTION OF MAN

The present Marxist conceptions of man are different from that of Marx himself. Marx took from Hegel the concept of the dialectic.[7] He rejected the notion of Spirit or Idea and, in its place, substituted Feuerbach's concept of matter and materialism, which now received its "dialectical character."[8]

MAN'S DEFORMATION AND ALIENATION

Marx also held that man suffered a deformation originating from defective economico-social relations. Man had become a servant and slave of these relations which are, in fact, his own creation.

The alienation of man constituted the basis for Marx's revolution. By his work, his government, and beliefs, man so alienated himself that, by himself, he is incapable of returning to a normal condition. He is now compelled to appeal to an uncorrupted class, *the proletariat*, which will enable him "to recover himself" and cease being a slave of human productions. For Marx, the problem of alienation flows fundamentally from the problem of religious alienation, although it is not exclusively limited to it.[9]

Hence, Marx's vision calls for a communistic community which will secure and establish by force new economico-social relations, in which man will become a free co-creator of human culture. In his *Das Kapital*, Marx subjected to penetrating analysis and profound critique capitalistic relations as the basis for the contemporary alienation of man.[10]

PROBLEM OF MAN

Marxism treats the problem of man from the point of view of his (1) ontological structure, and (2) axiological status as it is linked with the concept of law. The following theses concern his ontological structure:

A. Man is strictly a being of nature. Within a Marxist materialistic and evolutionary context, he is genetically the same as the matter of the surrounding world. Man is only qualitatively different from other creatures of nature.

B. Qualitative traits that differentiate man from other creatures of nature are:

1. *Consciousness*: man differs from the animals in that he alone possesses self-consciousness. Man "exists-for-himself" and his consciousness is reflective and universal.

2. *Work*: since man is a conscious being of nature, his work is purposeful. He transforms objective reality—nature, and society—the conditions of his own existence. Hence the human process of creation is "self-creation."

3. *Social relations*: man lives in union with other people, and this union is necessary for the preservation of being and of man's further development. Marx declared, "The essence of man is . . . the ensemble of social relations."[11]

Man is a "class being." He is incapable of existing outside of society. Work and consciousness are derivative elements in relation to the social constitution of man and, hence, "personhood" in the Marxist sense is a function of social relations. In the spirit of dialectical materialism, man cannot be understood as a spiritual being because this would lead to the fallacy of an idealistic understanding of man. Man possesses nothing independently and beforehand which is "his own," nothing "independently," nothing "personally." Prior to society, man of himself is a *tabula rasa*.[12]

CRITIQUE

Any evaluation of the Marxist interpretation of man would involve critiques of Hegelian pantheistic idealism, Feuerbach's materialism and the economic and social conditions of 19th-century philosophy of science. But independently of these critiques, we can state categorically that the Marxist theory of man is not an explanation of the human fact, which is given in prescientific common sense knowledge. Rather, it presupposes an already constituted image of the human phenomenon given in light of an already constituted complex of economico-social relations.

C. PSYCHOANALYTICAL INTERPRETATION OF MAN.

In this section, we shall consider the theories of Freud, Adler, Jung and others.

DEFINITIONS

The expression "psychoanalysis" normally means:

(a) empirical observations of psychical determinants of personality that do not permit themselves to be uncovered by an analysis of rational motivations, e.g., by introspection.

(b) methods directed toward the disclosure and examination of unconscious psychical activities for the purpose of psychical therapeutics, by removing disorders caused by these unconscious factors.

(c) a theoretical anthropological system which would already be a theoretical conception truly rooted in empirical observations but modelled on a hypothetically deductive theory.

A psychoanalytical model of man is already a theoretical interpretation of the "human fact," understood in some of man's important aspects of illness, i.e., the neurotic "I." We must therefore examine this proposed model of man, since Freud attempted to formulate a theory that would explain the entire man.

PSYCHOANALYTICAL DIRECTION

The psychoanalytical direction would differ from a psychology of consciousness in the following six ways:

1. Each psychic phenomenon possesses a determinate cause, which can be discovered and explained with the help of analysis.
2. That of which we are conscious is the result of suppressed desires.
3. Conscious psychic life is motivated by the unconscious, and it strives to realize suppressed desires.
4. Psychic phenomena are processes and actualizations of personal traits which germinally appear in childhood.
5. Biologically sexual orientation: personality is treated as having been determined by biological-sexual causes and the entire life is explained via this principle.
6. Social life is explained by laws which govern the individual. Society is a means of satisfying or restraining biological-sexual needs.

FREUD: LIBIDO AND FIRST THEORY OF INSTINCTS

The Libido Theory is linked (in its beginnings) with an attempt to explain psychic disturbances resulting from suppressed sexual energy seeking substitute outlets. Such neuroses as hysteria, neurasthemia, anxiety, and depression have as their immediate cause, specific "disturbances of a neurological economy" and, as their common cause, sexual disturbances.

The sex drive, *Libido*, appeared to Freud as the principal driving force of the entire human life. The Libido Theory appears especially prominent in Freud's so-called First Theory of Instincts, where he points to two fundamental drives in life. They are the sexual drive as a drive to pleasure, and the drive to self-preservation. Both drives express definite needs, and these can be removed only by their satisfaction.[13]

Freud maintained that a dialectical tension between the sexual drive and the ego drive of self-preservation passes through different phases: unconscious, pre-conscious and conscious.

Man must be regarded as a historical creature in whom sexuality develops from childhood and assumes many forms of expression important for understanding psychoneuroses in adulthood. Sexuality and neuroses of adulthood should be explained not only by repression and displacement, but also by sexual experience in childhood, in which the *Libido's* activity moves from the oral to the anal and genital spheres.[14]

SECOND THEORY OF INSTINCTS

Freud's Second Theory of Instincts is connected with World War I happenings which could not be explained through the activity of the *Libido*. Freud observed that soldiers who had been stricken with traumatic neuroses, tended to repeat past, even unpleasant, situations. Clearly, these cases contradicted Freud's psychoanalytical principles where the pleasure drive constituted the foundation of interpretation.

Freud therefore changed his theory by positing in the human "personality" the existence of two contradictory drives that mutually condition each other: *Eros*, the instinct of life, and *Thanatos*, the instinct of death.

Eros, according to Freud, is not a new invention, since it includes the previous *Libido*, as well as a portion of the instinct of self-preservation, i.e., *Ego*. (The instinct of death (*Thanatos*) would be the drive of organic life to return to the inorganic state from which it arose.) *Id* (it), *Ego* (self) and *Superego* are the regions of unconsciousness, pre-consciousness and consciousness respectively. *Id* is irrational by its nature and a great reservoir of *Libido* and death drive. *Ego* represents reason and health, and it controls *Id's* blind impulses. *Superego* represents moral and social demands, and it is the source of so-called moral conscience.

CRITIQUE

Freud's psychoanalytical theory was constructed to explain many facts of human life. But these facts can be explained differently from what Freud postulated. In actuality, he quickly encountered dissidents within his own circle: Adler and Jung.

Freud's errors were of two types: (a) he often mistook cultural phenomena for biological instinctual phenomena; and (b) he placed all the emphasis on the erotization of a situation when it may have been purely developmental.

DEFICIENCY OF PSYCHOANALYTICAL MODEL

Most fundamentally, Freud's psychoanalytical model of man is seriously wrong because it denies the *one, subsistent, substantially-personal subject of activity, who is man.* Man and his consciousness would be something secondary, something that has arisen from the dialectical (and sometimes mechanical) interplay of impersonal forces. He would be a combination of forces called instinct. Consciousness in man would be something merely historical.

If we admit, as we do, the acknowledged ontic unity of man, then Freud's explanation of consciousness by an appeal to instinctive and prepersonal powers and their natural mechanism of activity, must be rejected. Further, Freud's use of unconsciousness, struggle, and accumulation of impersonal forces, is the old Hegelian concept of dialectical evolution, from thesis through antithesis to synthesis. We find here the foundation for the evolution of the *Id* as a power of the inorganic state, which is common to the entire universe.

Man would appear as a particular place for the struggles of various powers, but he would be only a "moment," a "reflection" of the whole, which is the power of the inorganic state. This is the position formulated by Hegel. The denial of the subjective-ontic personality makes it impossible to accept Freud's model of personality as the model for the universal understanding of man.[15]

This does not mean, however, that the Freudian model is useless and that his investigations have no value for science. It only means that this model is inadequate in relation to the "human fact." It allows for the achievement of certain therapeutic actions and shows itself to be restricted and incorrect because it omits the essential trait of man's subjectivity.

ADLER

Adler denied Freud's foundations for neuroses and insisted that the starting point of the evolution of neuroses is a threatening feeling of uncertainty and inferiority, a feeling which begets a compulsive need to find some kind of purpose which would make life bearable. Constant and exaggerated use of psychic media (furnished by thought, will, and action) on the subject begets neuroses.[16]

JUNG

Jung explains neuroses in yet another way and thereby modifies the psychoanalytical model of man. According to him, Freud placed his emphasis on the objects, while Adler held that the subject was of paramount importance. Jung proposes a *via media*, i.e., that human behavior is conditioned as much by the subject as by the object.[17]

HORNEY

K. Horney disagrees with all three opinions and holds that neurosis arises from social frustration, which is the product of urban civilization, of competition and anxiety caused by certain forms of social life.[18]

FROMM

E. Fromm explains neurosis as a specific kind of relation of the individual to the world and to himself. He holds that "man's most compelling problems have to do with the needs society has created in him. These, not sex or aggression as such, create his greatest difficulties . . . So he uses certain irrational methods of relating to the group: sado-masochism, destructiveness, automation conformity."[19]

CONCLUSION

The common danger of the psychoanalytical theories is to conceive man as a set of relations of certain powers or drives, chiefly biological and sometimes social or cultural. These models can be used validly only when they are accompanied by a philosophical method that shows man to be a subsistent personal being and who directs, more or less consciously, his psychic activity.

D. PHILOSOPHICAL IMPLICATIONS OF STRUCTURALISM IN THE AREA OF ANTHROPOLOGY

C. LEVI-STRAUSS AND STRUCTURALISM

Lévi-Strauss, the most representative of structuralist thinkers, holds that objective human language contains within itself everything which *de facto* was expressed and became a cultural property of mankind, as well as everything that can be expressed by man. Hence language is a structure which embraces all spiritual possibilities of man. "Linguistics thus presents us with a dialectical and totalizing entity but one outside (or beneath) consciousness and will."[20]

The difference between reflexive or rational and spontaneous and uncontrolled thought loses its ontic reason, since in both forms of thinking, the sense comes from an objective system of signs, which man expresses independently of the particular historical *stadium* in which he finds himself. Language as a structure which contains this system of signs and anthropology can be understood only through an analysis of linguistic structure.

Structuralism would thus reject historical thinking. It would also reject the subjectivity of man, since Lévi-Strauss refers to the "supposed totalizing continuity of the self which seems to be an illusion sustained by the demands of social life." He also disqualifies methods of analysis of our own "I," which does not exist because it is only an interiorization of objective language.

To summarize, according to Lévi-Strauss, we are searching for the most universal structures which will explain the general human relations which ethnology reveals. General, human, social relations which constitute the area of anthropology are understood and explained through objective linguistic structure that is capable of explaining even the feeling of the ego, since, at the foundation of things, it is only an appearance and interiorization of language. But even if the limits of language are the limits of thinking and of culture, there are more fundamental structures than that of language. These are inert matter and the law of accidentality that govern it.[21]

CRITIQUE

Lévi-Strauss himself does not hesitate to point to the ultimate consequence of his position, namely the negation of transcendence. As a consequence, K. Jaspers' notion of transcendence, which is based on human consciousness, must be rejected because structuralism denies the existence of the human subject. Man is ultimately "cancelled out" as a human subject because he is objectively reducible to the structure of language. The model of intelligibility for man is not conscious being, but an unconscious structure.

Little wonder, then, that where consciousness is denied so radically, there is also a denial of history, which can be reduced only to objective structures, to "mytho-logy." Christianity in particular, as a history of redemption, becomes an a priori mythology.

Ultimately, objective linguistic analysis is reduced not so much to an analysis of sense or meaning but rather to an analysis of the very structures of language, of its syntactic aspect independently of meaning. It is a gigantic all-embracing structure of nonsense which finds its ultimate justification in acknowledging the law of accidentality as the ultimate model of intelligibility. Transcendence is denied and agnosticism reigns supreme.[22]

II. CONCEPTION OF MAN AS A SUBJECT MANIFESTING A SPIRIT

The second set of postures emphasize the spiritual side of man. We shall examine these under three headings: A. Descartes and Post-Cartesian Heritage, B. Some Existentialist Conceptions of Man, C. M. Scheler's Vision of Man—The Reverse of Power and Value.

A. DESCARTES AND POST-CARTESIAN HERITAGE

Ancient and medieval philosophy traditionally divided beings into living and non-living. (The soul was the first source of life.) Descartes, on the other hand, divided beings into conscious and nonconscious. Life became a purely material process and the soul, which lost its union with life, also lost its union with the body. The soul became a "thinking thing" and the body became subject to mechanistic laws.

HUME

D. Hume denied the intelligibility of the human soul's existence (perhaps even its existence). He likewise denied the Principle of Causality and the idea of substance.[23]

KANT

I. Kant undertook to correct Hume's scepticism. Kant first distinguishes between sensory knowledge which takes place within the framework of a priori categories of space and time, and rational cognition which, through judgment, classifies and unites the data of experience by using the a priori categories of the understanding. Causality and substance are the two most important categories. Being in itself, however, is unknowable.

As a subject, man is the condition of the object. Judgment is but the ability to unite what is a reflection of the unity of the very self. For the creation of the "object" is an activity of the understanding: object is that on whose conception the variety of a given experience is united.

But the activity of the understanding (transcendental analytic) demands its completion by reason in the dialectic, since what we know by understanding is only fragments of being in itself. Reason integrates the fragmentary results of understanding under the three Ideas of soul, universe and God.

The Idea of the soul, however, is given us as an a priori Idea which can never be verified; nor can we ever be freed from it. The same applies to the Idea of God. That which is useful in science is the "I," but it is only a form of unifying images a priori. However, we have no image of the soul, and hence we understand it only as a function, not as a substance.[24]

FICHTE

Kant's philosophy of the subject is continued in the thought of Fichte and Hegel. Fichte began the conception of the Hegelian dialectic. Fichte held that the affirmation of the "non-I." when I understand and affirm my "I," I assure myself that being "I," I am different from "non-I." In a word, affirmation of self postulates the antithesis "non-self."

HEGEL

As an absolute idealist, Hegel attempted to achieve a synthesis of these positions by way of the Absolute Spirit which manifests itself in man. Hence the opposition between thesis and antithesis results in a synthesis which, in turn, is the thesis of a further antithesis and even of a higher synthesis. Hegel also held that the dialectic of thinking was not only a logical form, but it was also something objective and ontological: a form of being. Thought and being are the same. The entire evolutionary process is a dialectical evolution of the spirit.

HEGELIAN TRIAD

The Hegelian triad is as follows:

1. *First Stage*: the "objective spirit" finds itself as "being-in-itself." The philosophical discipline answering to this stage is logic.

2. *Second Stage*: the spirit finds itself in a state of alienation. The spirit, as its own antithesis, takes on the form of nature, clothed in space and time. The discipline here is philosophy of nature.

3. *Third Stage*: the spirit in the synthesis returns to itself. It is "in-itself-and-for-itself." This stage is studied by the philosophy of spirit.

The ultimate triad is composed of Art (thesis), Religion (antithesis), and Philosophy (synthesis), which "constitutes a larger state in the development of the Absolute Spirit, its self-knowledge as a subject-substance of the whole reality."[25]

CRITIQUE

Hegel's anthropology is nothing else than an application of dialectics to psychology. Understood in this way, psychology is to reveal to man the "self" as a spirit, whose passing through dialectical differentiation is the "very heart" of the totality. As a pantheism, Hegelianism denies the reality of a subsistent subject of existence. Man is only a "moment" in a dialectical process. Hence Hegel's model completely fails to explain the "human fact."

B. SOME EXISTENTIALIST CONCEPTIONS OF MAN

Existentialism represents a reaction to Hegelianism, which treated the human subject as a moment and aspect of the dialectical development of the Idea. While Marx sees the liberation of man from alienation by means of the proletariat class and revolution which will lead to a classless society, Kierkegaard sees this liberation through the experience of his own existence on the boundary of nihilism and Christianity. Man feels himself condemned to nothingness, but he regains himself through faith in Christ.

HEIDEGGER

M. Heidegger's conception of man was influenced by Nietzsche and Dilthey. Nietzsche's concepts of "beyond good and evil," slave morality, meaningless existence, and superman (*übermensch*) left their imprint on Heidegger's thought.

Dilthey's thought influenced Heidegger in two ways:

1. Dilthey replaced a mechanistic way of thinking wherein psychic life is picture as composed of psychic "atoms." Dilthey sought to investigate individuals in their historical conditions. Man is studied in the context of his "totalizing" mutual conditions.

2. Heidegger criticized Dilthey's historical reason as a theory of cognition and insisted on the "time aspect" of man's existence. As an ontologist, Heidegger is interested not only in the historicity of the concrete man, but "man in general."

BEING OF BEINGS AND DASEIN

In his *Sein und Zeit*, Heidegger searches for the meaning of being by studying the concrete given man (*Dasein*). Since man reveals the meaning of being, he acts as a catalyst or agent, in whom being (*Sein*) manifests itself. In the historical process of creating ourselves, we are the first form of an aspect of being, and hence we can ask questions about the "meaning of being."

The fundamental concepts in Heidegger are: *Sein* (Being) whose sense we must "read" and which normally manifests itself as a *Seiende* (particular or limited being) and in a human, concrete historical *Dasein* (man). The task of metaphysics is to attain *Sein* by means of a phenomenological analysis of *Seiende*. As a *Dasein*, man is a "being-in-the-world." He finds himself in the surrounding of what exists as "beings" (*Seiende*). That which exists is constituted by (a) *Dasein*, historical man and (b) existing objects of which man makes use. We discover the world not in cognition but in use.

While man meets other existing objects and also other people, the most important way of being is that of his own conscious *Dasein*. Here man discovers *Sorge*, a concern about his own *Dasein*, and this begets *Angst* (dread).

Man is a being-toward-death (*Sein Zum Tode*). But death itself cannot be experienced. The presence of death stands before man in the existential experience of dread—death is a passage from *Seiende* to *Nichts* (from being to nothingness.)[26]

CRITIQUE

Heidegger's thought can be adversely criticized on many points. Nevertheless he calls our attention to the fact that man, as a concrete, conscious being (who is in the world and in history), cannot base himself on the traditional Aristotelian model of *substance* which, of itself, is atemporal.

Another important moment in Heidegger's thought is the emphasis on man's Death, which is linked with the temporality of human experiences. It is connected not only with the termination of temporal human existence but with a kind of "tension-toward-death."[27]

JASPERS

K. Jaspers' starting point in his analysis of man is existence itself. I am fundamentally different from the being of all things because only I can say: "I am." For "my" situation as a being is unique, since I understand myself as existing. My existence—in auto-affirmation—can never be objectivated. It is original; it transcends objects. It leads to the grasping of a "pure consciousness," which postulates the existence of an absolute consciousness.

The moments of the transcendence of consciousness are seen best in border situations as, for example, death, suffering, guilt, war. To experience border situations is the same as "to exist." The transcending consciousness reads the world like a cyphered absolute spirit, and metaphysics is the reading of the "cyphers of the world." For everything that is finite is only a symbol of infinity. The history of man is a basic cypher in the foundation of things, and the sense of the cypher opens "the doors of faith." For Jaspers, existence is, above all, something non-factual, even non-objectivated. Man appears essentially as transcendence.

C. MAX SCHELER'S VISION OF MAN—
THE REVERSE OF POWER AND VALUE

Early in life, Scheler was influenced, in turn, by the idealists, then by Husserl and phenomenology; and, after his conversion to Catholicism, his ethics of value was "colored" by Augustinianism. Nine years before his death, he moved on to a metaphysics of his own, which argued against his formerly accepted Catholic outlook.

LOVE PRECEDING KNOWLEDGE

In studying the relation of man to the problem of cognition, Scheler advances the thesis (already known to St. Augustine and Goethe), that we can know truly only that which we have already loved. Before man became an *ens cogitans* or *ens volens*, he already was an *ens amans*, for the order of love precedes the order of knowledge. Man's unique position in the world depends on his ability to love. Through this ability, man creates a bridge between his nature and a new world, a world of value and, through it, of new possibilities. It is only through love that man can become a perfect being, a completed being, and thus escape the "blind alley" of his own nature. He can thus arrive at the kingdom of the spirit.

Scheler held that man's development can and should be understood as the self-development of God. "Man is that unique place in which God realizes himself but, at the same time, this same man is a part of this transcendental process."[28]

THE SPIRIT OF MAN

Scheler held that it is due to the spirit that man differs fundamentally from the animal. The spirit is a state which is independent of physiological processes. Man can go against his physiological and animal drives, which the animal can never do. Man experiences the "objectivity" of things, their essence, and he forms the "personality" of his spirit, which is apprehended as an "object." The animal possesses "consciousness" but not "self-consciousness." Man does, and he can grasp himself as an object. Only man has the ability to choose suicide. He can "objectivize" his life and "throw it away." The animal can never do this.

Scheler believed that there exists in man a *centrum* of activity, which he called "person," and which creates itself through the opposition of man's organism and his surroundings. In the *centrum* is found the spirit and its will, understood as a continuum, which transcends himself and the world of objects.

But what *is* this spirit which inhabits the *centrum* of human activity? Is it some kind of subjective being? Scheler's answer, which here refers to Kant, is negative. The spirit is this unique "something" which, of itself, cannot "subjectivate" itself; it cannot become "that which is." The spirit can only be pure actuality, a fulfillment of act and not "that which" is some kind of subject.

Scheler disagrees with Freud on the question of the drive in human life. Freud held that the drive constitutes the essence of life. The drive is the fundamental mover of human psychic life, and all spiritual experiences are only a sublimation of the drive. Scheler, on the other hand, holds that the spirit manifests itself by suppression and sublimation, at the same time by the ability to say "no" to the reality of drives.

The spirit, however, does not possess its own ontic base; of itself, it is powerless. It cannot become a subject. It is grasped only as a function.[29]

REVERSE OF POWER AND VALUE

Scheler contended that the ancient Greeks were wrong when they postulated that the order of function indicates the order of substance, which would be the source of the function; and, hence, asserted that the higher the manifestation of the spirit, the more powerful the substance as a source of spiritual functions. He believed that the opposite was true, i.e., there exists an inverse proportion of value and power. The higher the value, the less power it possesses. The higher values live at the expense of the power of the lower ones.

As the highest value, the spirit is of itself completely powerless; and if it does have power, it derives it only by a sublimation of greater powers from lower values.

Hence the highest spirit, the kind that God is supposed to be, is omnipotent; while a pure spirit can be only completely powerless. Scheler is a theoretician of a powerless spirit and of an inverse proportion of power and value. The lowest drives, almost purely material ones, possess the greatest powers and must be used in order to nourish the higher values.

CRITIQUE

Scheler's thought can be characterized as an "anthropologico-cosmic pantheism."[30] While he does emphasize the specificity of the spiritual and, therefore, man's distinctiveness in relation to the world of nature, his position, nonetheless, is directly contrary to man's fundamental, direct self-conscious experience. For we affirm ourselves as subjects in the act of subjectivation. Further, an analysis of the "ego" as an agent of my acts shows the character and nature of man. Above all, the process of the spirit's manifestation against the background of a denial of biological drives cannot be treated as the birth of a spirit from matter. Neither can it be treated as the birth of an immaterial spirit and consequently, as the kind of being which does not possess traits that are indigenous to matter. Finally, as we have already indicated, Scheler's spirit is not a subject; it is only a function of actuality. It lacks an ontic base. Of itself, it is powerless. It can never become a subject.

CHAPTER IV

THE ONTICAL STRUCTURE OF MAN

This chapter which studies the ontical structure, or, we might say, the *being* of man, is divided into five sections: I. The Point of Departure—the phenomenological "given" II. The Self—A Subsistent Subject III. Soul Organizing Matter (The Form of the Body) IV. The Immateriality of the Human Soul V. Immortality.

I. THE POINT OF DEPARTURE

At the beginning of the analysis of the nature of man in realistic philosophy stand certain data obtained in the immediate experience of the human subject, wherein I distinguish in myself all that which is "mine" from that which constitutes my self, the "I." The original human situation in which we are conscious of ourselves, in which we feel precisely as human beings, performing "our" acts—is immediately given to us in self-cognition, the knowledge that I exist as "myself" who am the subject (in acts of subjectivization) of all that is "mine."

A. "MINE" AS POSSESSIONS

Most often we speak of "mine" when we have in mind results of our "work," of that activity which, while remaining within me (immanent), also transcends "me" to some "thing." "Mine," in this broadest, purely external sense, appears as a designation of the external objects of our productive activity or other appropriations, all that which is called "possessions." In this sense a house, field, forest, money, clothes, all objects of external use, can be "mine."

To say this relation of belonging is external is to call attention to the fact that it sometimes "comes" to me as an already constituted being, and in any case it certainly does not "construct" my being. One can break off this sort of relationship in various ways and not thereby diminish one's be-ing.

The "I" understood in this way can be called the "phenomenological "I", i.e., a dispositional center related to external things. Man, in relation to the world of external things, is their disposing "possessor." Things constitute for him a certain pyramid of value, as Heidegger said; they are useful and subject to man. Hence, there must arise within man in relation to the world of things one dispositional center, a single center that does not permit man to become lost in this world, but to use it for himself. The center disposing the world of *things* is this phenomenological "I," to be distinguished from the "I" as the subject who subjectivizes "my" *acts*.

We conceive the phenomenological "I" also as an individual "object" subject to time and a definite place in space: some "James X" is the "center" disposing possessions. "Mine" and "I" in this context are understood purely externally, as two "objects," one of which happens to be also a "subject."

B. "MINE" AS "MYSELF"

In addition to "mine" understood externally as belonging to "me," we should distinguish the other types of that which we call "mine," which correspond to the "I" understood as the subject of acts of "subjectivization." Here physiological functions must be distinguished from psychic functions and, among these latter, the more concrete functions "fused" with organic changes, such as sensory cognition and emotions, from the higher, more spiritual, psychic functions, and these both in the area of cognition as well as desire.

PHYSIOLOGICAL FUNCTIONS

Let us first consider physiological functions, such as eating, breathing, muscular activity, moving, sleeping, etc. Having these in mind, we say: "I am breathing," "I am eating dinner," "I am going for a walk," "My head aches," "My leg hurts," etc. In the statements just cited, we notice above all a direction of this type of function to a single "center," to the same subject of the functions, which subject is also the performer of those functions. The subject and performer of the physiological functions, called the "I," occurs here as an "I" in a different sense than that which occurred in the first instance, when to my "Self" was opposed "mine," understood in the sense of "possessions." This "I," which appears as the subject and performer of physiological functions, no longer appears as an externally defined object, but as a conceptually indefinite physical-bodily "center," and as a kind of focal point with which all functions are connected; either by being somehow radiated by this center, or radiated and performed at the same time.

These physiological functions are on the one hand distinguished from "me," together with their organs—it is "my" head which aches, and the aching is "mine"; on the other hand they are inseparable from me, they are ways of "being me," and the cessation of "my" functions annihilates me. Since however, "mine" in this sense manifests itself as connected with the structure and function of some material organ of "my" body, it is commensurate in its ontical structure with these functions; this "I" is in some sense material, though it is not identified with any organ.

Here the question arises: how is the ego to be conceived, if it is a subject of material functions? As yet it is some cognitively indefinite and undoubtedly material "I."

But is it only material? If the "I" existed as a material subject, if there were not in man other functions beyond purely material functions, then there would really be no grounds for raising the problem of the ontical dichotomy of the "I" and "mine."

PSYCHICAL FUNCTIONS

We also perceive occurring in ourselves activities which definitely are not a function, as least exclusively, of bodily organs, These are the cognitive and appetitive functions. For the sake of precision, it is necessary here to distinguish the cognitive functions more closely connected with the activity of a material organ by reference to the content character of cognition. We differentiate sensory cognition from so-called mental cognition. Sensory cognition such as the sight of colors, the hearing of sound, impressions of scent, taste, touch, warmth and cold, of weight, etc., is closely connected with a definite sensory organ, e.g., the eye, ear, taste buds. Impressions of this kind, recognized as "mine," are directed toward some "center," toward that "I" which is in equal measure the subject and performer of cognitive impressions. I feel that I am essentially the same subject, "I," one who eats, who breathes, as the one who "sees," "hears," and moreover—who "thinks," "loves," "hates."

I can also take as the subject of my cognitive attentions the functions of thought, manifesting themselves in concepts and judgments. For whenever I "think," I constantly perceive that I am the same subject, the same "self," which is the subject of both physiological functions as well as sensory-cognitive functions. My most sublime cognitive functions, moments of some intellectual ecstasy, contemplation, understanding of some law, moments of creativity in which I actively intervene in the existing course of events, all the moments of human "spiritual" life recognized as "mine," are also performed through that same, identical "I" which digests, breathes, feels pain. And I do not feel more "myself" when I think than when I eat, or go for a walk, or breathe. Furthermore, it is sometimes precisely "my" physiological functions that allow me to become more conscious of "myself," of my "I" and its character, than the lofty acts of contemplation. Only let my head or my heart begin to ache and I distinctly feel the threat to "myself" and the ontical contingency of that which I call "I."

But in all of "my" acts, both "material," as well as purely "spiritual," I notice without great difficulty that they are directed toward the same "center," toward the same "subject," of which we are conscious as the "ego," the "I." The "Self," therefore, as "center" and performer of "my" functions stands before us as something that at the same time can be both material and immaterial.

This description of the fundamental human situation found its place in the *Summa Theologiae* of St. Thomas Aquinas. In an article entitled "Whether the Intellectual Principle is United to the Body as Its Form?" Thomas says: "We must assert that the intellect which is the principle of intellectual operation is the form of the human body. For that whereby primarily anything acts is a form of the thing to which the act is to be attributed." After a systemic justification that activity is act (and act in the Aristotelian system is form) he expresses himself characteristically; "It is the same identical man who perceives both that he understands intellectually and feels sensorially, but sensory feeling does not occur without a body."[1] Hence, Thomas appeals to the inner experience in which we perceive the *identity of man—the ego* which is immanent both in acts of intellectual cognition, as well as in sensory cognition occurring with the help of a bodily organ.

II. THE "SELF"—A SUBSISTENT SUBJECT

If the data of immediate experience continually make known the ego as the subject, performer, and unique "center" of "my" functions—vegetative, animal, as well as spiritual-cognitive, then they thereby point to a single subject, "me." The "I" as the center from which all my functions flow, and toward which they are directed, is spontaneously recognized and continuously confirmed as the permanent subject of those same functions. In fact, if someone does not have "consciousness of oneself," if someone is not *compos sui*, he is not recognized as a human being performing his acts, and in legal action he is not considered responsible. Hence, to be "conscious of oneself" is considered to be a preliminary stage of the normal psychic life of man. There is really no difference between "consciousness of oneself" and the ascertainment of the factual existence of the "I" as subject.

The immediate experience of one's "I," i.e., the concrete affirmation of its existence as a subject—performing functions recognized as "mine" can also be confirmed by an indirect way of philosophical explanation. For, starting from the fact of the existence of somatic-psychic functions in man, it is necessary ultimately to explain them. Therefore, either "my" functions of this kind are subsistent beings, in themselves independent and autonomous; or they are dependent, subjectivized beings, ultimately existing through the existence of a subject. Only the second alternative is conceivable, namely; the functions recognized as "mine" are not independently existing beings, but are only emanations of the "I," i.e.; they are beings, indicating a subject, and their existence without the subsistent subject would be contradictory.

BERGSON AND FREUD

If we were to accept the hypothesis, suggested by Bergson, and also appearing in the works of Freud, that our functions, especially the higher psychic ones, are only a so-called "stream of consciousness," then it would follow that each act of consciousness, each act of will, or any unsubjectivized act whatsoever, is an autonomous being, incommunicable to another being. Each such act would thus be an example of what classical philosophy calls a "substance." That which is called "a man," would be, in this case, only an accidental unity of some kind, in which various and independent acts that exist independently, converge by themselves. Each of these acts would be a separate being. The essentially single human being would disappear. And there would be as many subjects and separate beings as there are separate acts of consciousness and psychosomatic acts.

Such a state of affairs, however, is contrary to the facts immediately accessible to us in inner experience. "I" feel and constantly co-ascertain in inner experience that I am a single being whose acts are "mine." Further, certain absurd consequences follow from the contrary hypothesis. For instance, we should not regard an individual as responsible for his acts; one would have to deny the individual as the subject of laws and as a member of society.

Therefore both immediate experience, as well as a consideration of consequences, points in a convincing way to the real existence of a single "center," a single "I" as the unsubjectivized subject of acts of the somatic as well as the psychic activity of man.

JASPERS AND HUME

A particular confirmation of the subsistence of the ego, emphasized by Karl Jaspers, is the affirmation of personal existence in the judgment: "I am." He noted that man alone in the whole of nature can say: "I am," i.e., he has consciousness of the existence of himself—an ego. This occurs "from within." When I affirm that "I am," then that judgmental affirmation is an act of the intellect, but an act that does not represent any "contents" in the sense of attributes. Everything that is "mine" represents a definite content, able to be expressed in the form of an enumeration of the appropriate "attributes" of things; it is "characterized." On the other hand, the affirmation "I am" does not represent any definite concept, any definite collection of attributes predicated of a "thing," but is the primary, pure affirmation of one's autonomous existence.[2]

David Hume, who thought that the only things of which we are directly aware are "sense data" (he called them "impressions" or "ideas"), naturally denied that we are aware of any ego or self, or even that any such thing exists.[3] But we ascertain the "I" not through an impression or idea, but in the existential judgment: "I am"—"I exist." All possible ideas referring to me are ideas of my psychic or psycho-somatic acts. These acts, however, are only emanations of the "self-existing "I;" and they are not the same as "I;" whereas the judgment, "I am," is a confirmation "from within" of one's self-existence, i.e., a confirmation of that which is called "substance." The "Self" always appears as a "contentless" performer and an existing, precisely self-existing, subject.

ARISTOTELIAN SUBSTANCE

It is true that the model of Aristotelian substance, understood statically and transferred unequivocally to man, would be artificial. Yet the intuition of Aristotle is closer to the truth than the phenomenological description of human "fate-destiny" somehow constituting the "meaning of man's being." For in applying the concept of substance to man it is not at all a matter of some "reification" or "objectification" of the vital human ego. There is something exceptionally valuable in the concept of substance; namely, the expression of the possibility of self-existence, the possibility of a being, which is no longer an attribute of something, whose existence is an original act constituting that something as a real being, the bearer of many attributes. Precisely as an indication of the real identity of a human being, despite his many-sided variability, we call man a "substance." This in no way means that man does not change, even in the structure of his substantial qualities. For through his acts man can so rationally and freely modify his qualitatively substantial endowment, that they attain their precisely substantial-personal, unrepeatable expression. To be such a subsistent subject existing in oneself and for oneself is "to be man."

III. SOUL ORGANIZING MATTER
(THE FORM OF THE BODY)

In previous considerations we arrived at the conviction that there exists (subsists) an ego understood as the "center," as the "subject" of physiological as well as of psychic acts. For both physiological acts as well as psychospiritual acts (of the same order as intellectual knowledge and intellectual desire) are truly "mine," are therefore an emanation of a single "center." And so this center, which we call the "I" or the "ego," manifests itself at once both as material as spiritual. At the same time, taking stock of "my" particular material organs, and even of "my" whole body, one cannot say that it is really the "I" in the strict sense, because every organ of my body, and indeed my whole body, is "mine." Consequently a difficulty arises: how is the "materiality" of the ego to be understood so as at the same time not to deny its spirituality as the bearer of specifically spiritual acts, i.e., of intellectual-cognitive acts?

This question has long fascinated philosophers, and since the days of Aristotle a theory of the soul has been constantly improved whereby one could, from one side, explain the subsistence of the human ego; and, from another, indicate its immaterial and material side.

But what is the relationship of the "I" to the human soul? One cannot say that the soul simply is the ego. First of all, we do not experience the soul as soul (in its classical understanding; the form of the body and the source of intellectual functions), but we experience the "I" in each human act.

Indeed we arrive at the notion of soul only as a result of a systematic philosophical analysis and explanation of the "I." The ego, by contrast, is given to us from the existential side, in the immediate cognitive experience. The ego thus given to us refers to the whole of our human being, i.e., to the fact that we exist and are the way we are, and that we express ourselves in "my" material and immaterial acts.

The ego thus given to us, however, is subject to systematic philosophical interpretation, just as all facts given to us immediately in cognition are. The philosophical interpretation relies above all on the manifestation of those ontical functions that do not contradict the ontical fact originally given to us for explanation. Hence, the first matter that demands philosophical explanation is the possibility of this being that appears as essentially one (the experience of the identity of the "I" in "my" variable and multiple acts of various contents) and also "composed" of many factors, acts that do not integrate.

Hence, the relation of multiplicity to unity in our experience is very specific: we have a feeling of the identity of the "I," of its fundamental, essential unity. (In general, we construct the concept of ontical unity after the model of the unity of ourselves.) This unity expresses itself in the multiplicity of "my" atomic acts, maintained by that single "I." The essential unity in multiplicity is noncontradictory only when a single act has the potentiality of being expressed in multiple "structures," actualized finally by a single act.

Consequently, the inner experience of one's ego as subjectivizing "my" contents is noncontradictory when, among these elements of experience, there is a unification expressing itself in the categories of act and potency.

We observe that our ego, performing acts of both material and immaterial content, is somehow "composed." If it is composed, however, then there exist ontical foundations actually manifesting themselves in "my" acts of both material and immaterial content. The composition justifying such diametrically different contents is a composition in the order of content—of a being where the act is form (in the human instance called soul) and the potency is matter, organized by the soul to be the body.

ARISTOTLE

If being basically assumes the form of substance, then one can rightly speak about the soul as a substantial form. Such a conception of soul already appeared in Aristotle against the background of an analysis of the structure of material beings, which arise and perish, are changeable and multiple. And so in metaphysics the fact of substantial coming-into-being as well as the fact of change is explained only through the composition of matter and form.

Obviously, the composition of matter and form is particularly suitable for the philosophical interpretation of essential changes of living beings, i.e., plants, animals, and humans. In Aristotle's system, changeable beings appear as composed of these two factors; with the qualification that form alone is "act," i.e., is the factor constituting the being, since it is the factor organizing and determining the being. In this system, however, each form (apart from the forms of the heavenly bodies) had to be completely material, and so a separate form could not exist. For Aristotle did not find in man any functions that would be the work of form-soul alone. Indeed, he discovered a special function, intellectual cognition, but he associated it not so much with the activity of the form-soul, but more with the activity of the "active intellect," which was supposed to be something different from the soul, since it, i.e., the active intellect, alone is "uncompounded" and "active."

Many Christian thinkers found this problem insolvable within an Aristotelian framework, and adopted Plato's position, or some variant of it, as apparently the only alternative. But Thomas Aquinas found another way.

According to St. Thomas, in normal ontical circumstances the act of existence belongs to the whole being composed of matter and form, and not to the form separately. But in the case of man, because of the fact that he possesses intellectual cognition and desire, which in their ontical structure and manner of activity appear immaterial and are the emanation of a material base, the act of existence does not belong to man as already composed of matter and form. His existence is the "act" of the rational soul and through the soul belongs to the whole man, and thus to his body.[4] Because of its natural immateriality, the human soul is a subsistent form. The soul, which alone is the form of the body, possesses its own act of existence, which it imparts to the body.[5]

Hence, if the composition of matter and form appears in all material substance, then this composition also appears in man, and in just such a composition the soul is the "form" of the body, together with which it constitutes one substantial being. And where there is one being, there is only one existence. Consequently man as one being possesses one existence. There is, however, a fundamental difference between man and all other material beings, insofar as the act of existence-life which man has, he receives not by reason of the composition of matter and form; rather he receives existence through the soul as an immaterial form organizing and animating the body. There is only a single existence of man, but he has this existence not as a result of material organization, but because it belongs to the soul. The soul subsisting (not temporally prior to or apart from the body, of course—we are concerned with ontical priority) imparts its very same existence to the whole body. If it were otherwise, man could not explain his acts, which, psychic, intellectual and bodily alike, are acts of man radiating from one center as from a single subject.

THOMAS VS PLATO AND ARISTOTLE

Why did this solution emerge for St. Thomas as the sole possible one? Perhaps this will become clearer against the background of Aristotle's and Plato's solutions, as well as a comparison of their positions with the immediate data of human self-cognition.

Aristotle's view agrees perfectly with the general conception of a changeable world. For if things are truly changeable, then they are changeable from within, entirely, which, after all, is given to us in everyday experience where we observe the corruption and generation of new beings. Man, therefore, being also a changeable being, coming into existence and perishing, is inwardly composed. But being inwardly composed of non-independent material and formal factors—in this case, body and soul—he exists as a consequence of this composition. Existing by reason of this composition, however, he does not have any functions independent of it, and consequently he does not have self-cognition, the experience of his own "I" as transcending the functions. The ego would not transcend these functions since, existing as a result of the organization of content, man would first have consciousness of the content, and only as a result of this cognition of what is called "mine," would he arrive at self-cognition, as by an inference. Man is, as it were, dissolved in his acts.

But Aristotle must be mistaken here, as a confrontation with the facts of self-cognition shows. I have perfect self-cognition of the fact that I cause, I perform, my acts; I transcend them, since I know that I cause them, that I am not wholly expressed in my acts, that I can substitute them for others. In a word, the moment of transcendence of the ego over the content of what is "mine" is self-evident in inner original, and immediate experience. Therefore we cannot hold that man exists as a result of the composition of non-independent factors, soul and body. Self-cognition contradicts this.

The Platonic model of man, on the other hand, is suitable to the extent that it emphasizes the moment of the transcendence of the ego over all that is "mine." For if man is a spirit residing in the body and using it like a tool, then the moment of self-recognition and the transcendence of the "self" over all acts, especially the material, is well emphasized. But this model is also faulty because in inner experience I well know that "I" am the cause of "my" acts, both spiritual and material. Material acts are not any less "my" activity than purely intellectual activity is, and this would not be the case if the Platonic theory were true. In fact, Aristotle's theory better explains this original fact.

The middle way out finally proposed by St. Thomas seems to be the most sensible and consistent with experience. Moreover, the denial of his solution is also a denial of this very experiential "given," and which we are trying to explain and not explain away.

In this formulation, the soul is the real form of the human body, in agreement with Aristotle. The body is a real co-factor of the human being, not just a stage for the drama of consciousness. Ontical existence, however, is bound immediately to the soul; this means that the act of existence actualizes the soul in the ontical order, and the subsisting soul organizes or "forms" the body for itself, the body being needed by it so that it can act, so that it can express itself and attain full development using its powers of activity. For the body, to exist means to be organized; the moment of the disorganization of the body is the moment of the cessation of the existence of a human body, and a return to the state of non-human matter. The body, organized by the soul, is the first "mine" of a special order. In it the soul is expressed for the first time, and through it, the soul comes in contact with the external world and has the possibility of self-cognition.

As a result, it is possible for man, in the inner, immediate experience of himself, to possess the cognition of the characteristic transcendence of the

"I" over all that is "mine," since in the ontical order the soul also transcends the body, possessing its own existence belonging to it by reason of itself. It is also possible to possess the consciousness of "my" material acts, since the soul, being the form or organizer of the body, is likewise truly the cause and performer of my acts having material content. The denial of any element of the explanation results in the denial of original experience. The solution proposed by Thomas seems to solve the main problem of man: his ontical structure.

The soul, therefore, is in certain aspects "material"—insofar as form animates matter and together with it constitutes a single corporeal human being. On the other hand, however, as the subject of purely spiritual acts (which will be discussed below), in itself, owing to its be-ing, the soul is a spiritual being, since it is ontically subsistent. But because the soul is the form of the body, in its inner ontical structure the soul is "incomplete,"[6] in that it exists in conformity with matter. As a result, we feel like "someone" bound to matter, despite the fact that the "I" cannot be identified with any material organ, or even with the whole body. This "materiality" of the ego flows from the essential conformity of the subsisting soul with matter.

In sum, although the testimony of our consciousness is correct according to which we feel like a material being, our feeling of ascendency over matter is also correct, because we do not simply identify with the materiality of our body, of which we are aware, and aware that it is "mine."

ACT AND POTENTIALITY

The essential unity of man, with the "two-sided" ontical dimension of spirit and body, becomes more intelligible in the light of an interpretation of a philosophical system employing the theory of act and potentiality. The "composition" of soul and body as one of matter and form or, expressing it still more generally, as one of potency and act, is—on this theory, the only possible and noncontradictory "composition" of human nature. On the one hand, we feel like a single being and we know that if ontical unity exists anywhere in the world, then it is realized above all in our very selves. Not only our consciousness testifies to this, but also the observation and analysis of the observable data of human activity, both physiological as well as psychic. Together with the unity, however, we experience that we are divided, that we are composed of milliards of parts of matter. The composition from numerous parts, however conceived, is only then noncontradictory, given the maintenance of the essential unity of the composed being, if this composition is conceived as precisely one of potency and act.

For if there were more actual "parts," and they are to remain "acts" i.e., independently existing parts, after the composition, there would no longer be an essentially single being. There would have to be as many beings as ontical acts. If, on the other hand, all the "parts" were something only potential, then there would be no being at all. And if there exists an essentially single being man, then his "composition" from spirit and body is possible only when there is a single act constituting be-ing: the act of existence being a property and belonging to the soul-ego as to form. And we are conscious of the unity of this act of existence-life as our single ontical act.[7]

The question yet arises, having its source in Plato, whether there is a possible greater number of "form-souls" in man. But if a particular being is supposed to be an essentially single being, and if we do not agree with ontological monism, then in an essentially single being there can be only one essential form. In man this form, constituting human nature, can only be spiritual form, as the subject of spiritual functions. Nevertheless, there is no contradiction in saying that one existing spiritual form is the form of matter as well, and would for itself also organize material life: vegetative and sensory.

Hence, man in his deepest "I" is a subsistent being, i.e., substance that subsists because it is spirit. The personal "I" embraces both spirit and matter; it becomes comprehensible ultimately through an appeal to the subsisting spirit, called soul.

Thus appears the solution of the paradox of our consciousness, according to which we feel as a "Self" different from everything that is "mine," even though this "mine" is the whole body; according to which we feel like one being: material and at the same time transcending matter, present in the world and present to ourselves.

HIERARCHY OF BEING

It is necessary to add, however, as Gilson rightly observes in *Elements of Christian Philosophy*, that within the sphere of the metaphysical structure of a complete being, the soul shares *with its body* the same act of being that it received from God. Man, as an ontological monolith, is truly one, owing to the unity of the existential act of being. Hence, participating in the very being of the soul, the body does not become the soul but, as something that receives the soul in the character of the subject, is raised to the level of an act of being that has soul as the principle and cause of the body. The whole universe, in the understanding of Thomas, constitutes a hierarchy of higher and lower forms, in which, so to say, the lower ascend beyond their levels by reason of the perfection of the higher. One of the consequences of this state of things is a certain kind of continuity of order imposed on the lack of continuity in the degrees of being, in agreement with the opinion of Dionysius, that the highest degree of a lower order always adjoins the lower degree of the immediately higher one. The often quoted observation of Thomas himself, that the rational soul is similar to a horizon or border line between noncorporeal and corporeal substances, finds its justification here. Why? Because, says Thomas, "the human soul is a noncorporeal substance, and at the same time the form of the body."

IV. THE IMMATERIALITY OF THE HUMAN SOUL

The general problem of immateriality is bound up with the concept of matter itself, and on the topic of matter there exists a whole series of divergent views.

TWO FUNDAMENTAL CONCEPTS OF MATTER

Taking under consideration investigations in the history of philosophy, one can advance the thesis that the different concepts of matter can be reduced to two categories: a *philosophical* concept related to Aristotle's idea of science; and a *"scientific"* concept, related to the idea of science developed in the "positivist" school.

In the first sense, matter is an element of being, one of its constituent factors, perceived solely intellectually against the background of the analysis of being as changeable. This conception of matter appeared in Plato and Aristotle, other philosophical systems presenting merely a modification of it. Matter thus conceived is an individuating agent, a multiplying principle, a potential, unknowable factor, a nonperfected factor.[8] Matter, however, does not reveal itself in immediate cognition. What appears in original cognition, is a changeable, multiple being, arousing wonder, being as an object given to philosophical clarification. The concept of matter originated as a theoretical justification explaining the changeable and multiple being originally given to us in cognitive intuition. In this sense, too, matter as a factor actually "justifying" change is at the same time the factor impeding the cognizability of the object. From the time of Plato, the conviction was generally accepted that this very matter impedes cognition and at times renders it impossible, whereas the withdrawal from matter, i.e., some form of "immateriality," is the foundation of worthwhile, scientific cognizability, such cognition being characterized by necessity, universality, and immutability.[9]

Matter in the second interpretation is an object of empirical, chiefly sensory, cognition. In this sense, matter is all which is cognized in a measurable way. Therefore, it is some kind of "temporal-spatial continuum," being precisely the object of the physical sciences, insofar as these sciences in the process of their cognition make use of sensory data, as well as of data obtained by means of various measuring apparatuses, and finally, of the intellectual "processing" of measurable data.

IMMATERIALITY

Having outlined these conceptions of matter, we are now able to construct a conception of immateriality, i.e., of spirituality. In the first case, then, we call the "formal" element in being, "immaterial." Aristotle, and in large measure Plato, understood immateriality in just such a manner. Immateriality thus will be: a) either that side of being that is the ground of the ontical identity, the immutability, and also even the universality—if we connect the concept of immateriality with abstractive cognition—of the only valuable cognition; b) or being itself, which, speaking in Aristotelian terms, is "pure form" (or in Platonic terms, "idea"). It was just such a conception of immaterial being that had already appeared in antiquity.

If we want to create an idea of immateriality bound up with the second conception of matter, then we would construct an idea of the kind of being that is neither an object of sensory cognition, nor even an object of any measurable cognition. It would be difficult to know anything about such a possible being on the basis of pure empiricism. For, on the basis of empirical cognition, one could only refuse to assert the *impossibility* of the existence of the kind of being that is neither an object of empirical cognition, nor of any cognition of the measurable type.

One can speak intelligibly about an immaterial being in this second sense, however, by reference to a somewhat modified first type of immateriality. For if Aristotle's intuition is correct in a general sense, then—according to the terminology of Aquinas—the "immaterial" side of a being is not so much "form," as the identifying element, as it is *existence* making being actual. For existence is the act of being; form is act in the essential order only. For it is not due to form that a being is truly something real, but it is due to the act of existence. If existence is an act of a simple substance, i.e., is an act of a self-existing form, then we can speak of the essential immateriality of a being; and then the whole being is truly immaterial.

ARGUMENTS FOR THE IMMATERIALITY
OF THE HUMAN SOUL

Relying on the ascertainment that the "ego" manifests itself as the subject and performer of psychic functions, one finds that it is necessary to analyze these functions themselves, and see whether they are material or immaterial in the manner of their very activity as well as in their products. If it is ascertained that some psychic functions are performed in an immaterial manner and the products of the higher psychic functions are immaterial in their structure, then there exists a foundation for the conclusion that the immaterial functions, emanated from the subject, are not the function of a material being, if the principle of contradiction holds; i.e., being does not come from non-being, spirit does not come from non-spirit.

It is also necessary to give careful attention to the fact that the characteristic functional connection with matter remains in agreement with the concept of immateriality. What is at issue here is the ascertainment of immaterial structures, and not the negation of their connection with matter.

First we should inquire about the possibility of "thinking matter." Locke judged that one cannot infer spirituality from the fact of intellectual thought, since no one knows whether God in his omnipotence would not be able to make thinking matter. In response to Locke it was observed that indeed we do not know the omnipotence of God and its limits in a positive sense; but, given the assumption of the rationality of the principles of cognition, one can assert the so-called "limits" of God's omnipotence negatively. Now contradiction is the cancellation of being; but only being can be the object of God's activity, so God cannot create a contradiction. Therefore if matter cannot at the same time be non-matter, matter cannot think. For matter (in either sense) cannot be non-concrete, non-individual, non-empirical. But the thinking of man through general ideas is precisely connected with non-individuality, with universality. Conceptual, intellectual cognition is universal, necessary, ontical, while matter-given to us empirically-is always individual, concrete, changeable, and temporal.

If we were to take into consideration the concept of immateriality related to the Aristotelian concept of matter, then we would call "immaterial" that side of being which is not potential and changeable from within, which is not the reason of the alteration of being. Now we know well that I myself am what I was several years before, and that I myself, am the same being, am continually the same center toward which I refer all my changeable, physiological acts, as well as purely psychic acts. In addition to the changeable element, there is in me a self-conscious element. Therefore, if in the "ego" we discover the human soul through philosophical explanation, then precisely the human soul as the ground of identity is the ground of the self-consciousness of the "Self." And it is not something ontically changeable or the ground of alteration, but, on the contrary, being the ground of self-conscious identity, it is thus the "immaterial" side of man.

If, on the other hand, we were to take the contemporary concept of matter, and, in relation to it, create a concept of immateriality, then we would call "immaterial" any being that is not a temporal-spatial measurable continuum. If, then, in the activity of our ego, we perceive the presence of such acts and of such a manner of activity, which precisely are not temporal-spatial, or changeable, then we will have the right to speak of the presence in us of acts immaterial in their content. In consequence, both the source of these acts as well as their subject is immaterial. The analyses of this problem can be conducted through an examination of the acts of intellectual cognition and, subsequently, of volitive activity.

CONCEPTS

Acts of conceptual intellectual cognition present a cognitive content detached from all the attributes of matter as a temporal-spatial continuum. For we form concepts distinct from impressions, concepts abstracted from matter and materializing conditions, general, necessary, universal concepts. And although these concepts refer to material objects, such as "man" for example, in their content there are no changeable, potential, spatial, temporally conditioned attributes.

> . . . It seems that intelligence, in pursuit of its aim, must transcend the phenomena of space and time. For beneath the particular, and the specific here and now, intelligence discovers the universal, the principle of unification and expresses it in the form of a personal judgment . . .[10]

ABSTRACT IDEAS

When we consider that we have ideas of immaterial "things," then the immateriality of the ego is shown even more conclusively. For if there existed in man only a material subject of cognition, then such a subject could cognize only what is material; what acts on it as a stimulus. Meanwhile, we understand such objects as "unity," "good," "beauty," "cause," "relation," "science," etc. We express judgments about these matters. No objects of this kind have anything in their structure that would be temporal-spatial, or quantifiably measurable in any manner. The objects, being in themselves immaterial, do not constitute a material stimulus for cognition; and yet they are cognitive, they awaken discussion, etc. Hence, the subject cognizing them is commensurate with objects of this type.

JUDGMENTS

The immateriality of cognition becomes clearer in the structure of judgments, which affirm the presence of certain attributes in the subject. In judgment there occurs a total and simultaneous grasp of the parts and the whole; there also appears the necessary perception of the belonging (or not) of the parts to the whole. This grasp of both the parts as well as the whole is a grasp not despite the "parts," nor by contact with the parts, but is total and simultaneous. Existential judgments in which we affirm existence also constitute an indicator that we are capable of grasping what in its nature is not matter.

SELF-CONSCIOUSNESS

The self-reflexive consciousness which accompanies all intentional acts is another indication of immateriality. As one modern writer says:

> In fact, to be ready to make contact is to be able to encounter and to welcome. Before we can welcome anything we must first withdraw into ourselves: that is, we must simultaneously possess ourselves and distinguish ourselves from that toward which we are moving, and this leads us back to a certain state of inwardness, which must be an awareness of and a presence to the self. Ready as he is to make contact, the knowing subject is not enclosed within himself, since he is capable of possessing being and of summing it up in himself in all its universality. Yet this capacity is linked to a deliverance from everything material, to the mind's situation beyond space and time.
>
> . . . This existence within oneself, unlike that of matter whose every part is external to every other part, is the privilege of the spirit, which is the subject of existence. To be within oneself, therefore necessarily implies a spiritually subsisting subject which is the source of all our intellectual acts, and for that very reason manifests itself as always present and disclosing itself everywhere.[11]

VOLITION

The volitive experiences of man are another sign of the immateriality of the human soul. Ordinarily, in a philosophical analysis of the act of love as a product of the human will, i.e., of rational desire, there are distinguished the objects of this love, the act of love itself, and the manner of its performance. An analysis of these moments of the act of love indicates a transcendence over matter and the presence of spirit as main factor of love.

Let us consider, now only in a cursory fashion, some aspects of this problem, subjecting to analysis the universal desire for happiness, and the concrete desire of good and love.

Philosophers have paid close attention to a characteristic division in this sphere. Blondel noted that the human will is always disposed toward something "more." No concrete wanting equals the constantly energetic capacity of the will, which is disposed toward infinity. (In Aquinas this division of the will was called "*appetitus naturalis*"—natural desire of the will, and "*appetitus elicitus*"—desire concretely brought forth in relation to a concrete good). At the same time, he observed that no concrete good constituting the object of an act of will appeases human desire, which on the strength of its inherent structure is directed toward universal good. This direction toward universal good is the natural desire for happiness, being the driving force of all concrete desires and at the same time concurrent with every emergent act of desire; the natural and never-extinguished desire for the Absolute: God. The richer man is in knowledge, the richer in material resources, the richer in love of others; the more often does the conviction accompany him that he has not possessed happiness, that the "something" that could satisfy him is always beyond him.

This division of the will into the desire for ultimate happiness and the desire for concrete goods testifies that the subject itself (man, soul) is in its nature infinitely receptive. The desire, unceasingly flowing from us, for an infinite happiness transcending all partial goods, indicates the source-subject, which must likewise transcend in existence material conditions amid which it finds itself.

SELF-MASTERY

Still another sign of the immateriality of the essential part of our "I" is the possibility of self-mastery. Only a spiritual and immaterial power can say "no" in relation to itself, and master its inclinations, because such mastery presupposes full reflection over oneself, and, simultaneously the grasp of oneself and the object of one's aspiration. Acts of reflective self-mastery, in the full sense of the term, cannot be observed anywhere in nature apart from man.

Hence, the fact of the immateriality of our ego-soul appears to be rationally justified. While it is possible to take these reflections further in relation to the concrete ways of man's activity, as Marcel does in his works, and show the increasing transcendence of the human spirit over matter, the signs shown here of man's transcendence and of the immateriality of his ego-soul are sufficient in order to maintain the justified conviction that I am someone subsistent, a subject, and not just "something" that is the result of the organization of material relations.

V. IMMORTALITY

Linked with the analyses conducted here is another essential human aspect of extreme importance: immortality. For, keeping in mind the fact of the ontical subsistence of the human "soul" and also its immateriality, one can perceive the ontical foundations of the immortality of the human soul, of the ego.

For if the soul possesses its own existence—experienced in the subjectivizing "I" organizing the body for itself—then in the moment of the disintegration of the body, which exists by the existence of the soul, the subsisting and immaterial soul, as the subject of acts immaterial in their structure, cannot cease to exist. It would perish only if it were the result of the bodily organization. The essential ground underlying the immortality of the human soul is its subsistence, the fact that existence (ascertained in the judgment, "I am") belongs immediately to the soul, which at the same time is the form of the body.

If existence belongs immediately to the soul, and to the body only and exclusively through the soul, then the destruction of the body does not entail the destruction of the subsisting substance that is the human soul-ego. Thomas briefly notes: "That which has existence through itself cannot either come into being or undergo destruction, except through itself. For this reason too, the soul cannot come into being by way of generation, i.e., material alteration, since it has an immaterial existence; and likewise it cannot cease to exist by way of natural destruction."[12] There would have to occur a specific intervention of the Absolute, who would annihilate the soul, since the soul in itself, being in its essence an uncomposed spirit, cannot forfeit existence. Only the Absolute, therefore, is the essential reason for the existence of the soul, and only he—and only by acting contrary to the natural order,—could annihilate it. Consequently the context of the existence of the soul is not nature, which the soul transcends through its cognition and love, but is "Absolute Being" alone, God as the person with whom the human spirit, coming to know or contemplate nature, carries on a dialogue ascending unceasingly beyond nature.

We daily encounter the problem of immortality and thereby its germinal solution in the repeatedly posed question: Will we continue to exist after death? Such questions are raised not only in words, but in the whole of human rational activity. The very character of our cognition, the use of necessary, universal concepts, the character of our judgments in one way or another affirming being; the simplest acts and declarations of love, manifesting themselves externally with the help of the quantifiers "forever," "never;" the whole of creative and cultural work, attempting in the course of changeable and transitory matter to leave behind a lasting trace of our thought; in sum, all that is somehow a rational expression of man, is an expression of transcendence beyond changeable matter, or is at least the question: "Will we continue to exist when the changeable state of matter, entering into our ontical structure, undergoes still further, still more radical, alterations, called death?"

CHAPTER V

MAN AND KNOWLEDGE

This chapter, entitled, *MAN AND KNOWLEDGE*, is divided into five sections: I. The fact of Human Knowledge, II. Objective Non-Contradictability of Knowledge, III. The Subjective Non-Contradictability of the Act of Knowing, IV. The Process of Intellectual Conceptual Knowledge, V. Fundamental Areas of Intellectual Life.

> The primary and distinctive moment in which man realizes himself in the fullest, is in his capacity of knowing. In this sense, man can be called a "knowledge maker." Knowledge involves reflection with respect to both object and subject matter.

KNOWLEDGE AND CONSCIOUSNESS

Ever since the time of Descartes, there has been strong debate as to the exact understanding of the nature of human knowledge. Descartes attempted to explain knowledge as ideas in his consciousness. The Cartesian heritage is therefore deceiving because it makes human knowledge something subjective: man knows not concrete things in the external world, but only ideas in his consciousness. Intellectual knowledge, correctly understood, is *objective because it is of real objects existing outside the mind of the knower.*

DEFINITION OF KNOWLEDGE

Knowledge, correctly understood, is not a meaning which appears in consciousness; but it is the understanding of a concrete thing under the aspect of a grasped meaning. The meaning which presents itself in consciousness is also a sign subordinated to the thing. Between the existing thing and man (through his cognitive apparatus, chiefly his intellect), a specific bond called *knowledge*, is effected.

I. THE FACT OF HUMAN KNOWLEDGE

Human knowledge involves two aspects: (a) external utterance and (b) an understanding of the sense of this utterance. Obviously, understanding the sense is considered to be the essential factor of cognition itself. However, the character and structure of the utterance emphasizes the specificity of man's cognition.

External cognitive utterances vary greatly: in speech, in writing, in art. When I stand on the street and notice a colored spot moving and making a characteristic sound, I say "dog." As Gilson says, "The dog and man are concrete individual beings . . . whose actual existence can be verified by sense perception. But the very word spoken by the observer is also a concrete, particular, material thing. As such, it is a sound produced by the vibration of the vocal chords. Such a biological and physical phenomenon can be observed, measured, recorded."[1]

Just as the sound of the voice is something material and measurable, so too the inscriptions which are left on paper, clay, stone or wood are something material. The external utterance is a material sign of an inner experienced meaning.

The understanding of the sense of an utterance is human cognition. We use vocal signals as signs whereby we communicate to someone a determined cognitive content. As Gilson says, "*Meaning* or *signification* has no materiality . . . We can hear a spoken word but we do not 'hear' its meaning. We understand it."[2]

UNIVERSALITY OF CONCEPTUAL KNOWLEDGE

In our cognition we are conscious of contents which are really general and which do not contain within themselves particular, concrete, spatio-temporal attributes.

Such a general expression or a universal can never be real; i.e., a really existing subject despite the fact that in a sentence construction, it appears as a subject. Thomas Aquinas called attention to this fact (ST, I, q.13, a.12) when he said that in every proposition the subject and predicate are only symbols of this same thing, but something different with respect to an apprehended attribute. For example, in the sentence, "Man is white," the expression "man" and "white" refer to the same real being, but one expression means in the same subject-being, the combination of notes which constitute humanity and the other, "whiteness."

Conceptual knowledge, then, which presents itself in the form of universals, concerns being, and not only some sensible impressions. And because man is thus bound with being, conceptual knowledge is necessary and changeless. The involvement of judgmental knowledge with being is even more apparent. In predicative judgments, the word "is" performs the function of a copula and it usually expresses a truth because it concerns being. In existential judgments, however, it actually affirms the existence of being. For our knowledge expressed in such a judgment is a *specific, psychical grasping of objective, real, ontical reality*. Above all, a factual ontic state exists really. Such a type of knowledge expressed in existential judgments is a cognitive grasping of a being, immediately, spontaneously and primarily.

ARGUMENTS FOR THE EXISTENCE OF INTELLECT

1. If universals and judgments concern being, this points, in man, to the existence of a special cognitive power that is higher than the senses and representations, which cannot affirm being but only something sensible. This power is the intellect or reason.

2. If universals are the identity of inter-relational relations of different things, then this type of identity of relations can be the object of only a rational, essentially higher knowledge than that of the senses.

3. The sense or meaning of man's cognitive expression, and an understanding of this sense, demands the existence of reason (intellect) as the source of these concepts and judgments.

4. Whatever came into existence which previously did not exist, has a commensurate cause. And since we are aware of ourselves as the authors (or creators) of concepts and judgments within us, there exists, therefore, an undeniable cause of these concepts and judgments. This cause cannot be only an organic, sensible "apparatus" if the meaning of our statements is spiritual and immaterial in its ontic structure, and manner of functioning. Hence there exists a suprasensible, non-organic source which philosophy traditionally calls reason or intellect.

5. The existence of a reason which is different from the senses as the cause of our intellectual knowledge can be further established by an analysis of more specialized manners of cognition, such as conscience and self-cognition.[3]

II. OBJECTIVE NON-CONTRADICTABILITY OF KNOWLEDGE

If being presents itself as an object of our intellectual knowledge, we must determine how this "being-object" of human knowledge should be understood.

It is customary to say that the proper object of intellectual cognition is neither what is given us in sensible perception nor the cognitive forms of a purely spiritual, intellectual intuition. The object properly consists in contents given in intellectually cognitive forms which have been attained by way of abstraction from sensible perception, and these are called the sensibly cognized essences of things.

MATERIAL AND FORMAL OBJECT OF KNOWLEDGE

Usually a distinction is made between the material object and formal object of cognition. The material object is simply any thing whatsoever, with its entire ontic endowments, with all the traits it possesses, e.g., an apple, along with its weight, smell, taste, color etc. However, the same material object can represent a collection of various formal objects. In the case of an apple, its taste is the formal object of the human sense of taste, and color, of sight.

The formal object of human cognition possesses two dimensions: the first, "the *how*" (the proper object), the so-called essences of things that are sensibly cognizable; and the second, "the *what*" (the adequate object) is being— that which we know.

Man naturally tends to turn all objects of the human mind into abstract essences. As Thomas Aquinas says, the proper object of the human intellect is "that which a thing is." Since these essences are reducible to their definitions, the complex structure of reality is represented by a pattern of abstract notions. To conceive such notions, to define them to separate them by judgments: this is the normal intellectual activity of man. Philosophy has always concerned itself with analysis, description and classification of separate entities, sometimes called ideas. These ideas become better understood when they are studied in a setting of represented sensible perceptions.

But if "the how," i.e., essences, are the object of intellectual cognition, this does not mean that being reduces itself to essence alone. Thomas Aquinas frequently warned that essence is not the most important element of being. Rather, it is the *esse* (act of to be), the "be-ing" of being which is more fundamental to the actually existing being. There are, therefore, two elements to be considered: essence and existence.

SPIRIT OF ABSTRACTION

The spirit of abstraction, which substitutes definitions for things, defines and regards science as the creation of abstract concepts and their coordination. This error has had notably harmful effects in the history of philosophy. As E. Gilson points out, it is probably the most significant single source of political and social disorders, of intolerance and fanaticism, because it substitutes the definition for the defined; and nothing is more uncompromising than an essence, its quiddity and definition. For all abstract notions are radically opposed to concrete reality.

Such a position which affirms only abstractly-seen essences of things, is the foundation for all essentialisms; it is also responsible for the fragmentation of all sciences. In the history of philosophy, such a position objectivized "the how" we know and confused it with "the what" we know. Platonism is a classical example of such a confusion[4]

ESSENCE AND EXISTENCE

Being, as we have said, has two principles: essence and existence; moreover, a real essence can exist only when it is the essence of an existing being. Hence a real grasping of the essence is an actual grasping of being from one side; i.e., from the side of its content. This is why even our conceptual cognition puts us in touch with a thing, because it is in contact with an essence which belongs to existence. It is understood through the existence of this being whose essence it is.

In addition to conceptual knowledge, man also uses judgmental knowledge, and that of reasoning. The spirit of abstraction likewise affected these higher and nobler types of cognition, interpreting them as the mere production of new concepts.

PRIMACY OF EXISTENCE

In existential judgments, we affirm the fact of the actual existence of some concrete thing. The direct affirmation of some concrete thing is simultaneously an affirmation of being, given us in the most primary knowledge: being as the primary cognizable object (*ens ut primum cognitum*). In an existential judgment, the very fact or "act" of being is that which strikes us as most important in being itself. The fact of the being's existence is the foundation of the "be-ing" of a given being. Before I know what is the content of being, I first know that it *exists*. Hence the affirmation of the fact of existence is our most primary act of cognition—an act of pre-reflective cognition. It is only then that the next act of abstraction and of creating abstractive concepts can be accomplished.[5]

From the time of Aristotle, it has been observed that the foundation of intellectual abstractive operations is the sensible perception of the object. However, this act of abstracting from sensible data, presupposes the very fact of the existence of a concrete object of our sensible perception. Hence the human cognitive perception of the fact of a known being's existence is even more primary than the consciously sensible perception.[6]

Existential judgments bring us into contact with the very be-ing of being, and this primary affirmation makes possible the construction of concepts and of the issuing of judgments and reasoning. These existential judgments put us into contact with reality from the side of that which is the "root" of the reality of things (from the side of actual existence). Hence every kind of cognitive operation has its foundation in being, in reality. Without a pre-reflective contact with being which exclusively is the "nourishment" of our thought and knowledge, we would be doomed to idealism.

PREDICATIVE JUDGMENTS

Predicative judgments are completely different from existential ones. They are composed of subject and predicate, whose "soul" is the copula "is." The subject and predicate which appear as universal are two general traits of the very being whose component elements are evident in judgment as "subject" and "predicate." Hence every "real cognition" has simultaneously an essential and existential character. Being is first, but it is always; it accompanies all our representations. Cognition does not go beyond being, since beyond being is nothing.

We cite here a well known Scholastic example: that which I first see only from a distance is initially, for me, only something: being. If the object comes closer, I see that it is an animal, but it remains "being." If it were to come even closer, I would see that it is some kind of man and, eventually, that it is Peter. Being, therefore, is the first object of intellectual cognition, not only in the sense that it is already contained in the first known object, but also that it is contained in every known object. Hence every cognition is a cognition of being.[7]

III. THE SUBJECTIVE NON-CONTRADICTABILITY OF THE ACT OF KNOWING

Three systems of thought propose to solve the problem of the possibility of man's intellectual knowledge:

A. A system of innate ideas or a priori categories making valid knowledge possible;

B. A system of empiricism and, connected with it, a concept of concrete abstraction;

C. A system of empirical rationalism with the notion of universal abstraction and its non-contradictory elements.

The first two proposed solutions, which are diametrically opposed to each other, will be shown to be wrong, because of the absurd consequences that are linked with them. The third position avoids the absurd consequences, but its explanations will have a negative rather than a positive character; and, in this sense, it will recall the general solutions indicated through metaphysics.

A. A PRIORI SYSTEMS OF INNATE IDEAS
SENSIBLE AND INTELLECTUAL KNOWLEDGE

The problem of the opposition between sensible and intellectual knowledge arose almost concomitantly with the origin of Greek philosophy. Parmenides equated truth with intellectual knowledge and error with the way of senses. The way of intellectual knowledge leads to truth, because it is the way of being. Being manifests itself to the human intellect as an immediately given object of knowledge so that to think and to be are one and the same. Plato, St. Augustine, Descartes, Leibniz, Malebranche and Gioberti held that our intellectual concepts do not arise by way of an intellectual activity on empirical data but they are somehow given along with human nature. These concepts are innate or they appear at suitable occasions.

PLATO

Plato held that man as soul knew ideas directly before he was joined to the body. He knew them in previous incarnations (theory of innate ideas).[8]

ST. AUGUSTINE

St. Augustine, who accepted the notion of a soul using the body but also as needing illumination for knowledge of necessary, changeless and eternal truths, held that the source of these truths could be only God. And hence the existence of immutable truths in mutable minds is proof of the existence of God.[9]

DESCARTES

According to Descartes, there exist in us certain innate ideas. Some seem to be born with me; others come from without; and the rest are to be made by myself. There is a power in my intellect which, without the cooperation of material things, brings out the innate ideas, which are the objective representations of things. These ideas do not belong to experience, even though their use takes place jointly with sensible knowledge.[10]

LEIBNIZ

Leibniz held that it is impossible for one thing to have a causal influence on another ("the monads are self-enclosed and have no windows"). The soul, as chief monad, attains a knowledge of the world automatically on the occasion of sense perceptions. Acts of knowledge correspond to reality because of "Pre-established Harmony," whereby God so ordered the world that the activity of one thing corresponds to the actions of another.

ONTOLOGISM

Ontologism holds that the idea is not only a psychic human product but its own reality. Intellectual knowledge occurs through an immediate union of the knowing soul with its object, who is God himself. Ontologism maintains that our knowledge cannot refer to subjective ideas, since they are only modifications of our own psyche. Hence only something objective and eternal can be this object.

CRITIQUE

Obviously such false positions are due to a failure to distinguish between the mode of cognition and the mode of existing; and they lead either to a pantheism or an angelism and, ultimately, to a denial of cognition itself.

B. EMPIRICISM

ENGLISH EMPIRICISTS

From a certain point of view, English empiricism (Locke, Hume, J.S. Mill et al.) can be treated as a continuation of Descartes' ideas. Both Locke and Hume based their entire philosophical systems on an analysis of the epistemological point of departure previously proposed by Descartes. The difference is that Descartes believed in innate ideas, while the empiricists considered these ideas to be empirical in character.

LOCKE

Locke replaced universal concepts with general images, which he called "ideas." These general, hazy images lacked individuating notes and were the result of a concrete kind of abstraction; i.e., the separation of certain notes in a concretely saturated image. Such an abstracted image is general because it can represent and replace all the particular images of a certain attribute.

BERKELEY

While Locke held that general images are something fictional and created only by our mind and existing in it, Berkeley believed that such ideas exist only when our consciousness is aware of them. Abstraction is merely a function of attention whereby we concentrate our attention on certain notes of a representation.

HUME

D. Hume distinguished between concrete expressions, sensations and ideas. An idea arises from an impression, which is more lively and more permeated with concreteness. All ideas, both simple and complex, are concrete representations of singulars. Habit and association enable these particular, concrete representations to become as if universal and to perform the function of conception.

MILL

John Stuart Mill's empiricism held that the meaning of general terms depends not on some kind of general conception, but on a series of particular images, united in our consciousness according to certain notes or aspects. Hence attention and association of particular images replace abstraction and universal concepts.

TAINE

H. Taine also rejected the existence of universal concepts. In their place he advocated a kind of tendency we have to call things by a common term. When we think about something abstract, we have in our consciousness only words, accompanied by hazy and indistinct representations (images). On the other hand, what corresponds to an abstract concept is not the hazy representation but the word which evokes representations that belong to a class connected with the name. A substitute function of words, and mutual association of words and representations suffice to explain universal concepts.

RIBOT

Ribot, however, contended that the fact of knowledge cannot be explained with the help of such nominalistic assumptions. By distinguishing between meaningful and meaningless words, he held that so-called "universal concepts" are habits or individual dispositions that are formed in the area of consciousness. Hence a universal concept is composed of a series of elements: habit, memory of prolonged characteristics extended from representations, and an activity omitting changing characteristics.

CRITIQUE

In sum, a priori rationalistic theories held that the intellect is a specific power or quality of soul contacting directly a spiritual or ideal object. The second group of theories denied the existence of the intellect as distinct from a sensible apparatus, especially of representations, of a cognitive power. Neither group of theories deals with the fact that our abstractive, intellectual cognition is intimately connected with a sensibly representational cognition.

We must therefore seek a middle course, which affirms a connection between intellectual knowledge and sensible sources, and also points to the "structure" of the subject of knowing acts; i.e., the intellect.

C. STRUCTURE OF THE INTELLECT
ARISTOTLE AND THOMAS AQUINAS

Extreme rationalism and extreme empiricism have failed to explain satisfactorily the fact of human knowledge. The most coherent explanation seems to be that of Aristotle and St. Thomas Aquinas, one which has been accepted by various thinkers over the centuries. This explanation involves three fundamental theses:

(a) The foundation of our human knowledge concerning its contents is found in sensible perceptions—otherwise there can be no contact with the world of reality.

(b) The contents of human knowledge testify that they come from a special, immaterial power, called the intellect, which differs from senses.

(c) We must accept an apperceptive power which makes possible (non-contradictory) the fact of knowing universals.

We shall now examine the contents of the three theses.

(a) *The unique foundation for the contents of human knowledge are sense perceptions.*

Aristotle pointed out that "there is nothing in the intellect which did not exist previously in the senses." And while the knowledge acquired by the intellect is essentially different from the structure of sensible cognitive acts, sensible knowledge is the unique and irreplaceable source of the contents of our cognitive life. Everyday experiences, as well as experimental psychology, confirm the complete dependence of our intellectually cognitive contents on given data of sensible knowledge.

A priorism and ontologism were rejected as unsatisfactory because they held that knowledge comes directly from the sphere of the spirit alone. Such positions would cut off our knowledge from the actually existing material world, which constitutes the source of the contents of our intellect. Hence sensible knowledge is absolutely necessary for our intellectual content.

MAN'S BODY AND SOUL

Further, man's structure as a psycho-physical being indicates that in the reality of the human functions of our psyche, there is an essential connection between the spiritual side of human cognition and its material side.

Man's union of body and soul, and his structure as this kind of entity, would be completely unintelligible if man did not draw his cognitive contents from sensible perceptions. In fact, the soul draws its benefits from this union. This can be achieved only in its proper sphere of acting; i.e., in intellectually cognitive functions in which the material-sensible aspect is involved. And since the body and matter do not enter into the structure of intellectual ideas, they are present only at the genesis and articulation of the intellectual structure of the ideas themselves.[11]

According to St. Thomas, sensible knowledge performs yet another function: the images (phantasms) actively impress their stamp on the intellect. We shall examine this instrumental causality of sensible knowledge below.[12]

(b) *The intellectually-cognitional contents do not contain anything material in them.*

Since we use universal concepts which are immaterial in their very structure, and these concepts constantly arise within us, they must also contain their own source or power which produces these concepts. This power is the intellect as the direct and efficient cause of concepts. The necessity for the intellect's existence as the direct source of our cognitional knowledge is something indisputable, if we are to explain why men know universally, really and necessarily with the help of judgments and reasoning. The intellect, which is directly responsible for our intellectual cognition and thinking, stands at the basis of the entire human culture.

The sensible aspect of human knowledge is essentially different from the intellectually-cognitive aspect. We attain sensible knowledge along with images under the influence of physical and psychological stimuli. Our senses are open to the activity of the material surroundings, but they never go beyond the limits of matter. However, by basing ourselves on this sensible and representational knowledge, we come to a self-awareness and a recognition of a spiritual content, or even of negation, of defects or of relation. Such a different kind of knowledge demands a separate knowing power, which we call reason.

ARGUMENTS FOR THE EXISTENCE
OF REASON OR INTELLECT

There are numerous arguments for the existence of reason as a special spiritual source of our ideas, and of the affirmation of existence, especially in judgments. A highly convincing proof for the existence of reason is our self-cognition. This is an instance of full reflection that grasps "oneself," one's own "I," insofar as it is the performer of cognitive acts and the objects and contents actualized through the cognitive "I." Self-cognition testifies to the experience of a cognitive realm marked by two extremes: "I" as the permanent performer of cognitive and other acts of mine; and, secondly, the "objective" contents that are gathered from the surrounding world and that intrude themselves on me, but which are never "I."

Self-cognition testifies to a spiritual source of knowledge, comprehending cognitive acts, insofar as they are accomplished through my own "I" and they affect "non-I."

Reason, as the source of intellectual cognition, manifests itself as "power," as different from senses and imagination, an automatic source of cognition.

A denial of the intellect as a source of our universal, necessary knowledge (of judgmental knowledge) would be to deny a phenomenon in nature which is MAN himself. On the one hand, we would note the uniqueness of the phenomenon of the "human fact" in nature. On the other, we would not accept any commensurable essential cause of this uniqueness.

All indications of man's uniqueness are reduced to the fact that man possesses a different power of knowing than animals, and this power is precisely reason, intellect, mind. These are different names for the same source of knowledge, which is a power capable of grasping, intellectually, being as it is in itself.

(c) *We must accept an apperceptive power which makes possible the fact of knowing universals.*

If this is clearly the case, then we must accept in man the existence of a power which is essentially connected with intellectual cognition and which makes this knowledge possible, and which acts in a stable and natural manner. From the time of the Greeks, this power has been called "agent intellect."

AGENT INTELLECT

Only Aristotle's and, principally, Thomas Aquinas' theory of agent and possible (properly *knowing*) intellect, enables us to avoid the positions of both sensualism and idealism. Abstraction is absolutely necessary in order to draw our cognitive content from sense impressions, to change concrete contents into universal ones, and to elucidate a necessary connection. For abstraction to become a reality, there absolutely must exist some kind of intellectual power, which will make it possible to perceive the intellectual, universal and necessary contents in given sensible representations. The theory of the agent intellect presupposes a vision of the ontic context of man's cognition.

Man's body and the surrounding material world constitute a kind of environment of human cognition. A thought, even though it is immersed in a material world, is not completely absorbed by matter. In fact, thought governs, dominates and orders matter for its own purposes. The problem of the possibility of knowing matter involves a twofold aspect: (a) immateriality of thought in its ontic structure and, (b) the materiality of the object of knowledge.

Matter cannot immediately influence the intellect, because a non-being cannot act on a being. If matter were to act directly on intellect and thought, then both would have to be material. But we have rejected this hypothesis.

Another possibility is that thought should act on matter and make it conform to its needs. But prior to its actualization, thought does not as yet exist. To hold that it does, would be to accept some kind of idealism; i.e., that thought exists before knowing, or that knowing does not consist of a union of object and the articulation of thought. Neither could we hold that the intellect "receives" content from reality. But we have established that our intellect is completely dependent on the content of the object of knowledge.

After having rejected two diametrically opposed propositions, we must finally accept the third. Matter, understood as a spatio-temporal continuum, cannot influence an immaterial spirit which has no extended and contiguous limits. Hence matter cannot influence the intellect as some immaterial source of knowledge. If objects were to determine their individual contents directly through themselves, then the intellect would know them individually, concretely, materially and mutably, just as senses know them in their sensibly cognitive act. For if intellectual knowledge does not show itself to be material in acts (conceptually-cognitive), then this proves that it is not matter that determines the intellect directly through itself. Rather, the intellect itself is active in relation to existing material objects: it itself uncovers immaterial structures in matter and thereby it itself liberates and somehow "structures" the immaterial in a given material object, so that it can now directly influence the intellect as a knowing power.

AGENT INTELLECT AND POSSIBLE INTELLECT

The intellect as *agent* constitutes intellectually cognitive forms; it constitutes them in sensibly-cognitional data. Hence the sense impression created by man who is knowing sensibly becomes subjected, as it were, to a "shining" by a naturally active (agent) intellect. This agent intellect reveals notes that are structural, necessary and separated from matter and hence it universalizes. In this way, the "de-materialized" impression can have an effect on the intellectually-knowing power called the knowing or possible intellect.[13]

Hence the sensibly-knowing impression formulated in and by man becomes "de-materialized" by the activity of human, spiritual-psychic powers. This same impression (image) is simultaneously "read" by the senses and, at the same time, dematerialized and prepared for "reading" by the intellect. This natural dematerialization of impressions, and especially of images, is performed by a psychical power connected with intellectual cognition. This psychical power we call the "agent intellect." This power, however, does not bring about the act of knowing, but rather makes knowing possible by constituting an object proportionate to intellectual cognition. For the object, as a dematerialized image, is able to affect the intellect and to determine it to know itself. The moment that the possible (actively-knowing) intellect unites with the dematerialized image—as already with an intellectually-cognitive form—the act of universal, necessary and essential knowing takes place.

The agent intellect, therefore, is a power that actually constitutes the object of intellectual knowledge. For in themselves, objects of intellectual knowledge as material things or only as representations or sensible images, are only *potential* objects of intellectual knowledge.[14]

Cajetan (a commentator on Aristotle and Aquinas) argued that because the object of intellectual knowledge in act does not exist of itself (only material objects exist), an actual object of intellectual knowledge must be constructed and produced. Hence there exists in man a natural power which constitutes actually the objects of intellectual knowledge. This power is called the agent intellect.

The essential function of the agent intellect is the production of intellectually-knowing forms, which can become the proportional object of our intellectual knowledge. Intellectual forms which are so constituted have the power, through themselves, of determining the intellectually-knowing power of the so-called "possible intellect." They enable the intellect to know precisely this object, which is presented by an intellectually-knowing form that has been freed from material and singular conditions.

In sum, the agent intellect fashions from the sense datum (image) an actual and dematerialized object of intellectual knowledge; and this is precisely why it is called an agent intellect. The possible intellect becomes moved and roused from its knowing passivity by the dematerialized form, which now becomes an actual object of intellectual knowledge. Hence the possible, knowing intellect, in relation to its object of knowledge, is "passive." It is in potency to knowledge.

PLATO AND ARISTOTLE

Aristotle did not know how to develop properly the matter of universal and conceptual knowledge. Plato had argued that there exist in the intellectual world, just as in the material world, actual objects of knowledge. These are the Ideas which constitute the object of conceptual, necessary knowledge. Aristotle rejected the possibility of the existence of Ideas "beyond things." This would lead to the absurdity of realizing an infinite series. Aristotle accepted a process of abstraction and the existence of two intellects: agent and possible (passive) intellect. The function of the agent intellect would be the furnishing of immediate and adequate conditions of knowing to the possible intellect, as its own intellectually knowing power.

Aristotle's explanations in the *De Anima* were so equivocal and obscure that they gave rise to numerous conflicting theories. Thomas Aquinas advanced a moderate position by holding that both agent and possible intellects are powers of the soul, and that there exists a spiritual faculty which possesses no bodily organ.

IV. THE PROCESS OF INTELLECTUAL, CONCEPTUAL KNOWLEDGE

ST. THOMAS AQUINAS' THEORY

According to St. Thomas' theory,[15] the entire process of knowledge involves the following six moments:

(1) Sensible knowledge is the foundation of every content of man's knowledge. (Experimental psychology testifies to the complete dependence of our concepts on appropriate sources of sense knowledge.)[16]

(2) Sensible knowledge, especially images, is subject to the activity of the agent intellect, which actualizes the object of intellectual knowledge in the given images. "To actualize" means the same as "to immaterialize an image."[17]

(3) The image which has been dematerialized by the agent intellect becomes the actual object of knowledge for the possible intellect. Hence it acts on the knowing intellect by impressing on it, its form or dematerialized

cognitive picture of the material thing. Prior to the "activity" of the agent intellect, the image is singular and material. Once it has been dematerialized and proportioned to intellectual knowledge, it determines the intellect to know that which, in its image, is expressed as a representation of the thing.

(4) If the intellect is in potency in relation to its object, and if it cannot by itself pass from potential to actual knowledge, there exists a proportional agent, which releases in the intellect the process of this knowledge. This agent is traditionally called "form." Knowing is an act of the knower, and not some kind of known thing. Therefore the known thing does not of itself act. Rather, it is the intellectually knowing subject who must determine himself to the knowledge of the non-subjective content. Hence the known object is in the subject, but only intentionally as contents.

The content of the object, therefore, exists according to the way the subject (man) exists. It is called an intellectually-knowing form which determines the intellect to the process of knowing this content. The form then is a determining and directing agent of intellectual knowledge. As a non-contradictable agent of an inborn process, it cannot become something conscious. Only the end of the process becomes conscious. This is the concept, and we can make it the object of our reflective knowledge.[18]

(5) The causative reason of this intellectually knowing form, according to St. Thomas, is the image, insofar as it is dematerialized. St. Thomas suggests that the image which is being dematerialized can be known in itself, as an instrumental agent. But the "light" of the agent intellect is the principal, actualizing agent in this activity.

The intelligible form is singular in existence and universal in representation. Being singular, it is also immaterial, since it originated in an immaterial intellect. At the same time it is universal in its representation.

(6) The intellect which has been "fecundated" with an intellectually-knowing form, achieves a knowledge of things which culminates in the production of a concept. When we say that the intellect knows the *essence* of a thing, we mean that we grasp a thing's attributes, usually in a sketchy way. When the human intellect knows the essence of a thing that is represented in an image, it recognizes this essence under the aspect of being, as *something intelligible* (knowable).[19]

* * * * *

This process of intellectual knowledge just outlined is based on St. Thomas' explanations. It accepts completely the reality of sense knowledge. At the same time, it acknowledges intellectual knowledge, which is genetically connected with sense information. Finally, it not only establishes the fact of conceptual knowledge but it also presents an organized theory explaining the process of intellectual knowledge.

V. FUNDAMENTAL AREAS OF INTELLECTUAL LIFE

Aristotle distinguished three activities of human life: (1) THEORIA (comtemplation) (2) PRAXIS (behavior) (3) POESIS (productive activity).

Aristotle and Thomas Aquinas held that this triple division applied to knowledge in the following way: if human knowledge is ordered exclusively to truth, it is called *theoretical knowledge* (contemplation); if it is related to activity, it is *practical knowledge*; if to an external production in matter, it is *productive science*.

St. Thomas further held that when we emphasize the structure of the object, we speak of *speculabile, agibile,* and *factibile*.

(1) *Speculabile* is the object of man's purely theoretical (informational) knowledge, whereby the knower strives to inform himself about the factual state of a thing. Truth is both the purpose and ultimate criterion of value of this knowledge.

(2) *Agibile* concerns itself with man's moral conduct. It actualizes itself in acts of conscience which direct moral decisions.

(3) *Factibile* directs creative, aesthetic and productive knowledge. It is connected with man's culture.

I. THEORETICAL INFORMATIONAL KNOWLEDGE

Theoretical informational knowledge is at the basis of other areas of knowledge. Prescientific or common sense knowledge is a kind of informational knowledge. Its characteristics are spontaneity and lack of organization and proper foundation, whereas scientific knowledge possesses its own methodology, organization and proportional organization.

In prescientific knowledge, man is rather passive, and reality acts upon him. His intellect develops, as if automatically, without any preestablished direction. And even if it is not an organized knowledge, nevertheless it is not completely uncritical, since it is ontically grounded and some kind of reality corresponds to its known contents. Despite the fact that prescientific knowledge lacks logical tools and it contains no organized positions, it does form the basis for everyday human life.

Theoretically scientific knowledge, on the other hand, is a methodical, reflected and directed knowledge. It is organized according to some model and proportionally grounded according to accepted theses. Scientific knowledge passes through two stages. The first consists in gathering information within the extension of a given science and under the direction of a master. The learner merely acquires information (he is "led") and makes no new intellectual discoveries. The second phase involves the making of personal discoveries which enrich mankind's universal understanding of the world.

Classical philosophy has defined scientific theoretical knowledge as "the correct use of reason in the sphere of the *speculabile* ." It is thus the work of reason as a discursively knowing power, which is directed by the very constitution of things. The *speculabile* as the object of theoretical knowledge contains the notes of (a)necessity, (b)immutability, (c)universality.

TWO THEORIES CONCERNING NECESSITY IN KNOWLEDGE

There are two classical answers concerning the objective foundation for necessity in knowledge: (a) Platonic-Aristotelian and (b) Kantian.

According to Plato and Aristotle, cognitive necessity is explained by the ontic arrangement of things. For Plato, the Ideas were "behind" a thing and were necessity itself. Aristotle held that the form, which organizes matter and constitutes the ontical contents of a thing, is the ultimate element which establishes necessary existence and knowability.

Kant held that the necessary character of knowledge flows, not from things, but from the structure of the knowing mind, which is then an a priori category. Hence the a priori category of necessity is a projection of our ego.

CRITIQUE

The realist position holds that necessary knowledge takes place within the limits of universal or analogico-transcendental concepts. These concepts disclose the non-contradictable, ontic agents of the fact of existence of analogically universal being. This is the area of philosophy.[20]

IMMUTABILITY AND UNIVERSALITY

Along with the attribute of necessity, philosophy has traditionally spoken of the immutability and universality of knowledge. Immutability, which has its foundation in things but is attained through the cognitive grasping of necessary structures, emphasizes the permanence and value of science.

Universality of concepts seems to be based not on the thing itself but on the human intellect which accomplishes the actualization. Through abstraction from material, singular notes, the intellect presents to us universal science when it is "anchored" in things.

NOUS, EPISTEME, SOPHIA

In theoretically informational knowledge, Aristotle distinguished three fundamental phases of development:

(1) *NOUS*, or the introductory phase, relies on the perception of first principles of being. In order to reason and accomplish various knowing operations, there must be a beginning, a "reading" of the fundamental intelligible contents; e.g., that what is, is, and that being is not non-being.

(2) *EPISTEME*. The second phase is called EPISTEME. In reality, it is "reasoning" in the widest sense. Different sciences have methodically-cognitive, organized and well founded steps which represent a kind of reasoning.[21]

(3) *SOPHIA*. The third and final phase, which crowns man's intellectually theoretical knowledge, is SOPHIA (wisdom); this can be recognized today as philosophy. This phase is the final judgment equally of the fact of knowledge, as well as of the most universal, analogical object of knowledge which is being.

II. PRACTICAL OR PRUDENTIAL KNOWLEDGE

Practical or prudential knowledge stands at the basis of all human conduct. This type of knowledge does not deal with reality as it presents itself in permanent, necessary structural aspects. It deals with *me*, as one performing actions. To accomplish something as a person, i.e., consciously and freely, I must first knowingly determine myself to action. Now human action is ultimately determined not through nature but through knowledge, which appears as a practical judgment, "Do this now, in such and such a way." Such a judgment presupposes a concrete knowledge of a changing situation, an acceptance of some kind of rules of conduct and of locating oneself as having to act concretely under all these concrete conditions.

There are three stages in this area of knowledge: (1) knowledge of principal rules of conduct, (2) act of conscience (practical reason), and (3) practical wisdom of experienced people.

(1) Knowledge of principal rules of conduct. These rules derive from a natural, rational law of acting, expressed in the form of a judgment, "Good should be done." This is an affirmation in practical language, in the area of prudence. It is a law of conduct which sets forth the whole order of morality.

(2) Act of conscience (practical reason) is improved through conscience, and forms a decision about acting or not acting. In every act of decision, there is a concretely-knowing moment that appears as a practical judgment, with whose aid we determine ourselves to this or that action. The union of the moment of choice of the practical judgment and the contents of a judgment, which determines the character of our action, constitutes the essential aspects of a decision.

This decision is a moral one because it is always related to a norm of human conduct. This norm is the good which is recognized by man, and it now takes on the form of duty that should be performed in the right manner. (This entire area is called *prudence*.)[22]

(3) The third stage is practical wisdom of experienced people. This type of worldly wisdom does not result from argumentation or cognitive analysis. It is testimony flowing from rich personal contexts.

III. POIETIC (CREATIVE, PRODUCTIVE, CONSTRUCTIVE) KNOWLEDGE

The goal of poietic (creative) knowledge is neither information about reality (area of informational knowledge), nor a realization of the good in the strict sense (area of practically-prudential knowledge). Its goal and basic criterion is beauty itself in the widest meaning, understood in a transcendental sense.[23]

Creatively productive knowledge expresses itself in the construction of new, intentional objects from the elements given us in informational knowledge. Creative knowledge stands at the basis of all kinds of cultural creativeness and it constructs all kinds of objects that belong to man's culture.[24]

Like informational and practical knowledge, creative knowledge also has three phases: (1) its purely creative and artistic phase, (2) its productive phase (creative ideas transmitted to a production in external matter), and (3) its phase of aesthetic perception.

(1) Creative and artistic phase. This phase is also called "artistic vision." In ancient Greece, artistic creativity was considered a special gift that cannot be learned. The artist was the chosen one of the gods.

(2) Productive phase. Art, understood as the execution or making of something in external matter, should be *recta ratio factibilium*, i.e., a right reason directed by the content of that which should be made. The technique of "incarnating" thought in matter has been named from its creative, productive, technical knowledge, art.[25]

(3) Aesthetic perception.

Ingarden explored the third phase of knowledge, i.e., aesthetic knowledge and the fashioning of an aesthetic picture within oneself, i.e., of the recipient. This type of knowledge has as its aim, the pleasure that follows from the knowledge of artistic works.[26]

In the aesthetic perception of beauty and in the construction of an aesthetic picture, there are three phases:

(1) initial emotion directing our knowledge to a given object so that it "excludes" the knowledge of other objects;

(2) a collection of cognitive acts concerning the artistic object in which we grasp an ensemble of coordinated elements;

(3) a personal pleasure flowing from a contemplative type of knowledge of an object, which is given us for an aesthetic "seeing".

CHAPTER VI

INTENTIONALITY OF
KNOWLEDGE AND CULTURE

The connection between knowledge and culture is beyond dispute. We shall now examine the nature of culture under the following three headings: I. The General Meaning of the Expression "Culture," II. Understanding of Intentionality, and III. The Intentional Aspect of Cultural Works.

I. GENERAL MEANING OF THE EXPRESSION "CULTURE"

DEFINITION

Overlooking a purely verbal explanation (*cultura* from the Latin *colere*, to cultivate), we use the term culture to denote everything which comes from man's activity or production. It can also be viewed as a transformation or "intellectualization" of nature. In the widest sense, culture can include everything which exists in nature as natural, and which is, or was, subject to transformation under the direction of the intellect. Hence manifestations of the human spirit, insofar as they are guided by the intellect, human work and activity caused by the intellect, and creations of material nature which have been changed by the human intellect: all these constitute the domain of culture.[1]

DIVISIONS

Culture can be further divided into so-called objective, subjective and functional culture, depending on what we submit to the productive or adaptive power of the human mind. Hence we have culture which is (1) *objective*: objects of nature which have been modified by human thought, (2) *subjective*: the human subject itself, to the extent that it is capable of being subject to the human intellect in a permanent or transitory way, (3) *functional*: human activities themselves, especially the act of the intellect, which can be further intelligently improved.

Culture can also be understood in the (1) biological sense, as furnishing man with some niche, which nature does not provide, and (2) eschatological sense, which reaches beyond to the Transcendent. Lastly, culture may be divided into culture which is individual, social, national; of the masses, state, philosophical, scientific, religious, literary, and artistic; of painters and musicians, agrarian, industrial etc.

II. UNDERSTANDING OF INTENTIONALITY

We shall now examine the question of intentionality which has been studied by F. Brentano, the phenomenologists and contemporary Thomists.

ST. THOMAS AQUINAS

The primary understanding of intentionality is connected with the philosophical and theological conceptions of St. Thomas Aquinas.[2] In Thomistic philosophy and theology, God is the only self-intelligible being, who possesses completely within himself the reason for his existence. All other beings have a participated or derivative existence, since their existence is imparted to them; it is as if they are an "influx" from the Absolute God. Thomas called this existence *esse fluens*, partial, flowing, not firm. He also called it *intentional existence*, as an equivalent of *existence by participation*.

INTENTIONALITY OF ACTIVITY

Along with the concept of intentionality of existence, St. Thomas also spoke of the intentionality of activity (especially in the case of efficient-instrumental causes). In such a case e.g., the activity of a pen in relation to writing, the instrument's activity is actualized by the influence of efficient causality.

St. Thomas also used extensively the notion of intentionality in explaining the cognitional way of existence of objects in the senses and in a knowing intellect. However, he did not concern himself with the question of the intentional existence of objects which result from the human cognitive psyche, e.g., artifacts.[2]

BRENTANO

F. Brentano (nineteenth century) explored the idea of intentionality. He called the cognitive objects which are in consciousness "intentional objects," since consciousness is directed toward them (*intendere*) and, as a result, he reduced these objects to psychical acts.

HUSSERL

E. Husserl protested against this position by emphasizing that the meaning or essence of an intentional being is, in no degree, reducible to psychical acts themselves. In Husserl's own words: "We understand under intentionality the unique peculiarity of experience to be conscious of something." (*Ideas*, I, par. 84) We must emphasize the great difference between acts of consciousness and the object which is presented in consciousness. Only the meaning which is presented in the acts is an intentional meaning or intentional object. Hence in an intentional object we must distinguish (1) that which is perceived (2) the manner in which it is grasped (3) the aspect under which we see it, e.g., as a whole, a part etc. Obviously, the intentional object is different from the transcendental object itself in relation to consciousness.

INGARDEN

R. Ingarden likewise referred to Husserl's conception and he developed his own theory in a series of works on aesthetics. Ingarden's analysis of intentional being includes three moments in sense perception. These three moments, however, are united in the one act of perception: (1) the moment of intention as opposed to "intentional," (2) the content of a non-evident conception (3) the moment of grasping reality. To these three moments there are added other moments, e.g., of hatred, love, desire, and repugnance that "formulate" the wholeness of the act.

Ingarden further holds that the structure of the intentional object differs from that of an individual and independent object. Two aspects must be considered here: (1) the contents of a purely intentional object and (2) the intentional structure of the intentional object itself. The intentional structure reveals itself when we are directing our attention to its "structure," reflect on it and thus pass from itself to its intentional equivalent. In its contents, the intentional object "is" exactly as it is conjectured. And precisely because all of this is thought about, conjectured and attributed, it constitutes a being of a purely intentional existence.

Ingarden also holds that intentional being is the weakest manner of existence in relation to real, ideal, and absolute being. Non-independent moments characterize intentional existence: of non-subsistence, derivation and non-activity.[3]

FOUR MOMENTS

Ingarden further maintains that in any intentional being, e.g., in some kind of artifact, we must distinguish four different moments:

(1) *The author's creative experience*, which is achieved through acts of consciousness which are characterized by an intention. This intention can focus on independent or eventually real objects or even those "constituted" as objects through an intention.

(2) *A physical foundation* which constitutes an intersubjective foundation of the identity of a given artifact, e.g., printer's ink or paper.

(3) *The work itself* or the intentional object and hence that which remained constituted as an object through the directive act of consciousness.

(4) *Concretization of artifacts*. Because the intentional being is indefinite, since it is only schematically outlined and has a suitable physical foundation for its identity, this being can be constructed by another person in another way. Concretization can be of two kinds: either cognitive or aesthetic.

CRITIQUE OF PHENOMENOLOGY

The phenomenologist's conception of intentional being is the result of penetrating analyses and description of the data of consciousness. To this extent, as a description, it adds a valuable *novum* to the history of human thought. Its weakness lies elsewhere: in its characteristic approach to reality.

As N. Moreau observes,[4] Husserl's phenomenology does not leave the area of gnoseology (theory of knowledge). Its theory of objectivity does not arrive at a contact with ontology (metaphysics). Husserl's gnoseology is not a theory of knowing *real being*. It is rather a *noezology* or a theory of thinking: *cogitatio* (cf. Cartesian idealism). This is why it "brackets" the real existence of the thinking subject as well as the real world. And at the very beginning of such a thinking, we are not dealing with a REAL AND ACTUAL EXISTENCE. Therefore in further analyses of the act of thinking and, through it, an analysis of the kind of being that appears in directing acts of consciousness, *it is impossible to reach factual and real existence*, which had been initially bracketed. And if we later speak of even an intentional existence, this "existence" will be understood differently than was the primary and everyday understanding of the existence which constitutes the factuality of the world, namely of an existence which is truly ontic in meaning.

NO REAL EXISTENCE

Intentional existence which appears in a phenomenological analysis can be characterized at best as a kind of "price" of a thought object in place of the object itself. A careful reading of the texts of phenomenologists on the subject of the character of intentional existence convinces us that we are not dealing with *real existence*. Rather, we are dealing with some kind of convenient selection of qualitites that is sometimes called either absolute, ideal, real or intentional existence.

The consequences of this statement are far-reaching in the area of metaphysics, where we are analyzing the undeniable elements of the existence of being. We are *not* dealing here only with some kind of "price" of a thought object, whose existence is bracketed a priori.

We must agree, however, that initially intentional existence does appear in acts of knowledge. Informational knowledge is the basis for creative, productive knowledge. Hence intentional existence, given us in a cognitive experience, is essential for understanding the intentionality of the creations of culture.

COGNITIVE MEANING

If intentional being is primarily realized in an act of human knowledge, we must differentiate between cognitive meaning and the cognitive act itself. Cognitive meaning is given me from the "outside"; it is always a "not-I," something which is "cast" at me. The known meaning objectively refers to the known thing, to a transubjective object. This meaning which is within men and which endures as a constant "non-I," does not differ from the real meaning of the thing itself. Hence the meaning of the cognitive act is recognized as coming from the thing.

CONGITIVE ACT

Besides the contents of the cognitive act, there exist acts that construct or "accept" some kind of meaning. These acts are "my" acts, since I make myself present, in some way, in these acts. They are the bearers of a known meaning which really exists only "in" my acts. The known meaning did not arise independently of acts of my knowledge. Neither does it possess an existence that is independent of the knowing acts. For real existence is the existence of something which is a "this" or "that" existing subject.

CRITIQUE OF INGARDEN

Hence we cannot agree with Ingarden that existence should belong to a set of cognized relations which are expressed in a thought object. The objection about existential monism is worthless, since a real and, hence, only subjective existence is different in every ontic case. It is not reducible to a second existence. The differentiation of the four ways of existence is, in relation to real existence—which the phenomenologists bracket in the beginning— something entirely equivocal.

For this reason, the intentional being possesses, in the cognitive act, its existence only as subjectivated in the human psyche. The meaning in an intentional being is objective; it is self-imposed from the object. In the case of man, it exists through the existence of the subject.

THE SUBJECT AND COGNITIVE ACTS

Our cognitive acts are the existing bearers and subject of cognitive meaning which—because they do not have their own objective existence—exist solely through the existence of the subject, i.e., man. The intentional meaning which is unreal through and in itself, becomes real through the subject. More strictly: *the existing cognitive acts construct in themselves the meaning in the presence of the influence of the existing meaning of a thing.* This content which performs the cognitive act, selectively chooses, as it were, and expresses the meaning in itself as in a subject. At the same time, it gives it a different kind of existence than it had in the thing itself. The intentional meaning in the act of cognition acquires an immaterial character because it exists through the existence of the knowing subject. Hence the structure of an intentional being appears differently in its existential character than described by Ingarden.

III. THE INTENTIONAL ASPECT OF CULTURAL WORKS

EXTERNAL EXPRESSIONS

Contents which originally exist only in the mind through thought can be expressed externally. We are dealing here with a linked system of signs, of which speech and everyday language are most primary and spontaneous. Meanings which are experienced in a cognitive way are identical with the content of things. The ability to externalize experienced conscious contents, in the form of signs and symbols, is an expression of man's psycho-material nature, for he is neither a pure spirit nor only organized matter.

In addition to speech and articulated signs, there are other external expressions of internal, living and conscious contents of the spirit. Human mimicry, gestures, song, dance, works of art, painting, sculpture, architecture and the like should be added to a system of conventional signs.[5]

Further, external manifestations of experienced inner contents may be of two kinds: (1) spontaneous manifestations such as shouts, speech, gestures or (2) the selection of a suitable, external expression-symbol after extensive reflection.

CONSTRUCTION AND PURPOSE OF SIGNS

The formal construction of the sign or symbol (i.e., of the fact that it expresses the qualities which constitute the intentional content), will determine the basic material to be used—whether paper, paint, stone, iron etc. In like manner, the purpose of the external expression (symbol), whether it be purely cognitive, practical-moral or aesthetic, will determine the way in which the material will be used.

CLARITY OF SYMBOLS

We have seen that the intentional contents differ from (1) the external conventional signs and symbols of internally experienced ideas and (2) the purpose of their use in relation to the essential character of the material in which we express our symbols. We must now consider that the formal structure of internal signs can be more or less clear in relation to the designated contents.

Creations of the human spirit are derived from the experience of inner psychical, intentional contents; and, at the same time, they are ordered to the human spirit as to a recipient.

CONCLUSION

Culture is an inner ordering of the human spirit and, speaking more precisely, of the development of human personality. Secondly, there is a hierarchy of value of cultural works, since works which are united more directly with the development of human personality, fulfill more fundamentally their essential destiny. In concrete cases, the hierarchy of these values is based on the decision which man makes when he selects those cultural values which are more intimately connected with the development of his personality.

If we seek to establish an analogical hierarchy of cultural values, then we hold that cultural acts within the area of the human spirit are higher than are non-spiritual ones.

Finally, the question of a permanent or non-permanent existence of culture is determined in the following manner:

(1) Cultural works which are objectivated in matter are subject to the laws of matter, i.e., of change, motion and non-permanence. They have no likelihood of a permanent, atemporal existence.

(2) Cultural works, which have come from the spirit and are assigned to the development of the soul, have a good possibility of survival through the spirit.

CHAPTER VII

MAN AND HIS FREE ACTIVITY

This chapter is divided into two sections: I. Freedom as a Fact of Consciousness, and II. Interpretation of the Fact of Freedom.

The first section is an introduction to the second, which consists of five divisions: A. The Human Being: A Spiritual, Material, Contingent Being; B. Feelings as Factors Intensifying Desire; C. The Will and Its Freedom; D. The Dynamic Structure of Free Choice; E. The Development of Freedom in the Human Being.

In the life of every human being there are many threads of activity, but only one moment of human action "severs" man from the whole of nature and sets him in opposition to it. This essentially human moment, decisive of the personal, unrepeatable, unique aspect formed "from within", is *decision*. Each of us decides from within what to do, or not to do, in relation to the various "objects" of our activity.

For some, the necessity of decision is so "dreadful" that they simply "decide not to decide", restricting the exception to compliance with or submission to some kind of system, and, concretely, to another person or group of persons who are supposed to take "in their hands" the burden of the decision and the responsibility. Escape, however, is futile, since from decision there is no possibility of evasion. When we decide to put our decision into another's hands, we thereby make a real decision about the "right and wrong" of the decisions of those who are supposed to decide for us. In addition, we form for ourselves the impersonal face of that system in whose name someone decides for us.

Moments of decision are therefore inseparable from man; they are in fact

88

nontransferable; they are that element which constitutes the human character of the individuals called *homo sapiens*.

I. FREEDOM AS A FACT OF CONSCIOUSNESS

The very fact of human decision and of its every experience reveals to each of us our inner freedom of activity and choice. Consciousness of this freedom accompanies us ineluctably in the process of making a decision.

Of course, the consciousness of the freedom of our decision is still not its justification or explanation; it is still not an answer to the questions: are we actually free in our decisions: and, *how is it possible* for us to be truly free in these decisions?

The question of the knowledge itself of the fact of making a decision is, however, rather complicated. The most frequently recurring misunderstanding in this matter is a tendency to treat knowledge univocally. For we already possess worked-out models or patterns of knowledge and explanation and we try to transfer them to our internal life, to impose them, as it were, on the moment of making a decision. But these are misleading, because the knowledge involved in making a decision has no clearly constituted object. All types of knowledge "immobilizing" the object have no place here, because there is yet no object but it is only to come into being as an outcome of "making a decision"; it is to come about precisely as a result of an inclination of the will.

ARISTOTLE

Aristotle realized this difference when he postulated a new type of knowledge, useful precisely for guidance in the sphere of the coming-into-being of human action, for the sphere in which a person "decides" about some act: in a word, for the sphere not of the theoretical but precisely of the *practical*. He borrowed this model of knowledge from Heraclitus, who called it *Phronein*, and thought of it as a deep, intuitive insight into changeable reality, for the sake of uncovering the fundamental law governing the "dialectical" world of mutually opposing forces and tensions. In the sphere of practical life distinguished by Aristotle, a person knows not in order to become informed about the necessary character of reality, but in order to act, to release from himself a human, unique, unrepeatable action. The general theoretical type of knowledge here would be of no avail, because I am to constitute a new, concrete being formed from my will, a being which is not at all necessary. Therefore, knowledge must find expression here corresponding to the context of the variable, individual decisions which we ourselves to some extent determine,

and in which, in the course of deciding, I am aware of my freedom of
deciding.

SCHELER

The specific consciousness of freedom in our acts of decision was emphasized by Max Scheler:

> That which is freedom, we understand only within the compass of our
> volitive life and never through theoretical reflection. Of all the contrasts
> between an affirmation of freedom and determinism, the deepest . . . lies
> in the dissimilarity of the fundamental attitude we are here considering:
> 1. whether we take an attitude of wanting, of acting, which precisely
> stands before some kind of serious decision included in the living drama of
> our acts—as if there, where the degrees of intention, of plan, of resolve,
> escape from the chaos of the inner agitation of mind and of the initial dance
> of thoughts and tend only toward increasing definiteness and resolution.—
> 2. or whether we treat the whole process from the outside as an
> 'object', as a stream of something that is happening, and then we divide it
> into parts, not looking into that inner living frame of acts and not experienc-
> ing those acts anew, as it were . . . Determinism knows nothing of the
> making of decisions, of the swelling of life from which they flow in an
> evident way, but establishes them as already completed and takes note.
> Then, in addition, it joins them together in their subsequent and causally
> conditioning processes, but it does not at all perceive with this the occur-
> rence of each of these processes from the side of life's inner activity.[1]

Scheler's sharp separation between the two kinds of knowledge makes
sense only within the limitations of his one-sided phenomenological method
and perspective. After all, differentiation is not the same as a separation; the
knowledge which accompanied us in the course of making a decision is still
that same intellectual knowledge (admittedly of a different type) which works
out a theory of this fact or process. If our knowledge were merely an external
inspection, like the visual inspection of some color or shape, then Scheler's
assertion, concerning the impossibility of a knowledge of freedom after the
process of decision is completed, would be justified. If, however, our knowledge penetrates the whole of our act of decision and its individual phases,
and if it is this same intellectual knowledge which accompanies the whole
"constructing" of the decision, then there seems to be no reason (apart from
possible preconceptions splitting up consciousness) why a given experience
would not be able to be placed in a network of theory regarding that very
experience.

Describing further the fact of making a decision, Scheler distinguishes the
freedom of the act of deciding from the idea of indeterminateness, which

entails unpredictability. A free person is autonomous, and thus his behavior exemplifies a trustworthiness, a consistent ability to do, regularly, his duty; in fact, therefore, a kind of predictability.

Scheler's observations here need to be balanced out by those of certain meta-ethicists who point out that true freedom escapes all necessity, even the constraint of the good as it stands before me in the demands of duty:

> . . . The absoluteness of duty does not determine me completely to . . . the good. If through the act I declare myself 'for,' that is my choice, my free decision, that is my act. If through the act I declare myself 'against', that is also my choice, that is also my act. The alternative of good, just as the alternative of bad, is an 'alternative of freedom'. The coerced act not only could not be either good or bad, it could not be . . . an act.[2]

SELF DETERMINATION

Therefore freedom appears in us—and of this we are conscious—as the ability of self-determination both for action as well as inaction; and both for action toward *this*, as well as toward *another*, object. We know the circumstances of our self-knowledge, that we do not feel coerced from without. And if someone tries to force us from without, we know, too, from our inner experience, how much our freedom "rebels" against such behavior.

At the moment when I make a choice, and through it the self-determination to 'this here' act, I am conscious of it, and I preserve this consciousness for a long time, sometimes in the form of the "remorse of conscience" that I myself determined to do just what I did; that I could have not done this, but precisely I myself wanted to, and therefore I did it. The decision comes from me; I who am the originative cause of this act which I myself form "within me." And so, bringing forth from myself this very act, I at the same time "become," I am "built." When I lie, I myself "become" a liar; standing in the defense of the weaker, I myself "become" a defender, etc. And so in practical behavior I in a way "create myself as a human being"; I form for myself, even through those deeds which I would never reveal externally, a personal face. The realm of free decisions is that only realm in which a human being "constructs" himself and by this transcends nature, which gives all other beings a determinate nature and a set way of acting. The person must "constitute" for himself his personal nature through acts of his free decision and be determined to that very way of behavior.

As Scheler writes:

> If we look without bias at experience then human life appears as an edifice composed of actions and endeavors running in phases. They are accompanied by the sense of determination, of passive compliance, of coer-

cion or behavior out of sheer habit. However, these phases run in free acts of various degrees, ranging from the relatively free act of will in the choice of direction of a street—in contrast to an automatic walk, to go just anywhere—to decisions concerning acts in which we 'radically change' our whole life and its innermost purpose[3]

The consciousness of the freedom of our decision, given to us immediately, is the fundamental fact in our moral, personal-human life. This fact, as fundamental for private life as it is for society, demands many-sided explanations.

II. INTERPRETATION OF THE FACT OF FREEDOM

The philosophical interpretation of the world acquires livelier colors when we focus it on the microcosm of the human being. Although it is true that the human being in large measure is an "unknown being" and, as Goethe remarks, "he is as strange today as in the first days of creation," still let us try at least to sketch in its most general contours that "nerve of humanity" standing at the basis of all culture, namely, the attribute of human freedom. Usually we speak of the freedom of the human will, but in fact what is in question is the freedom of the *person*, since the will is only a dependent element of the human structure. The concrete person is the one who acts rationally or non-rationally, freely or unfreely.

Therefore, in order to be able less inaccurately to clarify, and indicate the solution to, the problem of the freedom of the human being, it is necessary first a) to take into account the ontic aspects of human existence; b) to articulate the idea of freedom; c) to make an analysis of the dynamic structure of free human action; and through this d) to realize in what way the fact of human freedom, continually developing, is connected with the dignity (and also with the tragedy) of the human person.

In these inquiries we will employ the method suitable to classical philosophy. For the fact of the freedom of the human being cannot be interpreted apart from the more primary propositions of a system, since these facts are not the first and basic object of philosophy. They presuppose (in the explanation) a philosophical interpretation of being in general, and of the being of humans in particular.

A. THE HUMAN BEING: A SPIRITUAL MATERIAL CONTINGENT BEING

In wanting to know the nature of the human being better, we surely never stress too strongly his ontological contingency. The contingency of our being manifests itself not only in its very structure, i.e., in its complexity, divisibility, and transitoriness, but above all in the mode of its activity. Heidegger called human duration a "being toward death"; so too, the activity of the human being bears the mark of transitoriness and the tendency toward death. In intellectual knowledge, contingency appears in the possibility both of true as well as of erroneous knowledge, and in volitive aims, assumes the form of effective and ineffective, of good and evil desires, of spontaneous and free desires as well as of unfree tendencies marked by necessity.

One should not, therefore, expect *a priori* that human free choice would be ontically more perfect than the structure of the human being itself. As human contingency in the order of knowledge is manifested not only in knowledge that is aspectual, successive, but even sometimes erroneous, so too in the order of choosing, the diversified limitation of choice will be manifested.

ORGANIZATION OF HUMAN BODY

This limitation of freedom is accentuated all the more because the contingency of a human being concerns not only his ontological-existential side, but also his ontological-essential side, that is, not only his activity, but his nature ("human nature"). For if the human being is not a spirit "imprisoned" in matter, as Plato taught, but on the contrary a spirit being "liberated" through matter, a spirit which, as self-existing requires matter in order to be able to act and to achieve self-knowledge, then the mark of the determinism of matter will be expressed everywhere. The act of decision is that place in which in a most explicit manner the spirit is united with matter, the personal moments with the moments of nature. Attention should especially be drawn to the fact of the organization of the body itself by the human soul. For the human body is unique and cannot be placed on the same plane as the organisms of animals which sometime, from a biological point of view, are "more perfect," more specialized than the human organism. For only the human organism is a "body"; i.e., it is organized for the expression of the

---

*Such a general view calls to mind many factors of the Aristotelian conception of the human being which, in turn, seems to have been close to the Biblical idea according to which every person is more "body" than spirit, and the existence of the human being in eternity can occur only at that time when the body arises from the dead. Today in Christian circles, the creation of every soul by God being presupposed, we perceive an oscillation of thought between two conceptions of the human being: either as an embodied spirit or as spiritualized matter. Always, however, the human being appears as a composite being, a being who is one in the multitudes of elements constituting him, the unity existing not as a result of the organization of matter, but precisely providing that organization. The life of a human being is a unique existence, bound with the human soul through which, as through form, the whole being exists.

spirit and the possibility of the contact between the spirit and all that makes up the content of the world. The body is fundamentally ordered to the spirit and its affairs.

The body, therefore, as matter organized by the human soul, brings to the sphere of the spirit, a large "dose" of natural determinisms. Matter itself, being determinate, "transfers" its manner of being onto the manner of activity of the being of the human, of which it is an essential component.

UNITY OF ACTION

Understood in this way, the ontological structure is able to manifest itself in the specific activity of a human being. What should be emphasized here above all is the *unity of action*. The human being is a single entity, and all of his acts are characterized by unity. For they proceed from one "center"—"me"—and they have as their aim the unity of "me." At the same time, the functional unity of activity does not cancel the structural complexity and multiplicity.

This is clearly disclosed in knowledge. For we know that every type of thing which we call human knowledge composes one great "sequence" of my specific, conscious knowledge. And just as the stream of light penetrating into a Gothic cathedral through a many-colored stained glass window gives, thanks precisely to the structural composition, one picture, so too do we absorb cognitively, in a single, functional, cognitive continuum, the external world through the various sources of knowledge. Sometimes we accentuate the sensory-material side of knowledge, while at other times its spiritual-intellectual side. Always, however, there are in the acts of human knowledge, roughly speaking, two great cognitive structures: sensory and spiritual.

A similar thing occurs with the desires of a human being. For there are no purely spiritual acts-aspirations (spiritual feelings) without simultaneous sensory and material inclinations (sensory feelings). In connection with such a state of affairs, it is usual to distinguish in human volitive aspirations:

a) a system of neuromuscular movements, encompassing reflexive, instinctive, habitual movements. Alone in themselves they form a closed motor mechanism, which the will makes use of—without directly influencing its manner of performance—incorporating its energy toward purposeful aims or incorporating it in subordination to cognitive representations;

b) the cognitive representations, such as perception, images, ideas, and judgements, constituting also the element of volitive activity;

c) the group of sensory feelings-desires toward (or away from) the object.

The consequences of this effective intensity are observable motor movements in the organism;

d) finally, the essential, volitive element—an intellectual delight in the object itself, in which under the influence of the judgment of practical reason, the object is willed or wanted under a particular aspect.[4]

The structural multiplicity should not, however, obscure the functional appetitive-volitive unity, just as the view of a human hand in a dissecting room, where there are separated groups of tissues, should not obscure the actual function of the hand in the organism

B. FEELINGS AS FACTORS INTENSIFYING DESIRE

The question of feelings and their role in the psychic life of the human being invites extensive treatment. In a discussion of the mechanism of human activity and free choice, we ought, at least in the most general way, draw attention to the affective factor which so overwhelmingly intensifies activity, and sometimes even decisively influences the choice of what is desired, detested, or feared.

Just what is feeling in the human being? How does it manifest itself? What are its basic forms? What is its relation to activity? These are questions which should somehow be taken into account in an attempt to outline the role of feelings in our life.[5]

SOME DISTINCTIONS

Feeling is a specific appetitive-qualitative, psychic experience, being characterized initially by the acquisition or loss of the state of psychic indifference toward the "stirring" object. There arises a characteristic, appetitive movement "to" or "from" the concrete thing, more or less intensely felt.

The realm of desire is two-fold: intellectual and sensory. Feeling is connected with the sensory sphere of knowledge. Of course we do speak of "spiritual feelings"—of love, hate, sadness, anger, etc.—but these feelings, related to intellectual knowledge, are in fact acts of will, a subject to be discussed below. Feelings in the strict sense are acts of sensory desire and, as such, must be internally connected with physiological changes of the organism. As sensory desire, they comprise a specific synthesis of the psychic and physiological element. In addition, they are a manifestation of "originative desire"; i.e., they are connected with the knowledge of the subject, and in this they differ from so-called natural desire, which is an inclination of a being to its own proper good. Called "natural love" in classical philosophy, natural desire is the disposition of a being to an activity, and through it to some object, a good. The desire for food, for example, in the form of hunger, no more depends on any sense-knowledge-mediated response than does the impulse of an infant to suck. On the other hand, my desire right now to go over and sit in that shady spot is a response to a direct and discriminating sensory deliverance.

THE THREE ELEMENTS OF SENSORY FEELING

Ordinarily, three integrating elements of sensory feelings are distinguished: appetitive-psychic, physiological, and cognitive-sensory.

The appetitive-psychic element is characterized by a particular appetitive "movement." For just as a material-local motion brings the subject of motion toward or away from some object, so also the appetitive movement psychically inclines "to" or "from" a concrete thing.[6]

The physiological element of affective experience is physiological change:[7] a) more intense nervous and biochemical phenomena, e.g., in breathing, circulation of blood, endocrinous secretion, etc.; b) facial expression, greater or lesser muscular tension, gesticulation—as a result of which the whole configuration of the bearing of the human being is different—"body language"; c) the accompanying *voluntary* facial expression and intentionality produce symbolic gestures.

The cognitive-sensory element often precedes, but at times follows, the two initial elements. Feelings are united with impressions or images and accompany them. Not only does the quality of feelings depend on the content of impressions, but also, at times, their power. Focusing attention on the object awakening the feeling increases the strength of the feeling itself, and cognitive occupation with a different object weakens the former feeling.

Pleasantness and unpleasantness penetrate all feeling. Aristotle's explanation of this phenomenon, which has in no way become obsolete, observed that all acts of a sensory nature either are, or are not, agreeable. If sensual acts occur without impediment, they carry with them the quality of pleasantness; if, instead, an obstacle arises, then a painful and unpleasant moment follows.[8] For sensual acts are ordered to the good of sensory nature, which is the preservation of the individual and the species. Acts following this line are thus good for nature. The pleasure felt in sensory functions is that which regulates activities (especially in animals); pain, that which disrupts activities.

CLASSIFICATION BY GENESIS

Sometimes we experience bodily feelings which have their origin in organic changes, passing afterward sometimes into conscious feelings, satisfaction or pain; sometimes on the other hand, into sensory images, passing through the realm of likes and dislikes and finding their outlet in physiological reactions within the organism. Finally, there is the frequently encountered transformation of bodily feeling into sensory, when the process which originated in the organic changes is received through the sensory-cognitive apparatus and intensified.[9] Becoming conscious of the fact that I am hungry is an example of the first type; the second is exemplified when I experience a muscular tightening and a general repulsion as someone I dislike comes into view; the third when a vague and physiologically rooted sexual yearning becomes translated into an image of a (real or imagined) desirable partner.

THE FUNDAMENTAL ACTS OF THE AFFECTIVE LIFE

When we take under consideration the question of the formal objects of affective experiences, then we notice that we behave in one manner toward a concrete pleasurable good which is attainable without difficulty, and in another manner toward a good which is difficult to attain, one which must be won.[10]

Good easily attained is appealing, moving and guiding desire directly to itself. Attraction springs up. This is purely sensory *love*. Such concrete love is the first reaction when some concrete good proper to sensual nature stands before us. But when, instead of a pleasurable good, an unpleasant thing, a concrete evil, stands before this same nature, there arises a contrary act of affective *aversion*, specific dislike or even hatred.

Love and aversion, the initiating motion of affective life, can be converted into a further phase. For when a concretely appraised good is not yet possessed by us, then the original love is converted into *desire* (and sometimes longing, when that desire is constant and prolonged), and when we attain it— then satisfaction, a pleasurable state. A threatening evil, on the other hand, brings about affective flight, *repugnance*. But when this evil becomes real and unavoidable, it causes *sorrow*. Note that love, desire, and joy can exist without the second series, repugnance, aversion, and sorrow; but not conversely, since ultimately every feeling presupposes the original attraction, love.

ADDITIONAL OBSTACLES

The question of the affective life is complicated to some extent by the emergence of additional obstacles in conjunction with an attractive good, or when it is difficult to overcome a threatening evil. There follows a kind of appetitive restraint, and there springs up the concrete task of the conquering of constant inhibiting difficulties. If the possibility of overcoming the difficulties connected with the good is assessed positively, the person takes "stout heart" (in the spiritual order: *hope*); if the possibilities are assessed negatively, *discouragement* arises. Of course, this state develops further and leads either to *joy* or to *sorrow*, according to the degree to which the difficulty has been overcome. Unfulfilled expectation and discouragement turn into sorrow.

It is well known, however, that states exist in which it is hard to avoid an evil, awakening aversion. At such a time there stands before us the alternative: either this evil appears as possible to overcome, and then a feeling of *courage* arises; or else it appears as concretely impossible to overcome, and then *fear* arises. Courage and fear are particularly dramatic feelings, because of the threatening evil which can sometimes become present. As we know, a present evil produces sorrow. But it sometimes happens that present evil still does not destroy, still appears as possible to remove; and then one needs only to attack and overcome it. Then anger grows as a feeling destroying the former affective situation. Anger expresses a high degree of tension—like an explosion—and therefore it cannot last long, since it ends either in vengeance on the evil, and through this in an attained good causing joy, or in an unsuccessful act and sorrow.

Out of these eleven fundamental acts of the affective life (i.e., love, desire, joy, repugnance, aversion, sorrow; hope, discouragement, courage, fear, and anger) arise different combinations forming more complex affective states, the source of all affective states being the primary attraction called love. And while every subject has his own way or manner of affective response particular to him, still, there are certain general patterns of the manner of affective reactions, which are called the *temperament* of the subject.

THE WILL

Feeling acts are coupled with acts of will. Though analysis demands distinctions, there are no isolated states in our affective life. Rather, reason and the volitive life (the so-called higher or spiritual feelings) can activate our affective life; and with its help, as with a good tool, they can obtain a stronger means for the realization of personal goals.

Of course, feelings which precede the activity of reason (such as anger or spontaneous fear) demand calming, since they determine us too strongly to rash action. Accompanying and intentionally awakened feelings, however, assist spiritual strengths, give them greater power, and can also be conducive to the development of lasting, good dispositions in action. This role for the feelings in the personal life is called their essential "sublimation."[11] The process of sublimation and of the purposeful arrangement of feelings in our activity is long and arduous, but contributes to the harmonizing development of the individual. Feelings not trained and left to themselves, to their spontaneity, can result in a great deal of destruction, and they incapacitate or at least radically weaken our freedom.

C. THE WILL AND ITS FREEDOM

The question of the will can be looked at from a twofold point of view: a) the more general, and then by "will" we understand a particular way of acting, a certain manifestation of one's own "personality" and an expression of the character of our ego; b) the strictly philosophical, in the analysis of the ontic character of human rational tendencies.

When we look at the will as an expression of personality, it is really a synthesis of many different psychic states: imaginations, ideas, inclinations, desires, biological-unconscious dispositions. The psychic states of the person, together with the elements constituting them, are not loosely arranged side by side, but display a unity, and thereby point to an element or moment which organizes and gives to the person its own psychic mark—the "personality."

The will thus broadly understood does not, of course, exclude, but on the contrary, demands the existence of self-mastery. We experience the good known intellectually, and sometimes the resulting aim demands self-mastery; e.g., the serving of a sentence out of justice, or the apology of one person to another, demanding a humbling of oneself, etc. Precisely this spiritual-psychic tendency toward the good, organizing and not excluding, though sometimes transcending, various sensory-appetitive tendencies, is in the strict sense the will. The person constitutes himself through acts of decision, organizes himself as a psychic personality. Therefore one can speak of the existence in us of a power revealing itself in acts of the tendency toward intellectually cognized good.

TWO KINDS OF ACTS

In the tradition of classical philosophy there are distinguished, following Thomas Aquinas, two kinds of acts of will ordered to an intellectually perceived good: natural, emanated acts, and dictated acts.

Natural, emanated acts, have the will itself for their directed cause, and therefore they are called "voluntary" acts, for they have in view a perceived aim as good, toward which they tend directly from their source, the will. The fundamental act brought into being by the will is love, which can assume various forms, depending upon the good toward which it tends, e.g., the form of desire, joy, hatred, sadness, hope, despair, fear, anger, courage. These acts normally appear together with the "lining" of analogous sensory feelings. Natural acts brought into being directly by the will have the good for their formal object which, in concrete circumstances, is always a particular good. Good in its analogous generality, which is the object of the natural acts of the will directly brought into being by it, stands at the basis of the experience called "happiness in general."

Dictated acts are those originating from the will and performed by other powers of the human being, e.g., reason, the motor powers, the hands, etc. Note that these are subject to coercion. Voluntary acts on the other hand, are subject to necessity (in relation to the good in general but not in relative and particular good) but not to coercion.

THE WILL AND THE GOOD

It follows from this that our will, in relation to the analogously general good (which is our happiness in general) is subject to necessity. This means that we *cannot not* want good, if good is the formal object of the will. In relation to its formal object the psychic power cannot be indifferent. In relation to the good as good, we do not have any inner freedom, since all acts of will tend toward their object from the point of view of good, even at the time when we perform an objective evil.

On the other hand, the will in its freely formed acts cannot be subject to coercion, since these acts flow from an inner source, from the will itself, and they remain in the will itself. No one externally can command free inner acts of will.

Our freedom of action, called freedom of will, refers therefore solely to inner decisions directly formed within ourselves, in relation to the wanting of all goods that are not the necessary good, i.e., the analogously general good. For no concrete goods (even God, who appears to us solely indirectly in the light of conducted reflective discourse) can coerce the will to the necessary wanting of themselves. For every concrete object can appear to me cognitively as a limited object, "with shortcomings" in consequence of which I do not have to choose it. Hence, this freedom can be defined as *the rule of the will over its acts in relation to all goods that are not the infinite good.*

TWO KINDS OF FREEDOM

Thus conceived, freedom appears in the form of the so-called "freedom of choice" (*libertas specificationis*) and "freedom of action" (*libertas exercitii*). On the strength of the first, the will is not necessarily determined to the wanting of precisely this object rather than another. On the other hand, on the strength of the freedom of action, we can actually perform (or not perform) the very acts of the wanting of something. And so, thanks to the one and the other freedom, I can choose between objects "A" and "B" and even in relation to this same object, "A," I can want it at one time, and at another time cease wanting it.

D. THE DYNAMIC STRUCTURE OF FREE CHOICE

Before we come to a consideration of the "structure" of free human action, we will inquire briefly about those possible determinants of a human being, capable of cancelling out his free and independent choice.

In the history of philosophy and rational psychology, attention has been focused on a variety of factors determining a human being to necessary action. This action has been interpreted as only seemingly free as a result of the unconsciousness of the necessity of the determining factors. Determinism was proclaimed: theological (God in some way would determine beforehand the human will); psychological (the human being would be necessarily determined to some kind of greater or more attractive good); materialistic or physical (manifesting itself in some type of natural determination mainly as a result of the activity of the laws of inanimate or animate matter). All these, and other types of determinisms, limited or simply annihilated the possibility of the free choice of a human being.

Does a reflection of this kind contain certain pertinent intuitions, or is this view entirely erroneous?

What we must first do is briefly analyze the structure of free choice. Realizing the complicated nature of this issue and, therefore, of explanatory analyses, we will attempt to take into consideration a minimum number of factors, so as not to become completely lost.

It is clear that the human being performs choices, utilizing here those psychic sources of action which are proper to a human being as a human being—intellect and will. This does not mean that other powers do not play any role here; the acts of intellect and will presuppose the whole rich material of pre-psychic life. However, we are purposely limiting ourselves to the analysis of only those elements of free choice which ultimately determine the freedom of human decision. This does not mean that the consciousness of freedom experienced in decisions is the consciousness of absolute freedom; on the contrary, it is the consciousness of a very limited freedom, of a freedom that is often won with difficulty.

TWO FACTORS

A human act has above all two characteristic features: it is conscious; and it is performed with a sense of greater or lesser freedom. It is therefore an act uniting intellect and will as the ultimate, but by no means the only, factors decisive of the human aspect of our decision. But even when we limit our consideration to these two ultimate determining factors, there appears a difficulty; specifically how can one speak of freedom as "nondetermination" of human action, since reason necessarily "determines," by presenting for realization, some definite contents or definite plans? It is not satisfied with a merely general indication of the direction of activity. Rather, it examines the circumstances and analyzes the good which it is to obtain in the performance of a given act. And if this is precisely how the matter stands, then does not the intellect determine our will in detail?

MUTUAL INTERACTION OF INTELLECT AND WILL

Indeed the intellect enters minutely into the concrete determination of performing a choice of the will. Acts of intellect and will mutually intertwine and remain in a "dialectical" clasp with one another, forming one whole in decision. The relationship may be compared, however imperfectly, to the case of the cooperation of a strong, but blind person with a keen-sighted paralytic. The powerful blind person places the frail paralytic with sharp vision on his shoulders, and together off they go. The sharp-sighted paralytic fully informs the strong blind person of all he sees. Further, he fully examines the things and situations that become objects of interest for the blind person, but he is at the mercy of the blind one, who carries him wherever his own fancies point. And it could happen that the blind person learns from the one with sharp sight (who is unable to lie) about the existence of a pool of very filthy warm water. He gets into the pool in spite of the warnings of the paralytic, and takes a muddy bath to gratify his fancies. Or it could happen that he learns of tasty fruit in someone else's orchard. He goes to get it, ignoring all warnings. He demands only particular information about how to get into the orchard unobserved, and snatch the favorite fruit.

The comparison brings out an important point. Every intellectual indication of particular contents responds to some type of assent. The intellectual indication of content is especially important in concrete decisions which concern the selection of means to some end. This type of knowledge, called "phronetic" in the peripatetic tradition, is said to direct and determine me, in a practically indubitable way, to bring forth a decision concerning the performance of precisely this and not another act. This is not general theoretical knowledge, which would be of no use here, since it would not be capable of the determination of an individual concrete action. Consequently, there must emerge here a knowledge commensurate with the cognitive context, i.e., with changeable, individual decisions situated in a context of individual-changeable circumstances. This phronetic knowledge is called the "voice of conscience." It is the act of practical reason ordered to the sphere of concrete knowledge of that which does not exist, and which is to be done in order to exist.

Hence, the essential drama of the moral experience of a human being—of free choice—occurs not in the theoretical phase of the merely general intended act, or in the phases of its physical performance, but precisely in the moment of making a decision, i.e., in the moment when the person resolves to perform, or not to perform, some act, whether it be internal or external.

MOMENT OF FREE CHOICE

This is the moment of "free choice," the choice of some concrete means ordered to the realization of the general aim of human life. In the eyes of the great thinkers of the past, happiness, flowing from union with the final and objective good, appeared as the final reason of every human action. The fact that a person chooses this action, rather than another, demanded special justification and explanation. The choice of precisely this act, and not another, was considered as consent to the best *hic et nunc* means leading to the final end of human life.

In the moment of this choice, i.e., in deciding upon a deed, the above mentioned cognitive act is at work, which takes the form of a "practically-practical" judgment commanding what should be done and in what manner. Ultimately, then, the determination flows always from the intellect. Hence, the will and our choice (the act of the will) always follow a practical judgment of our intellect, determining us personally to the performance of "this here" act. And the will designates the final judgment of the practical intellect. Free will is exercised precisely in deciding which judgment of the practical intellect is to be this final judgment, ultimately determining us. The will can interrupt the process of intellectual inquiry and command: "I will have it so." It selects for itself the final judgment. And so, in the case of the person who is going to act, there occurs self-determination. And it must occur, if some act is to be brought forth in the person. The person, however, determines himself with the help of his rational powers of reason and will. But this, i.e., that he determined himself precisely this way and not otherwise, is regarded as the moment of the freedom of the person. Here is a schema which somewhat clarifies the relationship of the intellect and the will in the sphere of action.

Intellect	*Will*

I. THE ORDER OF INTENTION AS THE BASIS OF ACTION

1. A general-analogous grasp of the apprehended good	2. Love of the good as the general desire of personal happiness.
3. The intellectual vision of a concrete good.	4. The wanting of this good.

II. THE ORDER OF CONCRETE ACTION—
CHOICE OF MEANS TO THE END

5. Pondering over the means toward realizing the good

6. The approval or disapproval of the will.

7. Practical judgment about a concrete action.
   a) theoretically-practical judgment.
   b) practically-practical judgement.

8. Free choice of the will decisive of self-determination as the source of human action.

III. THE ORDER OF EXECUTION
OF THE FREE DECISION OF THE PERSON

9. The command of reason regarding the performance
   a) by concrete direction concerning how to do it
   b) by signalling the will to move the motive powers

10. The movement by the will of the motor powers of the person

11. Intellectual bliss from the attained end—*fruitio*.

12. Gratification of desire— *quietatio appetitus—delectatio*.

In this schema is shown the moment of the free decision of a human being who finally acts through his two psychic powers: intellect and will, mutually conditioning one another. Also illustrated in the schema is the preservation of the law of causation, in the form of the self-determination of the will through the practical judgment of reason.

Why, though, is the will able to decide "freely" that precisely *this* practical judgment will be the final judgment through which the person will be determined to a free action?

The possibility of free self-determination rests on the nature of our intellect and will. For if the intellect is ordered to being; if it has being existing in any manner whatsoever as its object of knowledge; then the person has a potentially unlimited range of knowledge. Now if we hold the metaphysical identity of being and good, we may then say that the person is necessarily ordered to unlimited, analogously general good. Every concrete being however, can appear to human reason as a being with some shortcoming, a being in some limited form. Each is therefore a limited good, a good not attracting necessarily. With respect to each such limited good, the person can cognitively and emotionally remain at a distance. In order that such a concrete good really attract the person and incline him to the choice of itself, it is first necessary that the person alone, through intellect and will, determine himself to the choice of precisely this, and not another good. The person must determine himself through a practical judgment to such an act, and not another; and to action rather than inaction. Therefore, freedom of action and choice enters into the very structure of human action—and the cancellation of this freedom is also the cancellation of the necessary and sufficient conditions of human action.

INNER FREEDOM AND RESPONSIBILITY

The justification presented here of the consciousness of the freedom of human decision, also confirms the spontaneous human conviction of the inner freedom of the will, confirms the human sense of responsibility, and confirms the intuitions of all morality.

Hence, according to the presented argumentation, one cannot agree with the thesis of radical determinism, in whatever form—theological, psychological, materialistic, or naturalistic—that the freedom of the will is only the unconsciousness of necessity. This is only an a priori negation of freedom explained with unascertainable hypotheses, an "explanation," moreover, which reduces the feeling of freedom to a kind of disease or illusion. This kind of explanation, however, immediately appears absurd and incomprehensible.

E. THE DEVELOPMENT OF FREEDOM IN THE HUMAN BEING

The theoretical conception of the freedom of the will sketched here, and its justification, are basically simple and general enough that one ought to be able to apply them to the concrete conditions of human life with the necessary qualifications. The human condition, as has been repeatedly emphasized, is not that of a pure spirit, although many textbook analyses of human freedom would have us think the contrary. But angelism is false since angels have a perfect will power. The human being is a contingent and material being; matter penetrates the human being, and the human being is one. If the human being acted entirely immaterially, he would cease to be human.

This does not mean, however, that the previously conducted analysis was faulty. But it took into consideration only the essential moments of human decision, which are the acts of intellect and will. These acts ultimately crown the whole complex of prepsychic and psychic processes, which must also be taken under consideration in analyzing the issue of the freedom of the will.

MATERIAL DETERMINANTS

After the ascertainment of the moment of freedom in human choice, more careful attention can be directed to the material determinants accompanying human choice. For example, it is possible to create conditions such that the normal function of the psyche is impaired: the subject must agree to the existing determinants, or face death. In such circumstances there are needed truly superhuman and heroic powers in order to choose freely the loss of one's life rather than submit to material determinants which one cannot control.

Furthermore, in the possible degrees of self-determination there also appears, like a "lining" of free human action, a degree of material determination. For everywhere that empowered potentialized material factors enter into play, there also exist their laws of matter and, amid them in some way also, determinism. Therefore each of our free acts always has an "unfree" side, because it also occurs in a material, and not purely spiritual, environment.

The function of our intellectual knowledge as well as the function of our aims-desires, is closely connected in us with our sensory-material substratum. And this substratum is found—being matter—in constant motion. Indeed, our spirit, penetrating matter, penetrates and unites the various phases of movement into one, but it nevertheless cannot rule out the essential function of matter which is continuous motion, unceasing change. Precisely as a result of this, we are not able to stop the course of matter and arrange it as we please, but we must make our decisions somehow "in the course" of the vehicle of our life, constantly running into the unknown. In virtue of this, too, our decisions and discernments are not all perfect acts of wanting and knowledge; they are connected precisely with the "course" of matter unceasingly flowing through us, the course over which we do not have full control. We decide in many cases provisionally, constantly postponing for later more thoughtful, more reflective and improved decisions.

SELF-LIBERATION

Therefore, in our activity we are free according to the measure of a human being. We can educate ourselves to freedom, i.e., to the making of decisions with greater and increasing independence from various forms of necessity. The development, however, presupposes action, the actual performance of liberated acts, through the actualization and development of our knowledge, reflection, through acts of self-mastery. Hence, through the conscious performance of free acts of decision, we can more fully control the dynamics of self-determination and thereby, in an ever fuller sense, create in ourselves a human, personal face open to the Absolute. In this sense, too, the saints can be regarded as those who reached greater proficiency in free decision, because they liberated themselves more fully from the material determinants of their wanting.

LOSS OF FREEDOM

It is necessary to turn attention to the possibility of the reverse direction of development. We can, submitting passively to the pressures of various kinds of determinants, gradually and imperceptibly decide to follow the stronger and more pressuring psychic impulse, and thereby resign from genuine choice, avoiding the more difficult alternatives. An especially threatening case of the deterioration of the freedom of a human being is public pressure organized by a power, such as that which took place in Fascist Germany, where the conditions for making free decisions were taken away. A human being, however, deprived of the possibility of free decision, or depriving himself, through passive submission to the surge of material determinants, of the freedom of choice, ceases slowly to be in a psychic sense a person, and becomes an "object," an element of the material world.[12]

HUMAN FREEDOM AND THE WILL OF GOD

In a chapter dealing with human freedom of decision, its construction and maturation, it is difficult to enter into discussion with various deterministic positions which, in the name of the preservation of order and neatness, throw overboard the possibility of the freedom of human decisions. But there is one theoretical difficulty which must be mentioned. It is connected with the maturation of a human being "toward freedom" and with the action of the Absolute on the world and on the human being. This problem was raised by Hartmann, who, accepting the freedom of a human being as a fact and as the foundation of morality, concluded to the impossibility of the existence of God. For the existence and action of God on the world would, he thought, cancel out the freedom of the human will.

Opinions on this subject flow most often from the inadequacy of our language in relation to transcendent reality. For we use an objective language, formed on the basis of knowledge of the material world. In the empirical sciences we have become accustomed to express contacts which take place between things in necessitating categories, and such a manner of expression assumed the rank of "scientific knowledge." But God and the manner of his activity are transcendental for human understanding. As Absolute, he is not at all limited to definite ways of acting—and such precisely are the freedom and necessity of contingent beings. The manner of activity of God is, after all, according to the measure of God, i.e., higher, and embracing at the same time necessity and freedom. Therefore the whole problematic of the determination of God in free human activity is basically only a linguistic misunderstanding stemming from an anthropomorphic theology.

CONCLUSION

Our personal freedom of decision is a primary self-conscious fact that is explicable and intelligible in philosophical interpretation. For freedom is a necessary aspect of the will as a psychic power that, through its free acts of love, enables us to live "for-another-person." The functioning of freedom, although difficult, can increase in our life when we rise above material determinants through self-mastery; but it can also decrease—when we decide to conform to psychic, social, or material determinants. Nevertheless, by making a decision, free in its core, we always bear responsibility toward ourselves and other persons, and also toward the person of the Absolute.

CHAPTER VIII

MAN IN THE PRESENCE
OF MORAL GOOD AND EVIL

The realm of morality constitutes an essentially human field of activity in which man is necessarily situated and from which, because of his own personal ontic structure, he cannot escape. A study of morality will enable us to understand more fully the meaning of human life as it takes place on the axis of good and evil. This chapter will deal with: I. The Foundations of Moral Being; II. Moral Being—the nature of acts as moral or immoral.

I. FOUNDATIONS OF MORAL BEING

For a fuller understanding of the problem of moral good and evil, it is best to break that problem down into three areas: a) man as a subject of morality; b) the constitution of things cognitively grasped—the object; c) the "eternal law" as the ultimate norm of moral conduct.

A. MAN AS THE SUBJECT OF MORALITY
The first and fundamental area of moral good and evil is linked with man, his structure, and his cognitive and volitional capabilities.

DECISION
In his ontic structure, man is a single and entire, undivided and subsistent being. Personal acts carry with them the stamp of a definite individuality. They are acts of "this-here" man who determines his own activity in a definite manner. The activity of a human subject is not a duplication of the typical functions of the "human species." Rather, it is an individual, unre-

peatable reproduction of an individual exemplar of personality, of an individual way of existing and of actualizing a potentiality which, only analogically and not univocally, constitutes every human individual in his act of be-ing (*esse*). In addition, in his consciousness man recognizes himself as the author of his actions. He feels himself as a single "I," a single distinct subject responsible for his own actions.[1]

We have argued above that the structure of the human being must be described in this way: the person really exists through a unique, unrepeatable act of existence which serves the entire "entity" by way of the human spirit that exists independently and is, at the same time, the form of its body.[2] Taking into consideration this composed structure of the human person, we can now turn our attention to the functional side of the person, where man's individual oneness is evident. The ontic oneness and subjectivity of man manifest themselves best in those acts which engage the individual powers of acting, i.e., those which distinguish the human individual in his relation to nature and to other persons. These powers of activity are the intellect and will. The human person expresses himself most completely in those acts in which the activity of these powers is joined together in one harmonious whole, enabling man to perform his own self-conscious and proper activity. Acts of this kind are called decisions.

Decision is the essential expression of a human person's autonomy. Through a series of decisions man becomes the author, the creator, not only of the object of his activity, but equally of his own "personality."

Consciousness and freedom, and hence, autonomy, are not "given;" they form and concretize themselves in activity. Human activities thereby take on improvements and a permanence in just the measure in which the subject is stabilized as an "acting person."

In turn, man does not acquire these habits independently of other persons. In this sense, man's autonomy is genetically and functionally conditioned by heteronomy in relation to the external world and especially in relation to other persons.

NATURAL LAW

The development of personal being in the direction of autonomy is the development of the capability of intellectual knowledge in its various forms, and of free choice of one's own good, most importantly of the kind of good which can become the object of personal love. It is also a development connected with capabilities of making a reliable decision, i.e., of the personal ordering for oneself of a known and loved good as the proper object of aspiration. In an act of free decision composed in this way, man recognizes, against the background of a concrete object, natural law. Natural law appears in the form of a practical judgment: "Good is to be done." At the same time, he accepts this law through an affirmation of this particular object as a good which directs him to a personal and, at the same time, a common good. Hence, natural law is "inscribed" in the rational nature of the human person, and it always actualizes and fulfills itself at the moment of a personal decision in the presence of "this here" good.

In such a decision man applies a law to himself, which is also (analogically) a law for other people. The guarantee of the objectivity of this law is the intellect which "reads" the necessary aspects of the object as a concrete good. Only in the light of the essential properties of human nature (an objectively knowing intellect and a will which chooses freely) as well as of common good, can a norm-law bind every man internally in conscience. It becomes a regulative law for persons only to the degree that it is accepted in an act of free decision, as an element which binds human autonomy with heteronomy, human individuality and independence with interdependence of nature and other persons. The acceptance of natural law in every act of decision is a basic and indispensable element for the development of the human person who acts "with nature" in the direction of common good.

RIGHT WILL AND SYNDERESIS

To make a decision in which the focus is on moral good and evil, natural law, responsibility, actualization of the person, is to have "right desire" (in Latin: *rectitudo voluntatis*).[3] Without the latter we do not even have, in a strict sense, a truly moral human act. The fact of right desire follows upon intellectual knowledge and a knowledge which specializes in the practical area and, hence, in the area which directs human conscious and free activity. We are speaking here of a type of knowledge in which we improve our vision of the natural law—"Good is to be done" by confronting it with fundamental areas of human life where acting and realizing good are important. The improvement of the practical intellect in these areas bears, in philosophical tradition, the name *synderesis*, human conscience.[4]

Man is born basically neither good nor bad morally, even though he is replete with hereditary inclinations, of which some are helpful in building moral good, and others are not. In addition, we can detect in man a kind of natural flaw which reveals itself in an internal disharmony, which Catholic theology explains as "original sin." In spite of this, man is, by nature, ordered to the knowing of truth as well as to loving the good (not yet "moral good"). At any rate, only this rectitude of the will, which is continually and endlessly forming itself by ordering itself to real and objective goods, gives a guarantee to the undertaking of morally good decisions or the avoidance of moral evil. However, it is not possible, practically, to seek first the rectitude of the will itself, rather than other concrete goods. This is so because the rectitude of the will constructs itself in us by and through the rightness of our decisions. Hence it is something dynamic in us; it can increase and diminish along with the increase and diminution of a morally good life, which life we may in turn define as a permanent and continuous choice of concrete, real and genuine goods.

What is the relationship between synderesis and "rectitude of will?" Synderesis, in the order of practical knowledge, is equivalent to the intellectual intuition of first principles in the theoretical order. Therefore in the order of action, synderesis will constitute the first foundations of moral life, which rests on the natural law of "realizing good." Good is the object of desire in the practical order; as a transcendental characteristic of being, it is therefore identical with the being which is the object of knowledge in the theoretical order. As in the theoretical order, being and the transcendentals (thing, one, truth, good, beauty) can be expressed in the form of first principles, so too, in the practical order, good appears cognitively in the form of a judgment. This judgment is the essential expression of the natural law: *good is desirable and it should be desired and be done; evil arouses repugnance and should be avoided.* This fundamental law-judgment is concretized in the first moral precepts that regulate the realization of good in basic, natural inclinations. Since we possess these very first principles in our psychical disposition as an application of the natural law to basic human inclinations, we possess, by the same token, an aggregate of first moral principles, traditionally called synderesis.

A lack of synderesis testifies to the inability of leading a moral life, and it is usually connected with some kind of psychical disorder. This sickness, clearly, is "graduated," but its most sensitive "barometer" is precisely the capability of a correct moral evaluation, particularly in connection with fundamental laws for human conduct.

On the other hand, rectitude of the will itself facilitates normal, correct functions of the practical intellect revealing themselves principally in synderesis. For rectitude of the will is the fundamental attitude of a person toward an actual good revealed by the intellect, toward a good which is suitable. For only a "suitable" good, that is, one that is ordered neither to "usefulness" nor exclusively to pleasure, can be recognized as an end in itself for human conduct.[5] Hence, a stable attitude of the will toward an actual good enables the intellect to perceive practical truth. For the will, since it is connected with good, does not obscure the intellect's field of view, but rather draws it nearer. Rectitude of the will, therefore, precedes the disposing acts of an intellectual intuition of the primary moral principles.

PRACTICAL REASON

In the tradition of realistic ethics, morality is called the relation of agreement (or disagreement in the case of moral evil) of the human act or decision with a rule of practical conduct. This relation is a "transcendental" relation, and hence inseparable from a human act. This means that as often as some conscious and freely-willed act takes place, this identically same act, even if it were not revealed externally and realized physically, is nevertheless the same moral act, since it is bound to a necessary and inseparable relation with the rule of conduct.

The rule of morality, however, or the rule of conscious and free conduct, is the human conscience—practical reason, insofar as it gives judgments. It begins with the primordial judgment, "Good must be done," and proceeds through the most varied particularizations of this judgment with respect to the concrete character of a good which can be chosen, and is the occasion of choosing the good. It dictates in a categorical way *hic et nunc* that one should proceed in this concrete instance precisely in this way, and not otherwise. The rules of conduct or practical judgments are obviously based on a vision of the structure of the concrete object as a good, about which we shall speak further on. And the final rule of man's conduct is the Absolute (Eternal Law) which having created man's nature and the world of things, is the ultimate guarantee of the rightness of natural rational inclinations to actual goods.

Between God's Eternal Law as the ultimate rule of moral conduct and concrete human prudential knowledge, there clearly exists a series of intermediates. We can mention, for example, society or various groups of people who are bound through mutual cooperation, who can indicate to each other mutually general norms of conduct in concrete, lived instances. And through this, they can educate themselves mutually in the moral order through common decision.

External intervention of the human community in the establishment of the rules of human conduct is not, however, the most essential element for moral activity. For the sphere of morality concerns basically only the interiority of man; it is precisely that necessary relation of agreement or disagreement of human decision with the rules of conduct.

Every fully human act is directed by the intellect with respect to the good; no conscious or freely willed human act can be indifferent in relation to good. Therefore natural law, which appears in the form of the judgment "Good must be done," is internally bound up with all human acts and with all "morality."

The good may be either ideal or actual. But if the good to be realized by an action is only ideal, and not an actual good, and if we judge it to be merely ideal, we are opposing natural law. As only an ideal, the good cannot be done. If we choose something as ideal in the sense of not being actual, we do not escape the moral order. The moral sense in such an act is negative, and the decision is morally wrong, since the good we are choosing cannot unite to the common good, which must be an actual good. The merely ideal good separates us from the common good.

The area of the subject which we have analyzed here and in which the entire "drama" of moral decision takes place, still demands a completion by means of objective elements which are connected with it, the so-called "objective constitution of a thing," in whose context human life and moral survival are effected.

B. CONSTITUTION OF THINGS

The second area which has a decided influence on moral good and evil is precisely the objective constitution of things. Man develops in a naturally communal environment. Without this environment, human life would not be possible. The objective constitution of things, that is, nature as society and as everything which was made by man in the cultural-creative process, is the necessary context of moral decisions. It demands a special emphasis with respect to the dangers of moral subjectivism.

According to "prescientific" and spontaneous knowledge, nature and society are not an accidental creation of elements assembled in a disorderly way; they have their objective laws and structures which manifest themselves in a more or less permanent and necessary activity. This conviction both grows and acquires fresh confirmation in a metaphysical analysis. One of the first and most basic philosophical laws established in the area of metaphysics is the thesis about the intelligibility of things. The point here is that being, both the existence of particular beings (taken analogically) as well as the essences of these beings, is somehow capable of being read by our intellect and, within certain limits, understood. Being is known by us when it expresses itself in the form of first principles; Identity, Non-contradiction, Sufficient Reason, Finality. If it is because of these principles that knowledge in general is possible, then since whatever we know is being, being in itself is rational and intelligible. The laws of being are the laws of our thinking. In other words, the intellect can carry out its cognitive operations only when it is specifically joined to being. Hence, rationality serves being.

Nothing, therefore, that we cognitively experience in a subject is independent of the objective constitution of a thing. For our intellect neither creates nor constructs the contents in an act of knowledge; rather, it "receives" them from the thing. In essence, our knowledge is the "receptacle" of the contents of the objective constitution of a thing. This is true in the moral sphere. In basic moral experience there is no danger of subjectivism since, in our really experienced moral life, we live by objective contents and laws of being.

ANALOGY OF BEING

In the arrangement of the things themselves, we should emphasize, on the one hand, the analogy of concrete beings, their uniqueness and specificity—in a word, their individuality. On the other hand, a profound, individual conceptual knowledge of concrete particulars is impossible; we cannot thus uncover individual ontic structures, inclinations and purposes. We must use universal, univocal concepts in the formation of "laws" as judgments about being.

Since the analogical state of existence reveals itself in the fact that being cannot be understood monistically but only pluralistically, every concrete being is different from every other, unique. Even within the extension of one class or "kind," there is no ontic univocity, but there exists a substantial, essentially concrete separateness. But separately ontical subjects create, through categorical, necessary and transcendental relations, a relative and analogical oneness and they point, at the same time, to their ultimate common source of origin, their ultimate ideal or model. For at the moment when we realize that multiple, changing, analogous being is rational and this rationality identifies itself with existence itself, we ask whether such an analogical being ultimately explains itself and its rationality. Must it not come from a being which is a pure intellect? When we observe that the essences of things are not the reason for their existence, and that their existence itself is generated and can be lost, we must admit that it comes from another being, who is Absolute Existence. And for the same reason, Absolute Being, as the source of all contingent and analogical beings, is most intelligible in itself.

NATURAL LAW OF PARTICULAR BEINGS

Individual finite beings reflect the intelligibility of their Source. Each is composed of the most various and diverse elements, harmonized into a unity of aim, an inclination to this and no other (general) activity. This ordering, for a given nature, of being to activity and through it, to a commensurate realization of good, can be recognized as a foundation of a natural law of particular beings. In every being, this law is specific, distinct and analogical, just as the composition of real relations that constitute being itself is specific, distinct and analogical. At the personal level, we say that each person's "call" is unique. However, in spite of the different, distinct existence of natural law so understood, we notice a proportional common or analogical inclination of various beings (in particular of persons), as existence itself is analogically common.

By grasping the natural inclinations to activity, and realizing through them goods suitable for a given nature, we can form a judgment-law about the nature of beings belonging to various classes. And in our conduct, and hence in a conscious and free decision, we must reckon with the nature of beings as found in their inclinations and purposes.

C. CONSTITUTION OF IDEA—ETERNAL LAW

The third area in which we arrive at a philosophical understanding of morality is in relation to the existence of the Absolute as the ruler of the world. According to St. Augustine, the Divine Law is the ordering of divine wisdom, insofar as it is the ultimate ruler of all acts and movements. It so created things that, as the result of their substantial construction, they hasten toward commensurate goals which have been assigned them. Philosophical knowledge, both metaphysical as well as ethical, cannot ignore Divine Law as the ultimate ontic reason of the structure, inclinations and purposes of really existing things.

St. Thomas Aquinas, in the *Summa Theologiae*, pointed to the Divine Law, and then gave a short, almost outlined explanation of Natural Law. He affirmed that Natural Law is only a "participation" in Eternal Law, though he did not explain any further on what this participation depends. In purely philosophical knowledge, however, we direct our attention above all to existing things themselves, and we point to God as a first and final cause of all existence and being. God is the ultimate cause of the intelligibility of things, and of their inclinations and purposes.

The Eternal Divine Law is the ultimate basis for the intelligibility of things and, thereby, it is also the highest law of moral conduct. Accordingly, we can assert that a failure to reckon in our decisions with objective natures and inclinations of beings is, in fact, a failure to reckon with Eternal Law as the ultimate reason behind the existence of things. In the same way, to reckon with the natures, the inclinations and purposes of things is an affirmation of the Eternal Law and an affirmation of God as the ultimate cause of contingent beings. For a transgression of the Eternal Law does not take place abstractly or directly in relation to God Himself. Rather, it takes place through the composition of things, with which we either do, or do not, reckon in our conduct.[6]

Having distinguished these three areas of moral life, we can in conclusion examine more closely the structure of the moral act.

II. MORAL BEING

In the theoretical order we distinguish a fundamental understanding of being in existential judgments: first, the clarification of the content of being in the form of "primary principle" judgments, such as Identity, Non-contradiction, and Sufficient Reason; then, the particularization of these first principles in the form of differentiated concrete judgments. Likewise, in the order of practical knowledge there is, first, the natural law, "Good should be done," as well as synderesis as the complex of first foundations of moral conduct. Natural law and synderesis are present "prescientifically," but they can be developed as a scientific "general ethics." Ethics, understood in this way, can then be the foundation for stating concrete judgments concerning proper conduct with relation to this or that object-thing.

THE PRACTICAL SYLLOGISM—SOME QUALIFICATIONS

To adopt the terminology of the ethics manuals, natural law, along with synderesis and the propositions of ethics, would constitute the major premise of a moral syllogism. The knowledge of the nature of the object in concrete conditions would constitute the minor premise. The conclusion of the moral syllogism would be a "practically-practical" judgment: "Do x" or "Do not do x."

This abstract schema can be deceptive unless it is understood that in a single cognitive function—as in one current of a great river—there stand out differentiated structures and currents which are dependent not only on the object, but on the knowing subject itself, on its structure, inclinations, behavior, etc. The question here, of course, is about practical knowledge, a knowledge which finds itself under a stronger influence of single perception than does theoretical knowledge.

In a person who is weighing a decision, cognitive sensible perception is further strengthened by the flow of the activity of instincts, so that the knowledge which is to warrant a proposed decision may be obscured or even nullified. In "premises" supplied by conscience there sometimes occurs a so-called knowledge of the nature of the thing, its internal relations, its purposeful relations, its relations to Eternal Law. But there can and usually does follow an immediate decision-act which, because of a diminished reflective consciousness, becomes a morally diminished deed.

ROLE OF IRRATIONAL ELEMENTS

A diminution of the moral character of the deed may also take place in relation to the pressure of our emotions and passions, which do not allow the intellect a calm examination in a situation. These diminished moral deeds are in fact the rule rather than the exception in human activity. To make a right moral decision we must train ourselves in self-control and reflection since the pressure of biological forces and a lack of spiritual control are by nature considerable. This is why we cannot underestimate the role of the irrational elements in the analysis and explanation of a moral decision. This means that in a concrete situation, it is exceedingly difficult to outline to what extent an undertaken decision was truly free, and to what extent the choice followed the overpowering of irrational aspects.

In spite of these qualifications, our analysis of moral good and evil should take into consideration ideal states which have been "distilled" from preconscious and unconscious pressures. If it did not, we could never grasp the essence of a moral choice and the nature of good and evil.

ELEMENTS OF THE IDEAL MORAL ACT

In an ideal moral act, then, working with complete freedom and consciousness flowing from a knowledge of the nature of the good which "stands before me" for choice, we can observe the following agreements or disagreements among the essential elements of our conduct:

1. Agreement of the free choice of the will with the act of the intellect, the "practically practical" judgment. This agreement exists always, except in cases of mental or emotional sickness, because a practical judgment and an act of free choice together constitute the one being of a moral decision.

2. The agreement of our practical judgment with the theoretical judgment about the "thing-good" or with a knowledge of the nature of the thing, its inclination or its purposes. Hence a knowledge of the object-good in the presence of which we undertake a decision is something very important for moral good and evil. I cannot "use" an object-good inconsistently with its nature, purpose, or inclinations especially when this object is a human person: I myself or my neighbor.

3. Agreement of the practical judgment with the Eternal Divine Law. This agreement comes about when the practical judgment impelling me to make a decision is in agreement with the inclinations and purposes of the thing-good indicated by the theoretical knowledge accompanying the decision.

Undertaking such a decision realizes natural law in a concrete case which discloses itself to me as a good. I actualize my personal potentiality by enriching myself with real good, affirming good objectively as the ultimate reason for the intelligibility of things.

MORAL EVIL

Concrete moral evil emerges in the lack of agreement between elements of moral composition. These absences present themselves:

(a) In the inadequate knowledge of a thing's nature, its inclination and its purposes. Even though in itself this is an intellectual evil and not a moral one, this lack of a cognitive agreement with the nature of things can bear the character of moral evil. The effort to secure a cognitive agreement must be proportional to the weight of the undertaken decisions.

(b) If, in a theoretical failure to recognize the nature of a thing-good, there is also lacking a correct practical judgment about our conduct in the presence of an observed good, then there is also no moral evil but only an intellectual error, insofar, clearly, as the falsity of the theoretical judgment was not due to the will.

(c) If there is a proper cognition of the nature of the object-good, its inclinations and purposes, and the practical judgment is not in agreement with the nature of that object, then there is a lack of agreement of our practical conduct with the object-good. At the same time, there is a lack of agreement of practical cognition with theoretical. This lack of agreement is a depravity from within man who makes a decision in the presence of an object-good which presents itself to him. This inner distortion of personality constitutes the essence of moral evil. It is an expression of disagreement between man's conduct and the nature of the being itself and its eternal and ultimate guarantee: the Absolute.

THE ERADICATION OF MORAL EVIL

Moral evil, as every evil, does not exist through its own existence but through the existence of the subject in which it resides. For this reason it cannot be, of itself, an object of any cognitive or active endeavors. For this reason, we cannot directly fight evil without simultaneously fighting, in some measure, the subject itself of this evil. For if evil is not a being, then only the subject-bearer of evil exists as being. Accordingly, a positive battle with evil is, above all, a battle with an already weakened subject who carries deficiencies, namely evil, within himself.

A total eradication of evil is possible only through the annihilation of the subject. Hence a direct and immediate battle with evil is an unsuccessful attempt to hypostasize evil. Meanwhile, the subject of evil is a being and thus good. A direct battle with evil would cause more harm than good because it would actually strike at being and good. Hence from a philosophical point of view, it is proper not so much to remove evil (for only that which exists can be removed), as to strive for good, including the entirety and perfection of the thing-subject. Evil can be "fought" through a healing of the subject and by providing him with goods which he does not possess. Perhaps against this background we can understand the theory of the Gospel precept of non-resistance to evil.

CHAPTER IX

MAN AND SOCIETY

INTRODUCTION

The chapter, *Man and Society*, is divided into two broad sections: I. Ontic Conditions for the Relation Between Individual and Society and II. Forms of Society and Man's Development.

The First Section is, in turn, subdivided into the following areas: A. An Open Ego, B. Dynamization of the Human Person and, C. Common Good. The Second Section comprises: A. Historical Point of View, B. Liberal Individualism and, C. Rejection of Extreme Models.

We shall now proceed to examine the complex relationship between man and society by posing a pivotal question: Does a society guarantee personal development? If so, under what conditions?

The answer to this two-part question will include: (a) an analysis of the ego—of a being that is open to a "Thou" and "we," (b) a study of the essential character of *society* and, (c) an examination of the basis for a social bond, which is called "common good."

This will be analyzed in the light of existential personalism.

I. ONTIC CONDITIONS FOR THE RELATION BETWEEN INDIVIDUAL AND SOCIETY

Contemporary philosophy has been increasingly preoccupied with the problematic of man in his social conditionings. The names of J. Maritain, E.

Mounier, M. Heidegger, K. Jaspers, G. Marcel, J. P. Sartre and others immediately come to mind. S. Kierkegaard had, in the 19th century, already rebelled against the pantheistic idealism of Hegel and tirelessly emphasized man's dignity and individuality. Similarly, G. Marcel condemned the "functionalization of man," whereby the human individual "in his own eyes and in those of others, presents himself exclusively as an agglomeration of accumulation of functions."[1]

Personalistic theories, especially those of Maritain and Mounier, distinguish between an individual and a person. Man's individuality alone, does not separate him with respect to a social group, but it subordinates him to this group in imitation of a biological cell to the entire organism. On the other hand, man as person surpasses the community which should be subordinated to him.

We are convinced that there should be today a renewed and better organized linkage of the problem of an individual's relation to society, with the tradition of classical philosophical thought.

A. AN OPEN EGO

The theory of personal being has a rich history and it extends to the earliest philosophical considerations of Plato, Aristotle, St. Augustine and the Church Fathers. Contemporary philosophers, especially the phenomenologists, give a better understanding of man as a subject, who acts both in relation to the world and to another person, who is a partner in human experience and, finally, in relation to a kind of community we can denote as a "we."[2]

MAN'S OPENNESS

Man's personal "openness" makes it possible for him to communicate in the order of being, with which he has come in contact through knowing and loving. Ultimately these activities find their expression in our acts of decision.

Although man finds himself immersed in a material world (Heidegger), he uses this world of things as a means for himself and his self-expression. In this development of his psycho-spiritual life, man uses things differently from animals. He communicates with the world under the aspect of his being. Unlike the animal, which knows concretely and only a limited segment of reality, man is open to *all* reality.

This "openness" places the world of things as an "object," as something distinct from the "I." It allows me to recognize the "I" not only as the center but also as the subject of my activity, through which I communicate with the world which is different from the "I." A lack of reference of the world to the

"I," an absence of an ontic connection, testifies to a "lessening" of both the "I" and the world in which we are immersed.

I-THOU

And yet, man does not consider the world in which he lives and the whole of nature as a partner of his dialogue. Dialogue, a mutual communication of intellectually known contents, takes place between "I" and "Thou," with the result that "Thou" is understood as another "I," a being in itself and for itself. A personal "Thou" possesses all those features which we distinguish in an analysis of self as a personal being.

I treat another person as an autonomous subject of all the acts of which "Thou" is the source and final end. "Thou" is another "I," with whom contact and communication are made, precisely because we recognize "Thou" as another "I." In a word, another "Thou" is an equal partner for "I," not as a world of things which is, for us, an impersonal world, an "It" (Buber).[3]

THREE AREAS

Our partnership with another "Thou" takes place in three specific areas of 1. Knowledge 2. Love 3. Freedom.

KNOWLEDGE

The very word "dialogue" indicates a communication of intellectual content. I can grasp the world by means of my cognitive faculties and then present or communicate these contents, by means of signs, to another person, another "Thou." The communication of known contents is human speech, which constitutes the essential means of interpersonal communication. Speech presupposes (a) an act of knowledge, (b) a readiness to transmit these contents to another person, and (c) an act of factual transmission through the use of a system of conventional signs.

By communicating through conventional signs, we can arouse in another's intellect the same meanings which we are entertaining. In the process of communication, "I" and "Thou" are open, both in relation to each other as well as in relation to the grasped meaning.

LOVE

Besides a cognitive communication of knowledge between "I" and "Thou," there also exists the possibility of communicating mutual love.[4] This love is understood not only as an attraction in a previously known object, not only as a dynamic disposition of another to do good and to communicate with him; but it is also an offering of an "I" to a "Thou." The moment of offering oneself to another person is the most sublime moment of the act of love, since it is an expression of the highest degree of existential communication. The subject, who is a person, offers himself/herself to another person and encounters, in the perfect act of love, a similar offering of another "Thou" to the "I." Hence there arises a "be-ing for another," through which the "I" loses nothing of his/her inner riches but, on the contrary, enriches himself/herself in everything the "Thou" has acquired.[5]

In the act of love, the personally-existential openness reaches its zenith: we have here the offering of the very person's subject (of the very being) who, while presenting himself to another person, adopts the manner of *being-living-for-another-person.*

FREEDOM

The possibility of both knowledge and of love presupposes a person's spiritual freedom. In cognitive communication, as well as in an act of love, there must be a voluntary willingness by a personal subject. No one can force me to one or the other. This freedom which is the basis for communicating with another person, demands a mutual trust, a respect for the freedom of the other person, and a real "encounter."

A self-centered and "closed" person, on the other hand, rejects all communication. In the place of dialogue, there is only a permanent monologue. The "other" is not treated as a genuine "Thou," but only as an "It," a means to an end. As Marcel observes, the "I" of such an egocentric individual becomes impoverished and constricted.[6]

In summary, a genuine I-Thou relationship makes possible a communication in knowledge and love through freedom. The "I" becomes enriched through the sharing of its being with a "Thou."

COMMON GOOD

I-Thou relations lead to a completely new form of interpersonal life, which can be called a "we." Contrary to inauthentic I-Thou relations which are only perfected forms of egoism, a genuine I-Thou relationship depends on significant and broadened values which form the basis for a new reality, a "we." Further, it seems that there exist such values that cannot be realized in a pair; these values are common to a larger number of people; for this reason they are called COMMON GOOD.

Different persons can participate in such a created or commonly viewed good and, by participating, they bring about their own internally personal development. Precisely because they have, as their aim, the development of their personal potentialities, it is impossible to develop them either in isolation or even as a pair. Hence there is need for the establishment of a social group, a community which will insure (1) the creation of objective values that surpass the potentiality of particular individuals (or groups I-Thou) and (2) the internal, personal development of particular individuals. In a word, the basis for establishing some kind of community is Common Good.

There are three categories of values which surpass the capability of particular human individuals. These are (1) cognitive, (2) volitional, (3) productive-creative.

(1) *SCIENCE*

Cognitive values stand at the basis of science, understood in a sociological sense and, hence, of various social arrangements which are ordered to a scientific knowledge and an objective development of scientific thought. All human welfare and progress are ultimately founded on cognitive, scientific achievements. The transmission of scientific progress to the next generation demands collective effort in attaining and consolidating theoretical achievements. For this reason, the value and good which flow from scientific knowledge are something universal and communal; they exceed the potentiality, production and attainment of one individual.

(2) *MORAL GOOD*

In like manner, such moral goods as a communal justice, living in peace and tranquility, and the like, need more than the good will of one individual. Only a society can effectively guarantee the achievement of an interhuman moral good.

(3) *CREATIVITY*

The entire area of creativity, which is linked with industry and technology, clearly exceeds the potentiality of an individual and his/her particular good. Everything that is the product of human work (both intellectual and physical), is a common good that transcends particular and individual goods. Above all, man's birth, his upbringing, his development and attainment of human perfection are possible only within the context of communal existence.

However, the development of the personal "I" takes place only through the "I-Thou" relation, which presupposes a personal openness. This is so because such a relation makes possible a communication in common good. If "I-Thou" relations have regard for another person as person, then "I-We" relations allow a participation in common good, which is the necessary means for authentic human life. It makes possible the ultimate fulfillment of the human person.

SOCIETY AS "WE"

The attainment of common good so understood must be respected by society, which is understood as a perfect expression of what is called "We." It is here that individual persons participate in common good. An authentic, human personal participation, which is the realization and expression of "We," demands that the participating persons be really responsible for the integrity of common good. It also demands that the participating persons can cause the common good to be (a) a form which would perfect an individual person, and (b) that this common good be realized as the ultimate end of human aspirations.[7]

Ultimately, society as the realization of "We," makes possible the personal development of man, the opening of oneself to an absolute objective good, namely the Absolute Being.

FAMILY AND SOCIETY

From different points of view, the family and society are the two most fundamental forms of social life, fulfilling the human category "We."[7]

FAMILY

In the normal course of events, the family is the basic social entity. It is the basic "We" in which "I-Thou" relations take place, where a person opens oneself to the world, to another person, and to common good. It is only in the family that man perceives common good and becomes a participant in a community, thereby creating the first "We." The role of the family, therefore, is of paramount importance.

STATE

As a perfect community, the state has all the means for taking care of the actual common good of the members of a national community. Today there seems to be a tendency toward a supranational community which would envelop all mankind into some kind of universal model of a chief political system. This system differs greatly from the character of communities which will enter into the composition of universal national community.

B. DYNAMIZATION OF THE HUMAN PERSON

PERSON-COMMUNITY

When we describe man as a social being, we mean that he can achieve the full development of his personal life only through the cooperation of other people, i.e., in a community.

The human person is a concrete, individual *compositum*, in whom material-sensible, as well as rational-volitional elements constitute a specific unity—a dynamic unity that underlies his/her entire development. And although the human person constitutes a certain whole and complete "world-itself," he cannot develop by himself. He cannot realize his potentialities which make up the fullness of a "personal" world without cooperating with other persons. Hence an independent, human individual "creates" himself in the process of interacting with other persons. By nature, man inherits only a disposition or natural inclinations which must be developed and transformed into a personal individuality.

Freedom constitutes one of the essential manifestations of a human being. A personal being actualizes himself from *within*. This, however, cannot be done without participation in common good and the help of other people. Hence for the actualization of personal life, for development of knowledge, love, creativity and of creating oneself through spiritual acts, a real participation in common good is essential as a basis for social life.

SOCIETY

Society is a kind of ecological (cultural) niche which makes man's biological and psychical-personal development possible. The psychological aspect, however, cannot be primary in the analysis of social being because psychical experiences already presuppose a corresponding subject and object—they presuppose being.

From a philosophical point of view, community is undoubtedly a certain actuality, a certain being. However, it is not an independent being as, for example, man or some physical, living being is an independent entity. Society can be understood only as *a group of people bound together with relations*. The relations which bind people (from the philosophical viewpoint), are not relations which constitute being in the substantial order. They are relations, which constitute a "social reality," a relational one, into whose "composition," enter particular subjects as *independent rational beings*.

There can be no substantial unity of a social entity without negating the substantial unity of individual human persons—which would be patently absurd. For, if a social entity is a gathering of people—of persons—then it can be understood only as a unity of relation among persons.

DEFINITION

Community is a gathering, a "bond" of categorical relations, binding human persons, so that they can develop the dynamism of their personality, for the purpose of fulfilling the common good of every human person. Community, then, is a natural creation which is necessary for the realization of common good.

C. COMMON GOOD

DEFINITION OF "GOOD"

We shall analyze the meaning of the two words "common" and "good;" and in our study, we must keep in mind the concepts of human nature and personality, with which common good is linked, and to which it is ordered as to its object and goal.

In the *Nicomachean Ethics*, Aristotle speaks of good as the end or goal of every activity.[8] The "good-end" of activity is in reality the object of the appropriate inclination of a given being. It is also called "desire." The end does not differ from the good objectively, but only formally. It involves a relation to an actual desire when we say that the good is "desirable." For good is being, insofar as this being becomes the reason of the desire. Briefly: being arouses desire because it is good, and since it is good, it becomes the goal of desire.

Man acts for a specific end only because the object of desire appears to him as worthy of desire—as a good and because of that good, man desires it—hence he "wants" it.

EXISTENCE AND GOOD

Existence is understood as the most perfect element or moment of being, since existence is the ultimate act of everything that is called a real being. For no perfection would be real if it did not exist. The existence (be-ing) of a being is that which ultimately actualizes all the potentialities of being that belong to the nature of an entity. If existence is understood as concrete and really existing, then we identify it with the good. The concept of the good stands at the basis of the justification of every activity, especially human activity.

DYNAMIZATION

For man, the good is the constantly fuller realization of the potentiality of his nature. In every other instance, there is another actualization, analogically understood. Man hastens "to multiply" his manner of existence, to enrich himself. These natural inclinations to a realization of man's essential status are ultimately founded in the Absolute Good, to whom every being and especially every conscious and free being is oriented. And this fuller realization of man's ontic aspirations in the area of knowing, loving, auto-determination is this good, which is the reason for every human being's activity. And in the sense of an analogically identical end, it constitutes common good.

From the standpoint of a person-subject, good appears as a foundation for human activity. The incompleteness, limitation and contingency of man's being testify to the "hunger" for a desired good. Hence the persistence of a lack of good testifies to an activity whose goal is a fulfillment of this lack. Only a suitable good can satisfy this lack.

DEFINITION OF "COMMON"

Only the good can become the common property of all people, for the character of this good designates human personality. For when we speak of common good, by that very fact, we also speak about the kind of good which concerns people as holders of a right to a personal development. Common good is attainable with the help of human acts as personal acts, which resolve themselves, above all, into acts of the intellect and free will.

Through these acts of the intellect and will, man actualizes himself and enriches his human personality in the areas of science, art and moral and religious enrichment. It is only in this order of purely personal good (attained by the intellect and will), that there can be no contradiction between the good of the whole community and of particular individuals as its members. And it is only in the concept of common good that there can be both a growth of the individual and of the whole society. Hence the goal of community is to make possible the fullest realization of common good, i.e., to create conditions for personal actualization to an unlimited degree.

MATERIAL GOODS

Clearly the actualization of personal good which is, at the same time, common good, demands such material means as food, shelter etc., which are needed for human life. Conflict can occur between the individual and the whole society concerning division and distribution of material means. It is the task of social powers to insure a just and equal division of material goods, as well as to organize work which will increase material means.

However important material goods might be, they cannot be recognized as common good in the proper sense. Neither can they be understood as the reason for the existence of law and social order. For material goods are only a means to a proper end. They cannot and do not possess within themselves the reason for an ultimate good.

HIERARCHY OF GOODS

A certain hierarchy exists in the order of material goods: there are goods of a higher and lower rank. Obviously vegetative human life is more valuable than vegetative animal life or plant life because it is involved in the personal life of man and there is no good beyond the individuality of the human person. Goods which sustain personal life are more valuable than those which provide more comfortable living etc. And just as in the order of nature we find a hierarchy of beings (where the entity of the Absolute is the foundation of everything) so, too, there exists a hierarchy of goods, for good and being are the same.

GOD AS HIGHEST GOOD

Hence the highest objective good is also the highest Absolute Being, i.e., God. This Good can be "attained" only through the personal acts of intellect and will. Since the highest Good can be the objective Good common to every person and the entire society, this very Good is the *raison d'etre* of society and its laws. Hence no society can issue any laws which would hinder the attainment of common good. Clearly any such decrees or pseudo-laws cannot, in any way, bind citizens in conscience.[9]

Human acts which border on common good or personal acts of knowledge and love enrich the entire community. Other acts, which deal with material, corporeal and external goods, must be subject to social control in order to insure their just distribution.

ERRONEOUS THEORIES OF COMMON GOOD

CRITIQUE

Some theories erroneously maintain that common good can be realized only with the common effort of all individuals together. Such theories which seek, within common good, both a suprahuman and suprapersonal good which an individual man cannot attain, are to be rejected. They deny the essential trait of personality, i.e., its "wholeness" or "completeness." According to these theories, the aggregate entity of a collective or some suprahuman formation would be a higher form of existence than that of an individual person. But there *is* no independent "fuller" form of existence than that of an individual person. Community is only a relational creature and it cannot usurp the place of a human being. If some kind of higher whole were to be placed above man-person, as a whole which could make him completely happy, then we would have a personification of a social creature— a totalitarianism. This is absolutely unacceptable.

INTERNAL BINDING FORCE OF COMMON GOOD

The binding force of common good is an internal one. A command imposed externally by a community which is neither understood nor respected, is immoral; it is a moral violence. To understand common good fully, we must see its essential character and the role of community in educating man for rational freedom.

II. FORMS OF SOCIETY AND MAN'S DEVELOPMENT

In this section, we shall seek to discover the kind of social organism which is not contrary to man's development as a free person. Three different models will be studied: *A. Unconditioned Supremacy of the Social Organism*, *B. Liberal Individualism*, and *C. Mutual Arrangements Between Human Individual and Community*.

A. UNCONDITIONED SUPREMACY OF THE SOCIAL ORGANISM

In ancient times, social organisms reigned almost supreme. Man was completely subordinated to the power and will of the whole. The human individual was "lost" in the state.

PLATO'S REPUBLIC

Despite the nobility of Plato's philosophy, his model state, the Republic, demanded a total and complete submission of man to the state. The "Wise Men" would thrust upon the people certain exemplars of authoritative happiness without regard to their free-will acceptance.

CRITIQUE

As K.R. Popper points out, Plato's concept of society allows little room for freedom in individual human activity. Plato locates man's freedom in branches of explicitly formulated law and an inexorably established social order. There is no longer any completely private life; everything is a social function.[10]

A. Kasia observes, "The ideal Platonic State was, in essence, a police state of unheard-of, severely executed moral-religious laws. The rulers should take every citizen of the state under scrupulous control and protection, without exception, from birth until death."[11]

The concept of a state which totally forms a citizen has never disappeared from the scene of history. Today various forms of fascism appeal to the Platonic ideal state for their justification. They regard the human person to be only a means of realizing the ends of government. In such a context, as J. Messner rightly notes, the human person can never be the end; his value is only that of a means for furthering the state.[12]

HEGEL

Like Plato who recognized only the totality as a genuine reality, Hegel (22 centuries later), accepted that only the "whole" is true and real. Individual persons are nothing more than dialectical moments in the evolutionary process of the whole. Individuals are completely subordinated to the community; they are merely its function. Society exerts (or attempts to exert) control over man's thoughts, his technical and artistic creativity. If he attempts to protect his non-conformist goals, he is known as an enemy of society and is destroyed by it. As a result, such societies inevitably bring back slavery.

B. LIBERAL INDIVIDUALISM

An equally extreme alternative of realizing the relation *man-society* is the theory which is based on nominalistic presuppositions. "Humanity" represents only human individuals; the family, individual members: father, mother etc. Society is a fiction; only people exist, of whom some have more power and others do not. Obviously, in such a context, there are no laws, no social obligations.

ROUSSEAU

J.J. Rousseau's "Social Contract Theory" is representative of the position that every man has complete freedom. (This is not a question of freedom of human decisions, of choice, but rather of the manner of man's existence.) Man is independent of everyone. He cannot be subject to anyone. He can be obedient only to himself and to his own commands. But because people desire to live more comfortably, they organize themselves into a society. And the social contract would reconcile the basic demands of natural law with a social association; thus, equality would be preserved.

Rousseau's notion of freedom is somewhat different, since it depends less on a manifestation of one's own will than on not being subservient to the will of another. To guarantee such a freedom, legislative authority must be exercized by all and only the *referendum* is uniquely the legal form of the functioning of authority.[13]

CRITIQUE

Such a conception of a freely united society, where every member is sovereign, leads to a denial of authority which is a formal element of every society. If individualistic liberalism were to be the basis for a social union of men, there could be no place for the realization of common good. There would exist only the good of the individual as the ultimate goal in itself alone, without common good. Such a state of affairs would end in anarchy or the ultimate annihilation of social existence and of all laws. Only the strongest individuals would rise without any moral scruples.

Proudhon foresaw another consequence of the evolutionary process of individualistic liberalism, namely that of totalism.[13a] In such a hypothesis, the human masses both are, and are not, the subject of sovereign authority, since they govern through delegates who act in the name of the masses. Such delegates battle among themselves and weaken the government. In the face of a debility of warring parties and delegates, there will arise strong dictatorial rule by an individual or a group, who will direct totally and wholly the community it rules.

As history testifies, such an individualistic democracy degenerates into a government of either one party that totally solves all difficulties, or of one race, or of one nation.[14]

C. MUTUAL ARRANGEMENTS BETWEEN INDIVIDUAL AND COMMUNITY

The extreme models which we have presented above lead to a denial of a human rational nature and they threaten a distortion of the development of human personality.

The following elements are essential for a satisfactory relationship between individual and society:

(a) an autonomous, substantial and self-contained personality which needs community for its existence;

(b) community understood as a relational being;

(c) common good which possesses its objective and subjective side and hence such a good that unites all to a common goal which is, at the same time, the goal of every individual.

Hence, *a community is a society of rational free persons who realize common good through acts of knowledge and love and creativity by being "for another."* Community, thus understood, is an accepted form of government "from within," through the consciences of free persons.

CRITIQUE OF HEGELIANISM

Community is therefore not a kind of autonomous substantial totality as it appears in Hegel's conception. Community does not exist through a dialectical unfolding of the absolute, of which people are only fleeting moments. A community is not above persons but, on the contrary, human persons exceed and surpass community. Despite Hegel's view, the real and autonomous beings are people, i.e., human persons. Society is only a relational association of these persons. Man does not acquire his be-ing from society but conversely the latter receives its be-ing from real individual people. Society has no real be-ing of its own.

Community is therefore really and fundamentally ordered to man as a person, since a personal being is the same as a free and conscious human being. A social structure which subordinates man and considers him only a social function is fundamentally wrong, evil and without a goal. Such a community is a servile community which deforms the personhood of its members, and persons are merely a means to the end of preserving the power of society.[15]

TWO OPPOSING THEORIES

There are two opposing theories of society: (1) the totality or the whole is truly being (Platonism and Hegelianism), and (2) the true being is the individual person. The first position holds that man is for the sake of the whole. The second maintains that the "whole" is really and basically for the sake of knowing, loving, free people.

CRITIQUE

Liberal individualism is a distortion and error in the social structure because it begets anarchy, domination by unscrupulous individuals, and a negation of common good. On the other hand, a position which holds that community is a being "in itself and for itself," totally disregards human nature. (Man is to be fashioned by society to serve its ends.)

AN EFFECTIVE CRITERION

Ultimately, the only effective criterion for an acceptable relationship between man and the state is the inner structure of a being which manifests itself in activity. This we call *nature*. When we examine human activity, we find a hierarchy of acts. The fundamental norm in determining this hierarchy is the common good of the activity of the individual and the entire community.

When we take into account man's personal immortality, the most valuable, most noble and lasting acts he can perform are cognitive-rational. Without question, these acts occupy the highest rung on the ladder of excellence. And because these acts permanently ennoble man and bind the person with common good, we contend that man is that "entirety" which is superior to society. This is so because such activity improves autonomous personal being as the highest "whole;" it endures beyond time and transcends material conditions, including death.

THOMISTIC EXISTENTIALISM

Both Aristotle and St. Thomas held that matter is the principle of individuation. For the Stagirite, who was influenced by Plato, the essential cause of being was form, which is universal and understood by itself and which, through individuation and intermingling with matter, becomes at all times universal.

For Thomas Aquinas, being is real not because it has form (it is organized through form), but because it *possesses the act of existence* (be-ing). Hence the question about individuation resolves itself into indicating non-contradictory elements of individuation—not as a being but as a strictly potential and receptive element which restricts the manner of an existing being. Such an element is precisely quantified matter which, for the same reason, is the cause of everything that can be called "individual."

ONTIC FOUNDATIONS

In this sense, we agree with St. Thomas' position that there exist ontic foundations which support both materially-circumscribed activities and, those activities which, transcending matter, are linked with the essential goal of the human being as a person.

Hence we should speak not so much about the individual structure of man as subordinate to the community and about personal structure as subordinating this community to itself, but rather about the *ontic foundations* of an individual and personal type. In this way, the theory of personalism is more closely identified with the character of human activity rather than with the manner of being. And the value of this activity will be determined by its connection with the goal as common good.

CONCLUSION

Man is ordered and subordinated to society and, conversely, society is ordered and subordinated to man; but from different points of view. Since man's dignity is the highest good, he is free and independent in the development of his personality and purely human actions. Concerning the division and just distribution of external, material goods, man is subordinated to the community. In this instance society has the authority and it rises somewhat above man who, in certain concrete cases, can lose his right to an uncontrolled use of material goods.

Since personalism is only a philosophical theory, it cannot become a social theory which would determine, in a concrete way, the organization of a given society. It is extremely difficult in practice to establish, without conflict, a relation of man-society. Nevertheless, we should keep insisting that man has basic inalienable rights. These human rights are his by reason of his personal human being and the goal of human activity. We should work strenuously to raise men's collective consciousness concerning these basic human rights (and duties), however difficult the undertaking might be.

CHAPTER X

MAN AND RELIGION
by Sister Zofia Zdybicka, Ph.D.

This chapter is divided into four sections: I. Introductory Perspectives, II. The Religious Fact (Phenomenon of Religion), III. Religion as an Area of Culture, and IV. Philosophical Formulation and Explanation of the Religious Fact.

I. INTRODUCTORY PERSPECTIVES

In his existential unity, man is composed of two ontic areas: matter and spirit. He both transcends the world of matter and he is immersed in the cosmos. He is equally a being in the world of things and the world of persons. Man is a "dynamic" being, i.e., one who develops and actualizes himself by entering into relations with these two realities. By his actions, man "creates" and transforms himself and he establishes values in two broad areas: (1) a material-biological sphere and hence the area of life-giving and economico-technical values and (2) a cultural sphere which satisfies man's psychic needs and includes all cognitive, aesthetic and social values.

A special type are moral values which define man's existence as a person and hence as a subject who comes into contact primarily with other person-subjects. These indicate a person-to-person relationship, as well as religious values which bind man with something which transcends the world of nature and of culture.

The purpose of nonreligious values is to develop a human dynamism which will shape the world in agreement with human measures. Religious

137

values, on the other hand, emphasize the fact that man is not only coexistent with other beings but he is coexistent with another personal "Thou"—the person of the Absolute.

QUESTIONS

Several fundamental questions must be asked: What is man's religious perspective, and what does it mean? Where does it come from? Again: Does there exist an equivalent of a transcendent reference and an object of man's religious activity? What is its nature?

In most general terms, the religious phenomenon is a relation between man and a reality distinct from him, namely, a higher and transcendent one. Hence the religious dimension of man presupposes reference to the real existence of a transcendent reality, which is the object of these religious actions. The question of man's "religiousness" is especially important because it bears on a determination of the final perspectives and dimensions of human life.

In fact, the great eras of human history can be identified by their differing relations to religion (Feuerbach). The Middle Ages, for example, considered religion as a principal value which permeated individual and social life. Today, because of the influence of Hegel, Feuerbach and Marx, religion is viewed by some as exerting a negative influence on man's autonomy and as hampering the dynamism of his development. We are witnessing today a conflict between two opposing kinds of humanism:

(1) immanent (atheistic) humanism, which considers man as a completely autonomous being, the most valuable of all reality;

(2) theistic humanism, which holds that man is a being of the highest value in the realm of created entities; his existence is immeasurably broadened because it is the ontic consequence of a psychological and moral union of man with a transcendent Being.[1]

The chief modern critics of religion (Marx, Nietzsche, Freud and Sartre), hold that it has no permanent, necessary and real foundations in man's nature. Religion has come into existence as the result of unfavorable and frustrating conditions of man's existence in the world. Once these conditions are removed or ameliorated, man can be freed from the bonds of religion. Thus the destruction of religion is essential to restoring man's dignity.[2]

In reaction to this improper interpretation of religion, there arose theories portraying the originality and irreducibility of the religious phenomenon to other spheres of man's existence. These provided a fertile field for the growth of phenomenology and the philosophy of religion. Their object was to discover and establish the essence of religious acts, of divinity, of holiness and the like. The adaptation of the phenomenological method to the philosophy of religion achieved spectacular results at the hands of R. Otto, E. Brunner, M. Buber, M. Eliade, R. Guardini, G. van der Leeuw and, above all, Max Scheler.[3]

PHENOMENOLOGICO-EXISTENTIAL METHOD

The phenomenologico-existential method strives to grasp acts of consciousness, their structure as well as the methods of constituting objective counterparts and meanings. This method has been especially successful in its analysis of man's religious experiences and his relation to external objective realities.

M. Scheler contends that religious acts grasp their object directly and intuitively. Hence they have an objective character; they do not create their objects, but *cognize* them. Divinity and holiness are not the products of man, as Feuerbach affirmed, but something that exists beyond man, something he discovers, feels and thinks. Phenomenological analysis enables us to determine the essence of religious actions, as well as the relation between man and religion and the transcendent object of such actions in relation to man.

Since the phenomenologico-existential method gives us only descriptive (albeit indispensable) knowledge, we must resort to a philosophy of religion. We need a more objective treatment of the phenomenon of religion and of discovering its final, ontically non-contradictable reasons.[4]

Accordingly, we shall first give a description of the phenomenon of religion from the viewpoint of both its object and subject, and we shall determine its relation to cognition, morality and the arts. Next we shall study the event of religion as a philosophical category. Finally, we shall show the ultimate non-contradictable relations of religion which are both objective (they are linked to the personal structure of the human being) and subjective (they are linked to the existence of a Personal Absolute and his relation to the world)—the transcendental participation of being.

II. THE RELIGIOUS FACT
(PHENOMENON OF RELIGION)

The history of human culture and religion supplies us with much empirical data, so that we can say with great probability that religion is inseparable from human life. Wherever man appears, he develops a religious activity. The universality of the appearance of religious acts is beyond discussion.[5]

A highly controversial issue, however, is the answer to the question: *What is religion and what are its ultimate sources?*

DEFINITION

In attempting to answer this question, we shall search for those elements that are common to all religions. But first we must define a "religious fact" or the "phenomenon of religion." In its original, basic meaning, a "religious fact" is man's very reference and direction to a transcendent reality. Prayer, sacrifice and cult are, therefore, religious acts or the realization of such a reference. A more precise description of the "religious fact" includes: (1) an indication of what constitutes such a reference and, hence, what is the transcendent object; (2) how is such a reference given to man (in what kind of human acts); (3) how is the religious fact related to other human acts (cognitive, moral, aesthetic).

An analysis of scores of ancient, mediaeval and modern writers discloses the following essential elements in the definition of a religious phenomenon:

(1) man's reference is always to some reality higher than man, which is defined as *deity, sacrum, numinosum, God* or "an object of worship;"

(2) an attitude of man toward this deity (faith, respect, fear, honor, certain responsibilities);

(3) a moment of active (redeeming) intervention of a transcendent reality in man's life.

In sum, *religion is a specific, conscious reference of man to something different and superior to him: it is a bilateral contact with someone who appears in a definite form and in a special human activity.*[6]

A. ANALYSIS OF THE OBJECT OF THE RELIGIOUS FACT FROM THE ASPECT OF REALITY—A RELIGIOUS RELATION

In the above-mentioned definitions, the religious object is designated in the widest possible terms as *mystery, sacrum, deity, God.* Since, for example, totemism, fetishism, animism, polytheism, pantheism and monotheism have different objects of religion, we must distinguish religion in a broader, and a narrower, sense. In a broader sense, religion is a reference to a superhuman reality, understood most generally. In a more restricted interpretation, religion is connected with a recognition of the personal character of the object in which man searches for the origin and meaning of life. The partner of a religious union can be a person, but not necessarily a most perfect person. (Man's reference is definitely to some *one* and not to some *thing.*) A decidedly personal and monotheistic character of the object of reference is found in Judaism, Islam and Christianity. Scheler limits the religious phenomenon to this type of reference only: "Only where the Transcendent 'Thou' surpasses the world as a totality—do we have a right to speak about a religious act."[7]

HISTORY OF RELIGION

The history of religion bears out the personal character of the object of religion. The religions of China, India and Greece speak of the personal deities of Zeus (Greece), Mithra, Varuna Indra (Persia) and Re-Harachte (Egypt), as well as those of Jinnism and of the religions of India and Japan.[8] Further, religion has always been treated as a search for the foundation of man's personal life. Man was searching for an answer to the question of the meaning of his actions and personal life.

Christianity brought about an exceptionally interesting moment in understanding the object of religion. It is the personal Absolute, who is simultaneously a community of persons. The Triune God is, for man, the ideal model of religious union. It contains in itself a relationship with a Transcendent "Thou" and, at the same time, with other persons in a horizontal perspective (one commandment of love of God and neighbor).

B. ANALYSIS OF THE RELIGIOUS FACT FROM THE POINT OF VIEW OF THE SUBJECT—RELIGIOUS EXPERIENCE

We have defined religion as a union of man with transcendent reality which justifies human life as a personal existence. We must now ask the question: In what way is this religious "reference to the other member" given to man?

Phenomenology of religion, and especially psychology of religion, have given much attention to *religious experience* as a path man takes to enter into a personal, conscious contact with divinity.

RELIGIOUS EXPERIENCE

It is difficult to determine the precise character of religious experience. As a personal experience, it involves all the elements of the human psyche (and even body): cognitive, volitive and emotional. Each experience is also unrepeatable and unmeasurable. Nevertheless, we can distinguish three basic phases which constitute this composite process: (1) contact with a religious reality, (2) the "taking over" of the activity by the subject which has been "struck" by the religious object, (3) actualization of the conscious bond with God, through the religious act directed toward the religious object.

CONTACT WITH A RELIGIOUS REALITY

Contact with a religious reality (*sacrum*) is a religious perception which supplies certain information about the religious object. It is analogous to cognitive and aesthetic perception in a cognitive, moral and aesthetic experience. The subject here is passive; it is the receiver. Activity is on the side of the object, which reveals itself, shows its presence, and "strikes" the subject and arouses it from its previous state. Both natural potentialities (cognitive and volitive-emotional) powers, as well as so-called "obedient" potentialities (in Christian theology, the grace of God) come into play here.

The chief problem linked with the first phase of religious experience is the manner in which the religious object manifests and reveals itself to man. All scholars of religion agree that the religious object is not directly accessible, in all its grandeur, to the subject. To express the cognitive transcendence of the religious object, the term "revelation" is used. All religions imply a revelation, either natural or supernatural, i.e., that the religious object in some way "speaks" about itself. These may be linguistic word-objects or oral word-signs which God "pronounces" about his existence and his aims in relation to man.

OTTO

According to Otto, the religious object (*numinosum*) is inaccessible to man in a conceptual type of cognition. But man possesses a special ability to experience or feel divinity. This feeling of *sacrum* is a special affection which results in man's search for communication with the religious object (*numinosum*).

The typical feelings which result are (1) a feeling of mystery full of fear, (2) expressing absolute inaccessibility, i.e., "otherness" of this *numinosum*, and (3) a feeling of complete omnipotence (admiration). There are two contrasting aspects here: one, a repelling element exciting fear; and the other, a very attractive and fascinating one.[9]

SCHELER

Scheler holds that the religious phenomenon begins only when a personal God is involved. Scheler agrees with Otto that, to describe cognitive perception in a religious experience, it is absolutely necessary to consider that reality which is linked with "revelation" and faith. For faith refers to precisely such a reality which is not directly accessible to cognitive perception. It is more a question of "hearing" God as one who reveals his presence and speaks to man who, in turn, responds in faith. Therefore faith has a character of personal involvement because it engages the will, which pursues good that has been seen (love).

Cognitive experience has a character of objective evidence or "vision." Religious experience deals with personal cognition conditioned by love. Hence God speaks and man responds in faith, hope and love. A personal God reveals himself. He is present in man who does not see him, but whose "voice" he can hear and respond to. The initiative must always come from the side of the object, from the side of the revealing God, and not from the side of man. Hence religious perception is dialogic in character, between an inviting God and a responding man.[10]

MAN'S ACTIVE PARTICIPATION

In the second phase of religious experience, man is the subject who has been "struck" by the object (God). Man now desires to enter into personal contact with God, and his interior and exterior acts are best described as an attitude of worship and respect. However, the ultimate aim of a final contact with deity is something more. Man desires a union with deity whom he acknowledges as the highest good, worthy of love. Man desires and pursues this union with it and wants to be absorbed by it.

NATURAL AND SUPERNATURAL CHARACTER

Man's activity here has both a natural and supernatural character. He prepares himself for dialogue by methods of interior purification, whether Hindu yoga, Buddhist, or Neoplatonic asceticism, or Christian asceticism and mysticism. In Christian mysticism, natural activity is reinforced by a special grace which prepares man for union with God. This mystical experience is the fruit of the Holy Spirit's activity in a properly prepared soul.

ACTUALIZATION OF A CONSCIOUS BOND WITH GOD

In the third phase of religious experience, there follows an actualization of the conscious bond with God through action directed toward the religious object. This final completion of religious activity takes place when the entire action of Transcendence (God) meets with a full "atunement" of man. The subject reaches a certain connaturality with God. Man is open to all aspirations for good. He reaches the state of passive (infused) contemplation.

SUMMARY

In all religions, but especially in Christianity, the religious experience develops from a passive acceptance of God's action (first phase), through various activities whose purpose is to free man from limitations and direct him toward God (second phase)—up to the state of actualizing the bond, the union which is a preparation for a full life with and in God, which is to be man's condition after death.

C. BASIC FORMS OF RELIGIOUS ACTIVITY— RELIGIOUS ACTS (RELIGIOUS DEED)

The basic religious acts by which man expresses his relationship to deity and actualizes his perspective as a "being-toward-Transcendence" are (1) prayer, (2) sacrifice, (3) cult (4) asceticism, and (5) moral perfection.[11]

PRAYER

Prayer constitutes the most basic and common religious act. The partner in a personal dialogue may be either some invisible power, or some other entity but it is always one who listens and responds. There must be a real awareness of a spiritual bond with a personal God. It is a dialogue between a human "I" and a divine "Thou."[12]

While prayer may assume the form of adoration, thanksgiving or petition, its basic task is the actualization of the spiritual bond with God. It is the greatest of human activities.

SACRIFICE

At the basis of every religious relation is love, which seeks union with God. Love is fundamentally a *giving* and not a receiving. Hence sacrifice as a giving of oneself appears in all religions, and its fullest expression is found in the Christian religion. The moment of the gift constitutes "being-toward-God," a union with him in love.

D. RELIGIOUS FACT AND SCIENTIFIC COGNITION, MORALITY, ART

The nature of the religious act can be understood better by contrasting it with cognitive, moral, and aesthetic experiences.

COGNITIVE EXPERIENCE

Cognitive experience involves contact with an object, which reveals itself to a knowing subject. Relations which constitute a cognitive act are personal-factual, and not interpersonal ones. Even if the object is a person, it is treated as a "thing" or a set of qualifications to be known, but not as a person with whom one establishes a personal contact. A religious act, on the other hand, involves volitional-emotional moments (love). It has a quality of involved personal cognition, which induces one to action.[13]

MORAL EXPERIENCE

In the first phase, moral experience assumes the form of an experience of duty. The subject recognizes that he should perform a particular act because this experience refers to moral values (moral good or evil).

In the second phase, the experience of duty and moral values moves to an experience creating a moral behavior, actualized in a moral act, i.e., a moment of decision. By means of an act which is in harmony with duty, man brings about goodness which enriches him and makes him "better" and more human. Moral experience, like religious experience, focuses on action. But in a moral act, human beings are its object and the very subject of the moral experience as a person. In a religious experience, however, the subject is directed at once to the Transcendent Person.[14]

AESTHETIC EXPERIENCE

Aesthetic experience is the result of a certain emotional state and it contains a set of cognitive acts, which grasp the qualities of the artistic object (its harmony of elements and the like). In turn, it evokes certain volitional-emotional states, expressing approval or disapproval (pleasure, delight or disappointment). The value of beauty and function of aesthetic experience bring no measurable material profit but they enrich man emotionally.

There is a great difference, however, between aesthetic and religious experience. The object of a religious experience can be only a Transcendence, a really existing and loving Person; and the purpose of religious activity is union with It. Hence religious experience focuses on action, leading to a real union (love) of God. The object of aesthetic experience, in contrast, can be every being—natural or derived from man—which gives the experiencing subject specific experiences. However, it does not fulfill a personal existential role. Religious life reinterprets man's entire life in view of its "being-toward-Transcendence."[15]

III. RELIGION AS AN AREA OF CULTURE

Religious experience involves a conscious cooperation with God in constituting a spiritual bond between human persons and a Transcendent "Thou." Although religion is a personal and individual matter, it demands the cooperation of other persons. Mutual help of human persons is absolutely necessary. In sum, religion is a cultural happening (objective sense), which includes an area of human knowledge and activity directed to a Transcendence. Hence the religious fact determines: A. A Set of Truths, B. A Program of Religious Activity, and C. Religious Institutions.

A. A SET OF TRUTHS

Every religion contains certain truths or common elements. (1) an ontic and moral *ideal*. (Every religion holds that there is a reality which is absolutely perfect and superior to man); (2) acknowledgment of man's insufficiency and guilt with respect to this ideal—human existence contains a *flaw*. (Man realizes that he needs help from the Transcendent Being); (3) a *"Savior"* or way of *deliverance*, from this unfavorable condition are indispensable elements of every religion. (In Christianity, this means supernatural salvation which frees man from sin and enables him to unite with God. Christ, the Son of God, is the means whereby religious activity should lead to a union of a human "I" with the Transcendent "Thou.")[16]

RELIGIOUS DOCTRINE

Religious doctrine or cognition differs from other types of human cognition, e.g., philosophical and scientific cognition. While the latter concern themselves with theoretical cognition (acquisition of information), religious cognition deals with living, practical truth. Likewise its ultimate source is always some type of revelation.

The most essential trait of religious cognition is the way in which religious truths are asserted. They are not attained through reasoning, or because of the object's evidence, but on the strength of trust in the person who presents the information. Faith is a special act of the will, i.e., of a power whose fundamental activity is love. This love further affirms man's personal reference to Transcendence.

RELIGIOUS KNOWLEDGE AND PHILOSOPHY

Religious knowledge differs from a philosophical knowledge of God. Religious knowledge is always conditioned ethically and it has a personal character. Philosophical (metaphysical) knowledge of God is attained by knowing the structure of reality and its explanation. It is natural and entirely neutral; it is always a direct and theoretical knowledge.[17]

B. A PROGRAM OF RELIGIOUS ACTIVITY

Since man is a person who has potentiality, he "learns" "to-be-toward-Transcendence," just as he learns "to-be-toward-another" man. Hence human society develops methods and patterns for religious behaviors; it organizes common prayer, sacrifice, forms of cult; it controls the principles of morality implied by the religious foundations.

C. RELIGIOUS INSTITUTIONS

Religious institutions are designated for social help for a human person in realizing his/her activity. The realization of the human person, even in one's direction toward God, is achieved through and together with others. And just as children are taught from childhood to know and love those near to them;

so too, one should learn "being-toward-God" even when one is not yet in a position to understand the character of this reference. The moment of rational verification of convictions acquired in childhood will take place later in life.

IV. PHILOSOPHICAL FORMULATION AND EXPLANATION OF THE RELIGIOUS FACT

Since the religious fact is a human fact, it must be interpreted within the philosophical framework of a theory of being, and of man (metaphysics and anthropology). Our considerations will therefore be examined under the following headings:

A. RELIGION—AN INTERSUBJECTIVE RELATION (I-THOU)

B. MAN, A DYNAMIZED PERSON AS A SUBJECTIVE BASIS FOR THE RELIGIOUS FACT

C. OBJECTIVE JUSTIFICATION—RELATIONSHIP OF THE WORLD TO GOD (ONTIC TRANSCENDENTAL PARTICIPATION)

A. RELIGION—AN INTERSUBJECTIVE RELATION (I-THOU)
In modern philosophy, M. Scheler achieved perhaps the fullest characterization of religious acts. According to him, these belong to human consciousness, as well as acts of thought, memory, will and the like. These acts have no empirical origin. They have a transcendent purpose. Only God can satisfy their aspirations.[18]

SACRUM
The immediacy of the experience *sacrum* is a primordial phenomenon. The idea of holiness is not reducible to any historical category. It is not subject to definition. The basic constitutive element of *sacrum* is infinite love.[19]

Although Scheler identified the *sacrum* with a personal God, he did not indicate any ultimate ontic sources of a religious relation. In actuality, the need for transcendence toward God is called for by the very personal structure of the human being. It reaches a conscious ontic situation of man in the surrounding world of things and persons, and its functions depend on the actualization of the human person in his/her fullest dimensions.

PHILOSOPHY OF THE SUBJECT

Contemporary existentialisms that emphasize the "subject" have contributed to a greater study of religious relations. They have revealed the multilateral "openness" of human existence, which is also an openness to something transcendent.[20] They argue that man realizes himself through communication with other personal beings. Man's subjectivity is thus formed in interhuman relationships.

MAN AS BEING-TOWARD-TRANSCENDENCE

G. Marcel says that man is a "call" to God; he is an invocation to God. While man is aware of being "rooted" in this world, he also realizes his distinctness from it. Because he is a personal being, man can choose the object of his cognition and love and thus he transcends the whole world of nature. As such, Heidegger holds that man is a being who is preoccupied with the meaning of his being. He asks about "being-in-general" and "being-a-man."[21]

He asks not only the "whence," but also the "whither" of his being. And because man fails completely when he is considered purely as a "project-in-the-world," the natural desire of his existence must be understood as an orientation toward a Transcendent Being, who is essential for the human personality. Man desires to see God. As Marcel observes, man is a thrust toward God, an invocation, a pointing toward God.[22] An "openness" of the human being to Infinity, points to a certain ontic structure and situation of man in the world which, in turn, explain the appearance of the "religious fact."

RESUME

Briefly we can say: man is a religious being because he is a thinking person. The religious posture is found in man's nature and his ability to think. God reveals His existence to us through our existence. As F. Copleston argues, religion depends on the experience of our contingency.[23] We realize ourselves only to the extent that we are open to other beings. By experiencing ourselves, we experience our own finiteness, dependence, incompleteness and contingency. We become aware of our contingency because we realize the limits of human experience—in the presence of death.

The human being who is not self-sufficient is aware of his/her contingency and the contingency of the external world. This primordial awareness postulates the existence of a full, Absolute Being who would be a justification and completion of man's personal life. The awareness of our own ontic status, of relation with the world of things and, above all, a postulated interpersonal relationship, leads us to recognize an innate desire for intersubjectivity with the Transcendent "Thou."

ONTOLOGICAL REFORMULATION
OF A PHENOMENOLOGICAL DESCRIPTION

1. The foundation for directing man to God is the contingent, ontic status of human existence. Man is not a primordial necessary being (existence does not belong to his essence). Hence he is a caused being. Knowledge about man's ontic situation, which is acquired in metaphysics, is given to man in his personal awareness of his "transitoriness," frailty and contingency. Hence this experience of contingency is a transcendental—it is the lot of all people. And the religious fact arising from this awareness of man's contingency is linked with the very nature of human existence. It pervades the whole of man and what is most essential to him; the human ability of cognition and love.

2. The goal of religious destiny can be only an absolute person. Because the capacity of man's cognition and love goes beyond contingent persons, he can be united only with a personal, fulfilled existence, freedom and love. We agree with Scheler that the end of a religious relation cannot be some kind of material being, some kind of personal dependent being. Only a personal Absolute constitutes an adequate "Thou" for human existence.[24]

HUMAN "I" AND ABSOLUTE "THOU" RELATIONSHIP

In view of the above, we understand a religious phenomenon philosophically as a relationship between the human "I" and the absolute "Thou." This relationship has the following notes:

(1) Existential: it is a real union, written into the very structure of man and demanding practical activity for its realization;

(2) Intersubjective: it occurs between personal beings. It has a dialogic-responsive character, i.e., of mutual meeting and mutual giving of oneself;

(3) Dynamic: it establishes in man a potentiality for "being-toward-God," which can be realized only through conscious and free activity. The religious bond created by religious activity involves both man and God. In Catholic theology, God's action is described as Providence, sanctifying and actual grace, and the special help of the Holy Spirit. These are a preparation for man's full union with God;

(4) Necessary: religious union with God is necessary so that man can truly become man. Likewise, since man attains his fullest develop-

ment through union with God, God cannot not desire this union because He himself is the "Author" of man's nature;

(5) Reversible: it is a relation between a human person with the Person of the Absolute. A religious act is completely directed to man; it is completely disposed to man's fullest actualization.

A religious act, as an experience and expression of a personal bond of man with the Transcendent Thou, involves the entire human ego. It is the most complete and most integrating experience by which man discovers and grounds his individuality most fully. Man becomes, to the highest degree, a person and a "spirit."[25]

FUNCTION AND VALUE OF RELIGIOUS ACTS

Holiness is the value which is achieved by religious acts. And yet holiness is not a separate category, like the transcendentals of truth, goodness and beauty. Holiness seems to be a value which is "built" on all the remaining ones. It consolidates them, and is essentially united with man.

Man is a being in the perspective of the Transcendent "Thou," who is a Pure Spirit. Religious activity is aimed at "spiritualizing" man. It involves a fuller subordination of the body to the spirit in an ontic sense, as well as in a moral sense, as a greater and more spiritual love, a fuller freedom and the like. If the value of holiness is a "spiritualizing" of man, then it seems to be more in agreement with the nature of the human person and the nature of the divine Person.[26]

In religious experience, man therefore actualizes himself as a spiritual being and, as it were, "divinizes" himself. Thomas Aquinas did not hesitate to call a human being "God by participation."[27] The entire religious activity of man is directed to such a divinization. "Being-in-oneself," "being-for-oneself," is simultaneously "being-for-another" and, above all, "being-for-God."

SPIRITUALIZATION

The entire process of the realization of man—creation of a human person—is a process of spiritualization. It involves the gaining of an ever fuller freedom in relation to the determining factors of matter. Man will gain an ever greater truth, goodness, love, interior freedom and the like. It is precisely because of his spiritual element that man has a relation to God and his union with God demands a certain connaturality and, hence, a "spiritualization." Such exactly appears to be the function of religious acts: the realization of man in his spiritual aspect.

In the process of spiritualization (sanctification), man is aided by special strength (grace). The religious act is achieved not only by personal activity of the subject, but it presupposes a special help from God. Encounter, dialogue, faith, love and hope in relation to a Transcendent "Thou" involve both man's activity and a special power (sanctifying grace) imparted by God.

B. MAN, A DYNAMIZED PERSON, AS THE SUBJECTIVE BASIS FOR THE RELIGIOUS FACT

INTERNAL AND EXTERNAL DYNAMIZATION

As a material-spiritual being, man experiences his existential unity (of his "I") and his subjectivity. This means that man is a "doer" of specifically human acts, namely intellectual cognition and volitional desire (love). As a substantial being who experiences his own identity, man is a *dynamized* being. He has certain dispositions and he realizes (actualizes) them in contact with the world and other personal beings. Man realizes himself as a person through acts in relation to his potentialities. He develops himself and achieves a fullness in the needs and limits of his nature. Dynamization (and hence actualization) of the human being, therefore, has a twofold dimension: (1) internal and (2) external.

INTERNAL

Man actualizes himself internally through cognition, love and freedom. Metaphysically, act is a perfection; potentiality, an imperfection. Hence activity—the act of the doer—is his actualization or his perfection. Man thus develops himself through the activity of intellectual cognition and deliberative desire.

Man's highest potentiality is his intellect as a cognitive power, and his will, as an appetitive power. The object of the intellect is truth; of the will, goodness. Man can know intellectually everything that exists, and he can love everything. His potentiality here is unlimited, because ultimately it is oriented to the Absolute.

TRUTH—INTELLECT

The proper object of the intellect is the essence of material things, and the intellect actualizes itself insofar as it knows the essences of these things. But since they are only caused, effected and derivative beings, man remains in the state of potentiality and inquiry as long as he does not know their cause: the Absolute Being who is Absolute Truth. Therefore none of the fragmentary truths actualizes fully the potentiality of man's intellect. A full actualization of the intellect's potentiality can take place only by a direct contact with Absolute Truth, who is the goal of human cognitive activity.

GOODNESS—WILL

Just as the human intellect is oriented to the knowledge of all truth, so is the will oriented to goodness. Man who knows everything, can love everything. He can unite himself with everything in an act of love. The adequate object of love for a personal being is a human person, who is uniquely capable of returning love and with whom a meeting and union can take place. But love of any relative good does not fully actualize the human potentiality. The ultimate Object, the ultimate Goal which can bring about complete actualization, is only the Absolute Goodness, God Himself.

An analysis of the cognitive and volitional acts of man as a dynamized person show that no contingent, finite being can be man's ultimate goal. Only the fully perfect Person, God, can fill man's need. Only a personal bond with the Absolute results in complete happiness for man. Neither is happiness understood here as a kind of emotional state. Rather, as Thomas Aquinas points out, it is a complete actualization of man's potentiality in a dynamic way; it is a union of man's intellect and will with the Person of the Absolute.[28]

HUMAN FREEDOM

"Being-toward-God" evidences itself in human freedom. Man is aware of his freedom in choosing goods, with which he unites through love. And so in a conscious and free way, man decides on the choice of Full Goodness, which is not apparent to him in its total distinctness as long as he lives on this earth.

The final end of man—union with the Highest Good and Highest Truth—objectively speaking—is not chosen by man. Man cannot not aspire to the full development of his natural potentialities. Freedom concerns the way and manner of aspiring to attain the ultimate end. Hence it concerns the means of attaining the end.

DYNAMIC CHARACTER OF DEATH

Contemporary philosophy has called attention to the dynamism of death as the end of self-actualization. (As long as we are living in temporal dimensions, we are not in a state of actuality.) The moment of death is the ultimate decision in relation to the Fullest Good. Death is therefore "the most important act through which man ultimately fulfills his existence."[29]

MAN AND COMMUNITY

Although community is a necessary condition of man's life and development, it is not the goal of a human person's potentiality. Since man is a substantial being and community is only a relational one, man is ontically the purpose of the community, and not vice versa. Hence the human person preserves his autonomy and freedom in relation to all social entities. This means that man can choose the means which lead to the realization of his ultimate end, namely, God. Man is aware of his freedom; he is not a function of the world, even though he is immersed in it. As a conscious subject, man transcends the world and dynamically directs himself toward God. Ultimately, he draws his subjective completeness and dignity from "being-toward-God" and "being-for-God."

RELIGIOUS ACTS

By a religious act, we understand every kind of conscious and free actualization which brings man, a potential being, closer to the Personal God: Pure Act. Hence religious activity is immediately and directly guided to the final goal and purpose of human existence and not to the means. Accordingly, the non-contradictability of the religious fact (i.e., the bond or relation between a human person and the Person of the Absolute), is the ontic status of human existence, which is personal and simultaneously contingent. The goals and limits of intellectual and volitional human acts constitute the possibility of coming into being of a union with the Transcendent Person. This kind of contact is realized in man's religious activity.

C. OBJECTIVE JUSTIFICATION—RELATIONSHIP OF THE WORLD TO GOD (ONTIC TRANSCENDENTAL PARTICIPATION)

Another broader and more widely existing foundation of an ontic union of man with God is the existence of God as a personal being, who is the ultimate efficient, exemplary and final cause of everything that exists. The existence of a personal Absolute is established in metaphysics, which we sketch below.

METAPHYSICS AND GOD

The existence of many changing beings—which are evolving and yet retain their own distinctness even though they are not necessary—indicates that their origin is from an Absolute Being, who is a Personal Being. This Being creates through cognition (according to a "plan" or "idea"; hence the world is rational), and in a free manner. Our factual human existence, as well as the existence of the world which is a collection of non-necessary and yet intelligible beings, would be incomprehensible and inexplicable without the existence of a personal and loving God. Only he, a self-knowing and free being, forms the basis for the justification, explanation and understanding that everything which is changeable or passing, exists actually. He is the source of the world's existence (efficient cause); he planned the world (exemplary cause); and he, above all, desired the world—loved it—(final cause). Hence the world was created out of love and exists by the power of participation in God's existence.[30]

We ourselves and the whole world are therefore united with God by means of necessary ontic relationships. There exists then a real, actual, and internal union between the world and God, who is the source of every life-existence. Whatever exists, exists in virtue of its participation in the Absolute. Therefore we can say that we ourselves and the entire context of existence, are religious, because we are really united through existence with God. In explaining the relationship between the world and God, the philosophy of being meets with revealed truth, which St. Paul expresses: "Because in reality he is not distinct from each one of us, for we live, move and exist in him."[31]

ONTIC FOUNDATIONS

Because man can recognize his ontic bond with God, he must, as it were, bind (*religare*, hence the noun *Religio*) with God through cognition and love. Man is destined to dialogue with an all-loving God. Man's bond with God (which reaches to the very "roots" of being), constitutes an ontic foundation for a supernatural order. Revelation refers to it as the order of grace, which gives a new dimension to man's union with God (adoption through grace in Christ).

TRANSCENDENTAL PARTICIPATION

The fact of transcendental participation (everything that exists, exists in the existence of the personal Absolute), constitutes the non-contradictability of the religious fact from the side of the object. It also indicates that only a religious fact—understood as an interpersonal union between a human person and the person of the Absolute—constitutes for man the only suitable and adequate type of religion. Only the personal Absolute and the Fullness of Existence, Unity, Truth, Goodness, and Beauty constitute the *sacrum* or *numinosum* in which man can believe, trust, love and aspire to unite with him.[32]

SUMMARY

As a result of our investigations, we can answer affirmatively to the question asked at the beginning: *Is man a "religious being" just as he is a rational, social and moral being?*

As a person, man is directed to the Transcendent "Thou," i.e., he is ontically united with God. Because of his personal "structure," man necessarily needs to enter into a psychological and moral union with God, and he actualizes these potentialities in a free manner. Hence the "religiousness" of man (religious dimension of the human person as a way of "being-toward-God") is not a variable, accidental and historically conditioned trait, but it constitutes a property rooted in the very nature of the personal being.

CHAPTER XI

THE PERSON—
AN EGO OF A RATIONAL NATURE

This chapter which studies the problematic of the person is divided into four sections: I. The Concept of Nature, II. Areas of Human Consciousness, III. The Primordial Fact of Man's Conscious Experience, and IV. Theory of Personal Being.

The concept of person is inseparably joined with the concept of being because the person is understood as the highest and most noble formation of being. Further, personal being can be a model of intelligibility and reality because it fulfills most adequately the fundamental traits of existence which in such a case consists in *subjectivity* and *subsistence*. These traits emphasize the be-ing of being, its autonomy, indivisibility, truth, goodness, "reasonableness"—in a word, the transcendental properties of analogical reality.[1]

There are two different approaches to the problematic of the person: (a) historical and (b) phenomenological. We shall proceed to examine each of them.

I. THE CONCEPT OF NATURE

EARLY GREEK THOUGHT

The concept of nature (*physis*) was one of the greatest discoveries in the area of rational cognition. Understood as a permanent structure and source of regular activity, nature was viewed by the Greeks as the basis for various activities and phenomena. Plato and Aristotle further stressed the primacy of

156

these universal nature-essences over individuals and henceforth philosophy had as its goal the explanation of the world via universal concepts that expressed universal natures.[2]

Clearly these universal concepts did not reach directly to the truly ontic and actual singulars. The cognition of abstract nature-essences had abstracted from life, motion, and change of particular beings. Hence it was inadequate for the cognition of a concrete living being, especially the spiritual life of a person. Nevertheless it was necessary to use concepts in order to grasp the various aspects of a substantial being.

Aristotle's analyses revealed that "first substance" (the real living Socrates) is different from "second substance" (the universal concept which we have of Socrates). Within the limits of "first substance," there can be perceived a kind of universal nature understood as TO TI EN EINAI. This nature and not the individual concrete being was to be the object of scientific cognition.[3]

CHRISTOLOGICAL CONTROVERSIES

In Christian times, Christological controversies occasioned the following question: What elements must be "added" to second substance, namely conceptualized nature, and what elements to substance as general nature, the bearer of TO TI EN EINAI, so that one or the other could become the real, particular Socrates? If indeed, as faith taught, Christ is true God and at the same time true man, then, since he is one personal being (as the Council of Chalcedon taught), he could have two natures as the source of his divine-human activity.

The Council solutions indicated the existence of such a unique being who, although he is a man, nevertheless he is not at all a human person, but exclusively a divine Person. In the light of the Council determinations, it was demonstrated that human nature is not automatically a human personal being because it was "taken over" and fully realized by the person of the *Logos* in the historical Christ.

Using Neoplatonic terminology, Christian writers sought to establish the essential constitutive element of the person. This could take place only in the area of "rational natures" and, hence, they searched for that which, in some kind of "total form" of an individual being, determines a person.[4]

The person was patterned on the model of an exemplar of a species of a rational nature. And although species is understood in itself, it "distributes itself" to individuals since it exists through singulars. The moment of "distributing" to another being, as to an autonomous subject, ranked as a sign of ontic incompleteness. Therefore personal being was understood as a "fulfilled" being, which cannot "communicate" itself with another being as with a subject. Thus ontic autonomy and subjective fullness became the characteristic traits of a personal being as expressed by Boethius' definition of person: "an individual substance of a rational nature."

ST. THOMAS AQUINAS

This partial solution was further clarified by St. Thomas who observed that only that element of a rational being constitutes a person which fundamentally constitutes being—and hence, an individual existence of this rational nature. For if Jesus Christ is only a divine Person and not a human one, this is due solely to the fact that he possesses only one existence, namely a divine one. Divine existence actualizes human nature, making it a real source of real human activities, which nevertheless were the "property" of the divine Person.[5]

DESCARTES AND CONSCIOUSNESS

With the appearance of Cartesianism, the problematic of the person became linked with consciousness, since only consciousness as *cogitatio* could constitute the essence of a spiritual substantial being; and only the human soul could be such a being. Consequently the question of the person was linked with various phenomena and forms of conscious life.[6] Accordingly, from the time of Descartes, there has been a turning away from the problematic of being, understood analogically, in the direction of the thinking subject and what he experiences in his consciousness. Consciousness and "areas of consciousness" became the privileged object of philosophical analyses.[7]

II. AREAS OF HUMAN CONSCIOUSNESS

MAN'S "REASONABLENESS"

The data of human consciousness differentiate man from all the other creatures. And hence from the time of the Greeks, "nature" has been understood as a determined source of activity. This nature is either a "reasonable" manner of activity by "going out of itself" for the purpose of entering the thing itself; or it is a conscious activity in the manner of comprehending that which manifests itself in cognition. In contrast to animals, man constantly transcends himself as a subject of activity. The goal of specifically human activities is not that of only an individual or so-called "species-nature." Man "goes out of himself" for the purpose of arriving at the very thing in itself. Through his "reasonableness," man attains the essential structures of things.

"Reasonableness" in intellectual cognition is connected with the intentional character of our cognition, whereby we attempt to apprehend the content of the thing itself.[8]

"Reasonableness" of human activity is found in acts of decision and free choice, which manifest a transcendence toward being. Love is the highest expression of this transcendence because it not only "leads us out of ourselves" but, as St. Thomas emphasized, it demands a "giving-of-oneself" to another person, to another "Thou."[9]

TOTALITY

Besides "reasonableness" we notice in ourselves, especially in the area of cognition, a total mode of apprehension. It shows that whatever we understand is always as it were something cut out of a greater totality. There is no comprehension of a thing which would exhaust our potentiality of cognition. Just as "reasonableness" is comprehending a being from the side of its content, so "totality" is a grasping of being from the side of its extensions. Both indicate being as an analogical reality.

SPIRIT AS FOUNDATION

The foundation which explains "reasonableness" and "totality" of our psychical acts is the spirit which manifests itself in these acts. Spiritual acts are simple, not subject to the laws of motion and change nor are they subject to physiological change. They are complete and they perfect the subject which produces them. Such acts give a kind of profile of a man; they denote a stable mode of activity and an organization and hierarchy which can be called "Self." Its fundamental characteristic would be oneness in the manner of acting.[10]

PHENOMENOLOGICAL "I"

Along with the self, we can distinguish in man and in the whole of his activity, his own "I," which is called the "phenomenological I." Having been "thrown into existence" involuntarily, man must establish in himself a kind of dispositional center, whereby he can use the things surrounding him. This dispositional center is called "phenomenological" because, by separating ourselves from things, we treat ourselves as a distinct center that disposes objects. This phenomenological "I" is not yet the "I" of a human being, nor the ontological "I" that reveals the be-ing and subjectivity of a person. It is precisely this "I" as subject and being that manifests itself in a philosophical analysis.[11]

III. THE PRIMORDIAL FACT OF
MAN'S CONSCIOUS EXPERIENCE

MAN'S SUBJECTIVITY

If we use a strictly philosophical method—namely the non-contradictability of facts or contents given in cognition—we find a twofold division of our experiences.[12] The cognitive experience "I" is completely different from the cognitive experience "mine." "I" is always present as a *centrum*, as a performer and subject of all my acts. As a subject, I perceive that all my acts flow from the *centrum*. But subjectivity is already a metaphysical category because to be a subject means the same as to be a being, because there is no being that does not exist as a subject. The experience of subjectivity is sometimes immediate, something which needs no proof. On the contrary, all proof as a psychic process presupposes the awareness of a subjective "I." The experience of "being-a-subject-I" in relation to my acts is indubitable.

Obviously the subjectivity (be-ing) of an ego is given only from an existential aspect: we know that we exist and we are aware of our existence as a subject who performs "my" acts. A direct experience of subjectivity from the existential aspect is not at the same time a direct cognition of one's nature. I can learn about the content of "I" or about my own "nature" only through an analysis of "my" acts. The ego is constantly present and conscious but only as an existing subject for "my acts." Hume erred by denying the subjectivity of the "I," and he held that the human ego is but another psychic habit. Max Scheler denied the subjectivity of every spirit which he claimed to be only a function. But functions and activities possess no subjective existence. In our cognition of a function, we human beings make it an object (*Gegenstand*) and, according to Scheler, a being. This is incorrect because to be a being or an existing subject is not the same as to be an object, especially in the Kantian sense. For in Kantian tradition, objectivity is something constructed.[13]

"I" AS TRANSCENDING THE CONTENTS OF MY ACTS

We avoid both errors by holding that the cognition of the content of that "I" which exists, and is, and is conscious in all "my" acts, depends on the recording of the relation of "mine" to "I," as well as on any analysis of the ontic structure of "my" acts. The constant testimony of our consciousness is that I am the source and author of both "my" spiritual and physiological acts. My "I" transcends the contents of "my" acts and it gathers them by integrating them into one being, by acting in a purposeful way from within.

In the area of human decision, "I" is as if most conscious, most subjective and as performing and creating "my" acts.[14]

In the act of decision through free choice, I perceive myself as causing a new being, which did not exist previously and for whose existence I am "responsible." There is also a conviction about the responsibility for everything that "I" perform.

PERSON

Keeping in mind the relation of a subsistent subjective "I" to the performance of "my" acts, we perceive a relation between man and nature, which is described in the classical philosophy of being. This subsistent "I" who is conscious of both "my" spiritual and corporeal acts is nothing other than the sought-after *person*, about whom St. Thomas said that he is HIS OWN EXISTENCE AND PROPORTIONAL TO A GIVEN INDIVIDUAL NATURE.[15]

As a subjective subsistent "I," given to us in cognition from an existentialist aspect, the person organizes and (as Aristotle and Thomas Aquinas express it), forms for himself *a concrete individual nature*, a concrete individual source of rational activity. Obviously this organization of man's individual nature is accomplished fundamentally through spiritual acts, although as a causing and subjective "I," the person is involved with the laws of nature when he is organizing and forming his body. However, man transcends nature and manifests his personal traits of activity, which are the consequence of a created personal "nature." As a subject that exists, the "I" transcends the contents of spiritual acts. Man chooses his acts and expresses himself through them.

The selection of suitable actions in an act of decision is precisely the creation of one's personal nature. It is the "construction" of a personal individuality. As the author of definite spiritual acts, I experience my personal existence differently than I experience the existence of other beings. Hence K. Jaspers correctly observes that I experience the judgment, "I am— I exist" differently than I experience the judgment, "You exist," "It exists." I experience my own personal existence as that of a person-subject from within. I affirm my existence by transcending the nature which I am organizing. On the other hand, I affirm the existence of another being (even a personal one), as objectivized, as a thing completely determined by its content. Conversely, I emphatically affirm to myself my own personal existence which brings into relief this "I" from an existential aspect.

MAN AS MORE THAN HUMAN NATURE

Christian thinkers who were influenced by the Greeks to seek persons through an analysis of nature as the supreme moment of nature's activity, were wrong. Man is not merely some kind of determined nature, some kind of "human nature" that is particularized in relation to the general "idea of man." Rather, man is, above all, a subsisting personal being, who is conscious, and who experiences as an "I"—a subject who organizes his own individual nature by producing acts, both spiritual and physiological. It is through spiritual acts, however, that I fundamentally form my individual "nature," as a stable source of activity with definite personal traits. And hence "human nature" is not so much given to me; rather, the transcending person "I" creates this nature from the accumulated elements of nature.[16]

SUBSISTENCE OF THE HUMAN SOUL

We have just described St. Thomas' theory of the subsistence of the human soul, in relation to the body whose form it is. Man subsists as a soul. He creates for himself and organizes, i.e., forms his body. Man is not the result of the organization of matter, but the organization of human matter is an essential formal function of a subsistent soul, which expresses itself in spiritual and corporeal acts as a subjective, subsistent "I." Therefore to be a being means to exist as an independent subject, i.e., a being which exists not only in himself but also *for* himself—he is, in the fullest sense of the word, a PERSON.[17]

Under the influence of nineteenth century thinkers, the model of a self-intelligible being, for science, was acknowledged to be the simplest material being. When such a model was transposed to all kinds of being, the most intelligible beings were the simplest kinds of material beings. On the other hand, beings which existed truly subjectively, i.e., personal beings, became something completely unintelligible and the epitome of unintelligibility would be the Absolute Being—God.[18]

IV. THE THEORY OF PERSONAL BEING

COGNITION, LOVE, FREEDOM

Classical philosophy emphasizes a twofold transcendence of the person: (a) in relation to nature—through spiritual acts of intellectual cognition, love and freedom; and (b) in relation to community, with respect to subjectivity of right, completeness and dignity. Hence it is not proper to separate, from each other, the moments of cognition, love and freedom, which mutually condition each other. By analyzing our cognition, love, and freedom, we are able to catch a glimpse of our ontic character. Viewed as one who acts cognitively through love with consciously experienced freedom, man is forming from within, his spiritual image and hence he acts *as a person*. By becoming involved inwardly (and therefore through some form of love), man freely disposes himself so that he is either receptive, or non-receptive, to a suitable informational-cognitive content.

St. Augustine frequently called attention to the role of love in cognition. For love of an object under investigation or motives of love in an examination, sometimes intensify a difficult process of examination. A human personal love is connected with a liking and spiritual giving of oneself to another person. Aristotle, Thomas Aquinas, Blondel, and Marcel have made substantial contributions to the understanding of the problem of love as a personal action. The highest possible act of love is the giving of oneself to the Absolute Person at the moment of death, understood in the active sense. In our personal life through acts of decision, we constitute ourselves as the source of activity. We affirm ourselves as an acting subject and we form our own personal image. Man's freedom and his acts of decision affect our practical judgments through which we determine ourselves to activity. Through freedom, I constitute myself the source of activity.[19]

LAW

As Max Scheler says, man can say "No" to his natural drives; he can "protest" against his natural acts. The three acts of cognition, love, and freedom complement each other. Three further moments point to a sign of a person's transcendence even in the subordination of creations of social life. The subjectivity of law binds man as a person with common good, which is ultimately identified, in an objective sense, with the Absolute. This Absolute is the ultimate object who actualizes man's potentialities to the fullest. Now to be the subject of laws is nothing else than to have a relation with respect to another person. The foundation of law thus understood is our objective subordination to the ultimate good; for each of us, in perfecting ourselves from within, can demand that there be no interference on the part of other individuals in this process. For the subjectivity of law is the primary and fundamental moment of transcending a human collectivity by a human person. This transcendency is possible only when man's personal being transcends the various forms of nature and determination.

PERSON AND COMMUNITY

Common good is also the ultimate foundation for joining together dynamized human persons in free personal societies. For community is indicated by the dynamization of the human person, whose full development is impossible without life in a community, because the perfecting of human cognition, love, and freedom would be impossible. The result of this perfecting is the constituting of a person as a "being-for-another-person," for acts of intellectual cognition and love develop and perfect themselves in a dialogue with a "Thou" of another person. This means that a person's life, his spiritual development and achievement of perfection as a rational being, are impossible without establishing his interior life on the level of a dialogue with the "Thou" of another person.

COMMUNITY

As an essential form of human life, community neither enslaves nor exhausts personal life. As a person, man transcends this community. And because he is a synthesis of person and nature, he strives as a person to subordinate community to himself. But as a relational creature who has a corporeal nature and is part of nature, he strives to be subordinate to the same community. The two real sides of the human being, i.e., the personal and the "naturalistically-natural," complicate things because it is impossible to rank man in a definite ontic context. If man as person were only a reflection of some greater "totality" (Hegel), then man would be subordinated to the "totality" and the transcendence of personal life would be cancelled at the very outset. If man were to be only a monad, which unfolds itself from within, then community would be only a meaningless margin.

We must recognize that man is a personal being whose development is accomplished in and for the subject. As a person, man has his own personal end which is not realized through community as such.[20]

TRANSCENDENT THOU

The third moment which is the dignity of the personal being is connected with the fact of religion. The real justification of personal human life is not primarily nature. Although man lives in the world, nevertheless he transcends this world in a spiritual order. He feels that he is a subjective being, distinct from the world. He also knows that his spiritual acts and inner spiritual life are not the accidental activity of the powers of nature. They are the life of the spirit.

This life of the spirit is inseparably joined with the "Thou" of another person, and becomes better understood by means of interpersonal relations. I always live in the context of personal principles. If I love, hate and perform acts of decision, then the fundamental explanation of such acts is not science which deals with things. The explanation is found only in another person, another "Thou," who gives foundation and meaning to human life. Accordingly, personal life structures itself as a form of "being-for-another-Thou" and, in its ultimate perspective, as the THOU OF THE ABSOLUTE THOU. This is precisely the fundamental moment of religion.

We can therefore say that man as a person is fundamentally a religious being because he is the kind of being whose *raison d'etre* of being and development is another person and, ultimately, the ABSOLUTE PERSON. Interpersonal unions which give a foundation and meaning to a personal life as being most worthy, make the same person SOMEONE WORTHY in himself/herself and usher in the moment of religion in the most essential sense.

In the last analysis, the context of a person's life is the TRANSCENDENT PERSON, in whom persons of human existence participate. As a person, man creates a nature for himself and elevates it to a participation in a person's being, as a manner of "being-for-another." Man creates himself through his personal acts unto the fullness of personal life and he joins other persons and, in the ultimate context, the PERSON OF THE ABSOLUTE, as the highest FULLNESS.[21]

CHAPTER XII

THE HUMAN BEING IN
THE PERSPECTIVE OF DEATH

Death "happens to" every human being. At the same time, death is an opportunity for the "acting person" to perform an ultimate, interior act. Hence this chapter will be divided into two main sections: I. THE FACT OF DEATH II. DEATH AS A PERSONAL EXPERIENCE

I. THE FACT OF DEATH

The focus of all questions in philosophical anthropology is, undeniably, death. Every human life inevitably tends toward death. Death is inscribed in all our acts, and it constitutes the "lining" of all our human experiences. If, as Heidegger accurately expressed it, a human being is a "being-toward-death," then an ultimate understanding of the human being achieves completeness only when we take into account the moment of death as a fundamental and necessary aspect of the texture of human life as it is lived and experienced. Before this question of death, all other questions pale, since they lack death's necessity and inevitability.

To be able to examine more closely the question of the death of a human being, one must first view this fact from without, looking at it insofar as possible as an objective observer. Then one must also take into account the moment of inner inspection; namely, the way we ourselves personally see our own death, so that against this background of death as a personal experience the process of death might be related still more to the inner structure of the human being.

166

A. THE FACT SEEN FROM WITHOUT

Human death is, in one sense, an obvious and natural fact. Every human being goes from birth through a period of maturation, aging, and finally to death as life's natural completion. Regardless of whether it turns out to be nothing but "successes" or nothing but "failures," life is an inevitable journey toward death.

AN IMAGE

From the biological point of view the life of a human being can be well represented in the great metaphor of a *Tauromachus*, as was magnificently done by P.L. Landsberg:

> The bull that enters the arena knows nothing of what awaits him. He rushes joyfully from the obscurity of his prison and rejoices in the vitality of his youthful powers. Dazzled by the sudden light, he feels himself master of the closed circle which becomes his world and which still seems to him a boundless plain. He tosses up the sand of the arena and rushes in every direction with no other sensation than that of joy in his power.—Thus the infant leaves the body of his mother and soon begins to play in a luminous world which still conceals his destiny and its attendant dangers.
>
> The first adversaries enter the ring. It is still a game. Combat is natural to the bull. The struggle intensifies his awareness of life and of his own strength. These little vexations at the beginning merely build up his anger. It is the rage of the strong which reaches full measure in this provocation. The struggle calls forth the attacking animal which lies hidden beneath his every day existence. There is nothing disagreeable beyond the limits of the game. But slowly a painful element is introduced. The game is rigged. The adversary is too cunning, he provokes and then retreats. Although the weaker of the two, the adversary becomes the stronger, because he is bad. The redness of the cloth becomes exasperating; it is no longer the happy pretext for a fight.
>
> Thus the adolescent at school and elsewhere has his first encounters with a guileful world against which the sincerity of his struggle is unavailing. But the fatigue of youth is not important.
>
> The fight only becomes serious for the bull with the entry of his enemies on horseback. From high above him the picadors strike at him with their lances and wound him from a distance. The bull attacks: he surpasses himself in his fury. His rage is now magnificent, blind and suffering; its frenzy secretly inspired by a despair of life, but constantly reinforced by a perpetual victory over this despair. It is the innocent old horse which suffers worst from his stubborn attack. The wily picador disappears when his bloody task is completed.—So does man enter on the real struggle of his life. He can never overcome evil. If he destroys any one of his adversaries, he will only

have destroyed an innocent. Here all are innocent; our adversaries are only masks for the evil which we shall never destroy.

At this moment the bull is still strong. But from now on his reserves are failing. He looks stronger than he really is. His grip on life is shaken. The wounds from the lances were deep and his blood is flowing. And now the action is held up by an intermezzo. He is to be decorated, and also wounded again. There is both respect and mockery in festooning this gallant fighter with bandilleros. And the heroic beast provides an almost comic pretext for the elegant dance of the bandillero, the man who garlands him with these lethal darts, and succeeds in planting his weapon, in spite of his own fears, thanks to the very grandeur and slowness of the driven bull.—Thus man in his maturity attains honor and success at the very moment when he is weakened by the wounds of life. And even worldly glory is only a more secret wound, a traditional and almost ridiculous decoration, a travesty of victory. For he has conquered nothing. No one is victor in this world. We pretend that he has been victorious, as if true glory lay at the disposal of man. This is indeed an insult. The bull, at least, does not believe in his new honors. Perhaps he has even the foreboding that the world only glorifies those whom it is about to sacrifice.

Then with the matador, the high priest of the mystery, death enters the arena. Behold it! It is the sword, beautiful, supple and inevitable, hidden under the terrible red of the cloth, but hidden only from the one destined to receive it. The others behold this death, and the weakened bull enters his agony, and in transcending this agony reaches a deeper, though not yet ultimate gravity after the tragi-comedy of the interlude. The tragedy begins, or rather the tragic significance of the whole spectacle is finally disclosed. A good bull remains dignified, a fighter to the end. I do not think that he still believes in victory. But though almost without intelligence, he is not without an obscure awareness of the approaching moment, an awareness which has been brusquely sharpened by the adventures of the past twenty minutes, which comprise a lifetime. There have been struggles and attacks, withdrawal and return, on both sides. There has been success and defeat. The combat has not rested on a purely physical plane. The matador, summoning up his will, tries to lead and dominate the bull, maneuvering him into the only position which will allow of a mortal blow. He waves the red flag of death, so that it masters the bull, compelling him to follow it, like a lover dying beneath the spell of a sovereign mistress. And suddenly the bull is killed. His massive body wears the sword like a last proud cry of despair. For a few seconds he seems to resist. But death comes, the death that has so long been present, identified with the sword, identical with its source, the matador who wields it. The dead animal is carried away, like a thing.—Thus we all come to death in this world. Every battle with death is lost before it begins. The splendour of the battle cannot lie in its outcome, but only in the dignity of the act. The definitive is the inevitable.

THE DEATH OF THE OTHER

This sort of general reflection on human destiny assumes a more painful and personal expression when death takes someone close to us, a partner in dialogue, in relation to whom we had shaped our life. The absence of the person occasioned by death changes the external situation—the very same house, the very same dwelling-place or surroundings, sometimes become "unbearable" for us because they testify to the constantly present absence of the person "filling" the environment. To a great extent our "interiority" also changes through this change of perspective, through what is more than just an absence of intellectual and emotional experiences of the partner. We notice that people, after the death of dear ones, become "different" in their outlook, in their love, in their opinions. St. Augustine recounts just such an experience vividly in his *Confessions*. In such a case, death has sown a desolation that is constantly present.

The death of a dear one affects us very directly. For if the "Thou" of another person is like an objectified "I," all that happens to the "Thou" of the partner affects me as well. The experience of the death of another person is in large measure the intrapolated experience of my own death, which awaits me in the world. But despite this I can, with the passage of time, become accustomed to the absence occasioned by the death of a close partner, since along with the passage of time there also occurs a process of rationalization. For we ultimately understand the objective necessity of the death of a human being as a natural, biological process.

The ancient Stoics took this "natural," "seen-from-without" perspective and made of it their whole philosophy of death. To the Stoics, nature explained everything, including death:

> But the time and the period is fixed by Nature; sometimes by your own nature or constitution, as when you die in old age; but always by the nature of the whole, whose parts being continually changing, the whole universe is preserved in perpetual bloom and vigor. Now that is always good and seasonable, which is conducive to the advantage of the whole. The termination of life, therefore, cannot be an evil to any one . . . Nay, it must be good, as it is seasonable and advantageous, and conformable to the order of the universe.

B. THE FACT SEEN FROM WITHIN

An understanding, and even a general acceptance of the fact of death, nevertheless takes on the form of a protest when it concerns personal death. The views of many theological thinkers also point to this, e.g., Hermann Volk: "Human death is frightening and mysterious, no matter how plausible it may be scientifically. For death is the downfall of what is bent on life."

Is it not a puzzling matter that in fact the real thinking of one's own death is not possible? I can imagine that I am on the death bed, that I have died, that I am lying in a coffin, that they are carrying me to the cemetery, etc. But in each such thought-experience (basically imagined), I make use of certain cognitive contents, which either radiate from me, from the ego, or somehow are established in the ego. That ego base of thought, the "I," however, is present everywhere, immanent and at the same time transcending its experienced contents, even if these are the contents of one's own death. I cannot really think of the nonexistence of the subject of thinking, since every act of thinking presupposes the immanence in this act of the very subject of thinking. An act of thinking is not possible without establishing it in subjective existence; and if death were the negation of the very subject, its annihilation, then the actual thinking of the nonexistence of oneself would strike at the existential foundations of thought itself, at the immanence of the subject in relation to thought contents. As a result I cannot, as I can with any other possibility, entertain the supposition with regard to my death that I am dead right now, at this moment. Hence, any thinking of mine about my own death is nothing but a constructional, artificial thinking, transferred from the view of other subjects and an imposition of that view on the "I"; with this qualification, however, that in thinking of our own death, we thereby affirm this "I" as thinking, i.e., surviving, because it exists in the experienced cognitive contents having to do with our own death.

OBJECTIFICATION

In trying to think of our own death, we must objectify ourselves, make a "thing" of ourselves, and somehow separate ourselves from the thus reified subject in order to be able to represent "ourselves" no longer with the "attributes" of life; to imagine ourselves as nonliving. This kind of cognitive objectification of one's death is not an authentic experience of it, if experience presupposes an affirmation of the existence of oneself as subject. Experiencing our death represented cognitively, we really experience it precisely as the death of "someone else."

Although we are not able cognitively to experience our own death in some isolated cognitive act, yet we constantly experience it in an "accompanying" way (just as a shadow accompanies our moving about in the sunlight) in our various cognitive-appetitive psychic experiences. And these are just the processes that must be considered, since their analysis provides informative material for the understanding of the human being as a "being-toward-death."

What is called "thinking about one's own death" is basically a thinking about one's own existence as its form fundamentally changes. We think of its ceasing to be in relation to the world but, changing forms and content, continuing to *endure* in other changed dimensions and contents unknown to us. And perhaps this is just where one ought to look for the grounds of the solution to the age-old experiential dilemma between the conviction concerning, on the one hand, the naturalness of the death of a human being; and on the other hand, the rebellion and inner nonacceptance of personal nonexistence. Death as a work of nature is something understandable, since it is the natural dissolution of that which is ordered toward this dissolution—and which, after all, is constantly occurring in us through catabolic processes. Given such a state of affairs, death would be a kind of radical falling apart and disintegration of the organism, i.e., of the body unceasingly organized by the living "I." Biological death is a necessary work of *nature*. It may even be painful, especially when it affects me in some way, but it is understandable.

Death cannot, however, be understood as referring to the *person*. After all, it is not only on account of the structure of cognition that I am unable to think my own nonexistence; it is also on account of the structure of personal being itself, which, subsisting, does not have in itself an inner ground of nonexistence, if the body exists through the existence of the soul. The human being as nature and the human being as person—here is the reason, on the one hand, of the naturalness of death and, on the other, of the rebellion against death and the fact that it is deemed the worst evil that can befall a human being.

C. THE ONTICAL FOUNDATIONS OF THE FACT OF DEATH

The inevitable fact of personal death, despite the cognitive and volitive difficulties we have mentioned, has always induced people to search for those ontical foundations which would explain to what extent the process and the very fact of death annihilates the human being. In large measure it was just this fact of human death that stimulated reflection upon the ontical structure of the human being.

THE WISDOM OF THE PHILOSOPHERS

Practically every ancient philosophy adopted a conception of human nature that "did not fear" death any longer; death was understood as something merely apparent. In this regard the attitude of Epicurus is typical: "Death is nothing to us; for the body, when it has been resolved into its elements, has no feeling, and that which has no feeling is nothing to us." Epicurus vehemently teaches that one should not fear any suffering after death, because with death the human being utterly ceases; the person's atoms are dispersed and the human organism perishes irrevocably. He stresses the nothingness of death: "We were born once; one cannot be born twice. Life passes away and will never again return. Not being certain of tomorrow, you put off joy for later, and meanwhile life is frittered away and each of us dies in the treadmill." And so there is only this short temporal life, which ought to be affirmed, since death ends everything.

The position of Aristotle and the Stoics was similar in its metaphysical expression. Seneca sums it up: "No evil is great which is the last evil of all. Death arrives; it would be a thing to dread, if it could remain with you. But death must either not come at all, or else must come and pass away."

A radically different solution of the problem of death against the background of a specific structure of human nature is given by Plato, whose considerations on this topic reached their high point in the *Phaedo*.

> So long as we keep to the body and our soul is contaminated with this imperfection, there is no chance of our ever attaining satisfactorily to our object, which we assert to be truth . . . We are in fact convinced that if we are ever to have pure knowledge of anything, we must get rid of the body and contemplate things by themselves with the soul by itself. It seems, to judge from the argument, that the wisdom which we desire and upon which we profess to have set our hearts, will be attainable only when we are dead, and not in our life time . . .
>
> 'Very well, then,' said Socrates, 'if this is true, there is good reason for anyone who reaches the end of this journey which lies before me to hope that there, if anywhere, he will attain the object to which all our efforts have been directed during my past life . . .
>
> 'And purification, as we saw some time ago in our discussion, consists in separating the soul as much as possible from the body, and accustoming it to withdraw from all contact with the body and concentrate itself by itself, and to have its dwelling, so far as it can, both now and in the future, alone by itself, freed from the shackles of the body. Does not that follow? . . . Is not what we call death a freeing and separation of soul from body?'

That ultimate victory of soul over body, which is the essential content of the *Phaedo* and of many of the other Platonic dialogues, constitutes the expression of the very act of philosophizing and of the profound hope a human being possesses on the strength of his or her own nature, on the strength of the structure of his or her psychic acts, which are constantly being incompletely fulfilled in life. In a way, Plato's view is not in accord with nature and inner experience, since neither he himself nor any of us has been eager to escape from the body—and *we* regard our body as a great good, not as an evil. Yet he greatly enriched the idea of the fulfillment in us of our spiritual acts. He brought into relief those moments of personal life that clearly transcend matter and that are the foundation of belief in an after-life for what Plato called "soul."

ONTIC IMMATERIALITY

The structure of the human being manifests itself through the structure of personal acts—intellectual cognition, reflection, love, decision. One can perceive that these are immaterial and as such testify to the immateriality of the ontical subject, which forms such acts from itself. The immaterial, ontical structure of the acts testifies to the immaterial structure of the subject itself, which, existing, causes and sustains these acts in existence. In accordance with the tradition of classical philosophy, we can call that subject the human soul. The soul is the ontical ground of our perceptible spiritual and immaterial acts, given to us immediately in inner experience—the "I" and that which is "mine."

The soul, being in itself a subsistent entity and imparting existence to the body, is the proper and essential core of the immediately experienced "I." And being an immaterial entity, but together with the body co-constituting the human being, the soul is at the same time the "form" of the body.

To remove the difficulties appearing in connection with the understanding of the term "form," I would like to stress that the point here is that a human being is not some sort of contingent conglomerate of spirit and matter, but is a single being compounded of two metaphysical components necessarily ordered to one another: soul and body. The relation of these components to one another is expressed in Aristotelian terminology as the relation of matter to form, or potency to act. What this means is that analogically the very same function that, according to Aristotle's system, form fulfills in some living body, is likewise fulfilled by the soul in the human organism. The soul makes this organism a true human body, i.e., the kind of organism that is essentially connected and ordered to spirit, to its activity, and to not only its inner "expression" but also to its inner enrichment, i.e., the actualization of the person.

The concept of the composition of matter and form, or more generally of potency and act, is not only a suitable concept but also the only admissible concept for the expression of the ontical state of the human being. For, despite the multiple composition of ontical components in the human being, there is really one being, one ontical existence. And wherever a multiplicity of ontical components can be distinguished with the simultaneous preservation of the unity of being, the composition of potency and act is realized.

If the soul is the form of the body, i.e., the human being's one act of being, then this means that it is not only the ground of the existence—of the life—of the human being, but also that it unceasingly organizes matter to be *human* matter—a human body. This does not mean, however, that the soul is altogether submerged and immersed completely in matter. It is not a mere "function" of matter, since it also performs specifically immaterial functions, which are the acts of intellectual cognition and acts of will. Acts of intellectual cognition and will have no attributes of the spatio-temporal continuum, nor are they changeable-potential in their structure. Therefore the immediate sources of these acts—the powers performing the acts of cognition and will—cannot be material bodily organs. Granted that sometimes the brain is spoken of popularly as the instrument of cognition, yet the brain itself is not an intellectual-cognitive organ. It is certainly a necessary instrument of cognition, just as for an artist an instrument for playing is necessary, e.g., a piano. This does not mean, however, that a piano concert is the work of the piano itself. For in the performance of psychic acts with an immaterial ontical structure, the whole human being participates, i.e., even matter, and in particular the human being's central nervous system. For in the human being we perceive a functional unity, which nevertheless does not rule out the structural-ontical difference among the components of the human being and ultimately the distinct character of the human soul as the subsisting subject for spiritual acts.

Having in mind, then, the fact of the ontical subsistence of the human soul and its noncorporeity, one can perceive the real ontical foundations of its immortality. For if the soul, as the essential factor of the ego, is subsistent being organizing for itself the body, then in the moment of the decomposition of the body and its total disorganization, the immaterial soul, as the ultimate subject of acts that are immaterial in their ontical structure, cannot cease to exist. It would perish only if its existence were the result of the bodily organization. But then the absurd would follow: being would arise from nonbeing; the body, which is not spirit, would organize itself in the form of non-body, i.e., "create" the spirit that manifests itself in all human cognition and wanting. Hence, the essential ground of the immortality of the human soul is its subsistence; that is, the fact that existence (ascertained in the judgment, "I am") belongs immediately to the soul, which is also the form of the body.

If existence belongs immediately to the soul, and to the body only and exclusively through the soul, then the annihilation of the body does not entail the annihilation of the subsistent substance which is the human soul-ego. Thomas briefly observes: "That which has existence through itself cannot either come into being or undergo destruction, except through itself. For this reason, too, the soul cannot come into being by way of generation, i.e., material alterations, since it has an immaterial existence; and likewise it cannot cease to exist by way of natural destruction." There would have to occur a special intervention of the Absolute, who would annihilate the soul, since the soul of itself, being in its essence an uncomposed spirit, cannot forfeit existence. The Absolute alone, therefore, is the reason of the generation of the soul, and the Absolute alone could annihilate it—and then only by acting contrary to the natural order.

EXISTENTIAL AWARENESS

We daily encounter the problem of immortality in the unceasingly posed question: "Will we continue to exist after death, and is our ego immortal?" These questions are posed not only directly but also implicitly in other expressions of human rational activity: the very character of our cognition in the use of necessary, general concepts; the character of our judgments in one way or another affirming be-ing; the simplest acts and declarations of love made with the help of the great quantifiers: "forever," "never"; the whole of creative and cultural work, attempting in the course of changeable and transitory matter to leave behind a lasting trace of our thought. Everything that is somehow a rational expression of the human being is an expression of a transcendence beyond changeable matter. These manifestations all pose the question: "Will we continue to exist when the changeable state of matter entering into our ontical structure carries out the still more radical alteration called "death?"

II. DEATH AS A PERSONAL EXPERIENCE

If philosophical reflection begins in wonder, the fact most conducive to wonder is our personal death. Keeping in mind the necessity of death, constantly accompanying us—like a shadow—one finds it necessary first to reflect upon the concept of death itself, and then to indicate those real forms of spiritual life which, with regard to their ultimate fulfillment, occur in the moment of death conceived as a personal act.

THE DEFINITION OF DEATH

Insofar as the "definition" of death is concerned, it is possible to set forth various propositions: a) one can speak of the clinical death of a human being, i.e., of the cessation of the functioning of the central nervous system, the heart, or some other important organs; b) clinical death can be distinguished from biological death, the irreversible cessation of the vital functions of the human organism; c) one can also conceive some philosophical or perhaps religious definition of the death of a human being as e.g., "the separation of the soul from the body." But this last presupposes that both the soul and the body are individual substance-things, separable from one another.

One can easily form an imaginary model of the "separation" of one thing from another thing but, as we have seen, that is not what is involved here. Such a definition says little or nothing since one must first determine the real relation of the soul to the body, i.e., one can understand such a definition only in the context of a system.

Can a non-systematic definition of death be found?

AN EXISTENTIAL CONCEPT OF DEATH

One can speak of death as the completion of life in time, and thereby of the attainment of that state of the human spirit in which the human being ultimately is constituted a truly personal being, capable of making ultimate decisions.

Let us assume for the present the hypothesis that the moment of a person's death is that particular moment in which change, and thereby time (as the measure of material change), is ended. There no longer follows a "transition" to a further temporal moment. In the moment of the death of a human being, therefore, we are dealing with the real, temporal end of "duration-becoming" (even if it is to be the beginning of a possible unchangeable duration). This particular moment in which the "fulfillment" of the time of a human being occurs is the moment in which all personal acts (i.e., acts of cognition and love) arrive at a completion. This moment, which will become the beginning of a new, unchangeable state, must be completed for fullness to occur, if it is to occur at all. Hence, too, the moment of the end of time is the moment in which converge, as in a keystone, the personal human acts continually begun but never ultimately completed (because performed in essentially changeable conditions) in the course of human life. And by calling that completion-finale "death," we avoid the system-related definitions of human death, particularly the one which defines it as the "separation of the soul from the body."

We also propose another hypothesis; namely, that only the moment of death as the moment of the fulfillment of all personal (cognitive and appetitive) acts of man is precisely that moment in which man becomes *fully* capable of making a decision in relation to his *whole* life. At death, we are proposing, the person makes an ultimate decision concerning the meaning of his existence, since only this moment of a human being's life is a moment in which his personality, understood in a dynamic, psychological sense, is fulfilled. This does not mean that a human being prior to the moment of the completion of his life is not a person. He is a person already in several senses; in a "potentialized" sense, in that he can continually become more complete; in an incomplete sense, in that he can always become more per-fect; he is a person in an ontical sense, which means that he possesses the circumstances of his existence allowing for personal realization. Beyond death, further development actualizing the potentiality of the person is not possible. Death, being the completion of the actualization of the person, presents thereby the culmination point in which all changeable acts begun in the course of human life find their fulfillment. The human being in the moment of death becomes perfectly enabled psychically to make his deci-sions concerning the meaning of human life, the affirmation of God, and his ultimate end.

Of course, when we speak of this moment of death, this does not mean that it could be experienced experimentally by someone. The experimental experience of death is incompatible with a return to the temporal, changeable conditions of duration. Consequently, such an experience of death must occur "after" the biological death of man, "after" the cessation of the mate-rial changes taking place in the human body.

ACTIVE AND PASSIVE DEATH

Still another demarcation is important here, namely the differentiation between death accepted passively, and death taken on actively.

Death in the passive sense is the decomposition of the human organism. Actually, decomposition is constantly occurring in the course of organic human life; the ultimate decomposition is biological death, the ultimate result of subjection to the laws of nature. The human being must undergo this death. This is the so-called "passive experience" of death, independent of the person and his psyche. The "passive experience" of death occurs beyond consciousness, and the famous aphorism of Epicurus can be applied here: "Death is nothing to us, since so long as we exist, death is not with us; but when death (in this sense) comes, then we do not exist."

But if a human being is a thinking being, and if spiritual life (cognition and love) is connected with the human ego understood as a soul that is to survive the decomposition of the body—then besides death understood pas-sively one must distinguish death understood actively, that is, death as a real experience of the human spirit. This experience cannot occur in conjuction with the co-activity of the brain, because by definition all material activity has already ceased. It can occur autonomously in the sphere of spirit, as the spirit brings to an end the changeable states and changeable activity of its powers. This kind of experience of death—transtemporal—still belongs to the human being, whose spirit completes the acts of cognition and love initiated and performed incompletely in the changeable, potential conditions of his life. This ultimate spiritual "expression of oneself," performed against the background of the completion of the changeable states of the psyche, is the moment of the making of ultimate decisions. This is death understood in the active sense. Without death understood actively, a human being would be a "thing," and not a person consciously experiencing the most important stages of his life. There arises, however, a question concerning what sort of spiritual acts can tell us something about death understood in this way.

THE COGNITION OF EXISTENCE

When we take everyday speech as the object of philosophical analysis, we notice that the expression "is," being a sentence copula in predicative sentences, fills an essential although mysterious function in the human intellectual cognition expressed in that speech. The character of our natural language bears witness to the fact that cognitively we apprehend existing reality— really existent being. In apprehending being we also apprehend, obscurely and imperfectly, the ultimate reason of being, which is the Absolute.

A mature human being in some way either "justifies" this imperfect and spontaneous judgment, ultimately affirming the existence of God (or denying it), or else he will resign from a justification. In the latter case he contents himself with fideism—the blind affirmation of the original and natural conviction that an Absolute Being exists.

HUMAN COGNITION

In connection with the philosophical interpretation of the spontaneous and original judgment concerning God's existence, related to the function of the expression "is" in our ordinary language, it is necessary above all to note the objectivism and realism of human cognition. Our cognition is a specific psychic grasp of the objective states of things, and not an arbitrary construction. This means that the cognition expressed in judgments has the attribute of truth; i.e., it is in accord with the factual state of things which first and foremost actually *exist*. We ascertain this in very simple and original existential judgments of the type; "John exists"; "This table upon which I am writing exists"; "My thinking exists." Even before I know what a thing is, I perceive that the concrete thing "is."

This original human cognition is so natural and spontaneous that we usually pay no attention to it. Instead we concentrate on the cognitive grasp of the content of the thing which occurs in a judgment in which the expression "is" again appears as its core; when, for example, I ascertain that "a human being is a mammal." We meet the expression "is," therefore, both in existential judgments in which we assert the real existence of some concrete, individual being, as well as in predicative judgments in which we ascertain the possession of some attribute (predicate) by a subject.

Though these two uses of "is" differ in meaning, we may nevertheless assert that in either type of statement the very expression "is" is conditioned by the cognitive grasp of really existing being, without which human cognition would not be possible at all. At the same time, the intellectual cognition of really existing being is the cognition of being that is merely contingent, changeable, i.e., not self-intelligible. Therefore it is the cognition of the kind of being that has the reason of its existence beyond itself in the Absolute. In other words the Absolute ultimately accounts for the fact that contingent being exists rather than does not exist.

Consequently, if all cognition making use of subjective-predicative speech is evidence of an intellectual cognition by us of non-self-intelligible being, there arises a need for a concrete and indubitable cognition of the ultimate reason of being, the Absolute or, in religious language, God. Without this cognition, our intellectual life would be unfinished in a fundamental and most important point. The human being as a person would no longer be a "someone" but an unfinished "something," not finding a concrete answer to that question which was involved in every act of human intellectual cognition.

If, then, at the moment of the completion of the changeable way of existence, i.e., at the moment of death, a person could not solve the existential questions involved in the whole of human cognition, then the human being would be an unnatural being. The whole course of human nature as a human being, the pursuit of the discovery of the meaning of existence, would be a pursuit never fulfilled. But since changeable duration merely gives rise to the whole of this problematic without solving it, only in the moment of the completion of this duration can this pursuit be fulfilled, if at all. Thus, if we are not to claim that human life is an absurdity, we must say that only when God, as the ultimate reason of being, stands concretely and intuitively before the human intellect, is human life fulfilled. This is the final, full, cognitive act to which the whole of psychic life is ordered.

DEATH AND THE WILL

We come now to the description and analysis of those volitive, typically human psychic experiences to which other philosophers have often drawn attention. We shall be concerned here with the experience of happiness and the experience of love against the background of concrete human decision.

A convenient point of departure is the description of the structure of what we call "will." Thomas Aquinas, and recently Blondel, carefully attended to a characteristic division in this sphere. The latter perceived that the human will is always disposed toward something more than it concretely wants. No concrete wanting equals the continuously living capacity of the will, which is disposed toward infinity. In Thomas Aquinas that division of the will was called "*appetitus naturalis*," the natural desire of the will, and "*appetitus elicitus*"—the desire concretely elicited in relation to a concrete good. In conjunction with this, he observed that no concrete good satisfies human desire, which is by nature directed toward universal good. That direction toward universal good is the natural desire for happiness, never extinguished by concrete goods. The universal desire for happiness, being the dynamic source of concrete desires and, at the same time, accompanying every elicited act of desire, is the natural never-extinguished desire for the Absolute: God. A human being is not always concretely aware of this. If, however, he is aware of his desire for infinity, he cannot "resign" from it, though atheists try to do this. On the contrary, if a human being becomes ever richer in knowledge, richer in material means, richer in love of others, then the conviction constantly accompanies him that he has not possessed happiness. That which can satisfy him seems constantly beyond him.

This division of the will into the desire for ultimate happiness and the desire for concrete goods can be explained as the derivation of infinite desire from the intellectual, cognitive apprehension of analogously general being (in which we obscurely apprehend God as the reason of being). Yet, as the natural desire for "something more," manifested unceasingly in every expression of wanting-desiring, it does bear witness to the fact that the subject itself is in its nature disposed toward infinite good. Now if this is a desire belonging to human nature as such, it has a chance of being fulfilled precisely as a work of nature (since nature is nothing other than this order of things to their fulfillment). But the division of desire into the desire for the infinity of an ultimate unnamed happiness and the desire for a concrete something will be overcome only when infinity and abstract happiness stand before the human soul, no longer as an abstraction, but as something concrete, and thereby as a real good drawing the human soul to itself. And such a "meeting" of the roads of abstract, infinite, and concrete, real desire is possible only at life's "finale."

GOD AS CONCRETE AND INFINITE GOOD

At the end of life, God can stand before the human spirit in order to show it that concrete and real good that, encoded, and appearing only under the evershifting veil of the changeable world, appeared to the human being's spirit during its journey through life. On the other hand, everything of value has pointed precisely to this good, which has influenced us through the succession of goods that do not satisfy the infinite desire of a human being. Therefore, human desire is divided until the moment of death. Then, in the highest moment of human life, God will stand before the human spirit as a *concrete* good and at the same time as the *infinite* good which, as analogously general good, as happiness in general, was constantly disturbing the human will. God, realizing concreteness and infinity, can actually appear before the human spirit only in the moment of the nonreversible finale of changeable human life.

Without this appearance of God, human nature would not have a rational ontical structure, since the pursuit of nature would be objectless, and objectless pursuit is not a pursuit of nature. If, therefore, we want to treat human nature rationally, then we cannot ignore natural inclinations. And if this is how the matter lies with human desire, then one ought to accept the fact that in the fulfillment of the human being's time, which is called death, God will stand before us in order to draw us to himself like a magnet, no longer through the world of changeable beings, but through his very self. The world of things and people prepares, enables, and suits us for this more intense adherence to him when he appears. Hence, death is the fulfillment of the natural desire of the human will. Only in this moment—if it happens at all—can there occur a total confrontation of human desires and decisions with concrete and infinite good, because in no other moment of human life is such a confrontation even possible.

LOVE AND DEATH

The works of many outstanding writers relate a co-occurrence of two states at peak moments of human experience: love and death are perceived as aspects of the same reality. The myth of Orpheus and Eurydice, writes Marcel in *Présence et Immortalité*, stands at the very heart of my existence, since only the deep experience of love allows for the possibility of the greatest accumulation of the spiritual strengths of our ego, strengths that are normally scattered and diffused. This accumulation of personal strengths in love permits the most expressive manifestation of "me"—of "my ego." For I only become conscious as an "I" when I set myself in opposition, not to objects-things, but as an "I" to another when, beside the "I," I perceive a "Thou" as a correlate. And, therefore, for a human being to be a human being, i.e., to be a conscious and loving ego, means basically to be a correlate of a "Thou." Hence, for a human being "to exist," "to be" precisely as a person, means "to-be-with," "to-co-exist."

The human being was born as a product of love and exists in love and for love. In the very heart of the personality, in the very core of the "I," is an enchanted inclination to a "Thou," thanks to which inclination and its realization through acts of love, we accent and develop our "I" evermore strongly. Without love our ego is weak, without support; moreover, it is not formed as a human ego, i.e., as person. The "I" of every human being has been formed in actual interpersonal contacts (which are always some modification of love). Hence, real bonds of love stand at the basis of an understanding of the existence of the human ego, since this existence as precisely human existence is expressed in love, i.e., in the union of an "I" and a "Thou."

An essential manifestation of love is the "giving of oneself." Nearly all thinkers, ancient, mediaeval, contemporary, but especially Marcel, have taken note of this fact that in the act of love we coordinate ourselves with the "Thou" as the object of our love, we give ourselves to the beloved "Thou." Through this act of the spiritual "surrender of oneself," we do not become impoverished but, on the contrary, we become fulfilled; we become a fuller "I."

If the human being is "built up" in his human existence through love for another "Thou" and through it reaches the fulfillment of his existence in assuming the features of "co-existence," then, we may ask, what is the basic factor organizing that existential "giving of oneself?" There can be only one answer: the limiting, individuating element, which not only exists in a human, conscious way but rather "is possessed," is our *body*. And if the body exists only through the ego-soul, then the manner in which the body exists is that of a "possession."

In Marcel's terminology, we are dealing with the famous distinction of "*être*" to indicate the manner of existence of our ego-soul, constituted in the dialogue of love, and "*avoir*"—the "possession" of that which is originally "mine" and which is precisely our bodily organism, organized by our ego, and existing by the existence of the ego-soul.

The body, then, on the one hand, makes possible the development of the spirit and, on the other, specifies its manner of surrender; unceasingly combining its development with individual, individualizing, atomizing forms of activity.

ABSOLUTE THOU

In the moment, therefore, when after biological death this form of limiting activity will cease, our ego will attain the condition of full self-expression in love for the transcendent "Thou"; it will attain the condition of full "giving of oneself" and thereby of full constitution as person, which is a cognitive existence for the love of, and union with, the absolute "Thou." Hence, if all the acts of love that we experience in life are acts of our ego's "giving of itself" to another

"Thou," then only death experienced actively (i.e., not the passive, biological death, conceived as the cessation of the functions of animated matter) creates the conditions for the outburst of personal love that ultimately constitutes the personal "I" in relation to the transcendent "Thou" as a concrete and absolute good.

Death and love, then, are the two sides constituting the human personality. Without the coming-into-being of the full conditions of love in the moment of death, i.e., in the moment of the cessation of bodily changes, all the impulses of great genuine love would be something pathologic and unnatural, rather than the work of a spiritual human nature. This liberating nature of love, freeing us from atomizing forms of existence, has been intuited by the great poets. In pairing love and death they intuited that love as a form of human existence conquers biological death. Moreover, they knew that only at the moment of the cessation of biological changes, can love attain the conditions of full self-expression, full freedom, and full constitutedness of the human personality. Without the real and concrete possibility for every human being of the eternal endurance of that which already now has appeared in biological forms of duration as transcending matter, the very acts of cognition and love, succumbing to change and time, would be yet another monster of nature. Death, then, experienced actively, becomes the factor ultimately making life meaningful.

One could thus analyze the various aspects of the psychic life of a human being and perceive death being realized everywhere in human existence, death understood from one side biologically as the cessation and passing away of determinate, atomized forms of activity, and from another—death as a liberation toward fullness, as precisely the fulfillment of that which transcends in human activity, of that which cannot be reduced to any purely material category. One could point here to such human psychic acts as the poetry and creativity addressed to a transcendent recipient who understands anxiety, sadness, tragedy, or the need of happiness and love; one could thoroughly analyze acts of human decision, which always turn out to be somehow partial, incomplete, not expressing the capacity of our ego and leaving behind themselves a feeling of non-completeness and ultimate non-self-expression, which is always "lined" with a certain "melancholy of existence." One could point to the conditions of human freedom, which is always freedom in a certain respect, determined also by material factors, as a result of which, freedom is more a postulate and point of destination than a point of departure in making ultimate human decisions.

One could finally point to that which St. Paul already once observed, that there exist opposite directions of development: biological and psychical. The biological direction goes from an original vigor toward a gradual diminution and disappearance as the years go by, whereas the developmental psychical tendencies, the so-called "inner man," develop and mature with the passage of time. And this notion is not refuted by the general ascertainment that an old human being is psychically less competent and sometimes becomes childish. For these sides of a human being are connected precisely with the decline of biological competence. In any case, the developmental tendencies of the biological and psychic lines are in different directions. With the crumbling of the "bodily home"—as St. Paul calls it—the moment of death reveals an inner, psychic, personal edifice.

In short, death may be seen as the moment of the full constitution of the personal ego. At death, human existence possesses the complete conditions for the concrete cognition of values, for the cognition of a transcendent, absolute person, and for entering into an ecstatic act of love. That act of love, as a fully cognized, fully free, loving bond with the transcendent "Thou," embraces, fulfills and perfects all the personal and transpersonal values that we attained in the changeable forms of life, values that we intuited or partially cognized.

A NEW MODEL OF DEATH

The "division of soul and body" has not proved an adequate model of death. The separation of the soul from the body is only one of the aspects of death, and that of death understood passively as the occurring dissolution in a man of his material elements, a dissolution over which we have no control or power. It "happens," but it is not caused by personal human acts and therefore cannot be experienced actively and in a free manner. In the passive experience of death we are not so much a person as a decomposing material object. And surely that is not what is at issue in the personal experience of death. What concerns us is an active free experience: *death as the completion of the changeable manner of existence*. In conjuction with this active conception of death, a different model will be useful, namely, a model of maturation and birth.

The human being in the embryonic state forms all of his organs for life beyond the womb, in the open world, life more subsistent and independent. Just so, our life already subsistent in the open world reveals a quantity of most valuable psychic activity which does not fit into the nature of the world, which unceasingly transcends the world of nature to the degree that the human being is forced to create for himself a special "ecological niche" (culture) in order to be able to exist and develop psychically.

Suppose the child in the mother's womb led a psychic, conscious life. Then the moment of its birth would be regarded as the moment of its death. For it loses everything at once in the moment of birth: nourishment, air, all the real conditions of existence. The cutting of the umbilical cord would be regarded as the ultimate act of death. And, meanwhile, in just that moment it passes into another manner of existence, independent existence. We can apply the same model of birth to death in which the human being is able for the first time to make use of the continually initiated, imperfect acts of his personal structure in relation to the infinitely extended cosmos and, above all, in relation to the transcendent "Thou." Just as the formation of the organs of the embryo points to their full employment in a life outside the womb, so the acts of the human psyche, acts of cognition, love, decisions, creativity, and rational work transcending the changeable world, organizing that same world, point to the full realization of all that which is now only begun, which is as though in an embryonic state.

The psychic acts now brought forth fit and prepare the psyche for the first cry of an independent existence, full of love and freedom. And that precisely is the experience of death by the human person, the personal experience, and not the so-called passive, biological one, which is only the experience of undergoing decomposition.

In such a perspective it is difficult to call death the "separation of the soul from the body," because—as Karl Rahner properly observed—not only do we not know whether it is possible to designate death in this way, but, moreover, since the days of Augustine and Thomas Aquinas, there exists a tradition according to which the soul, as spirit necessarily ordered to matter, cannot dispose of this relation without the simultaneous cancellation of its be-ing. If it were possible to speak of a separation of soul from body, then at the very most we might be able to speak of a separation from the "here and now" quantified body. And a separation in this sense, after all, goes on continually during our biological duration as the cells previously constituting "us" are sloughed off.

In this view, if in the moment of biological death more individualized matter in the form of body departs all at once, then our soul still does not thereby lose the relation to matter, because it cannot lose this relation. Rahner suggests that in the moment of death there would occur a much deeper bond of the soul with the cosmos than existed through the assimilation of nourishment, a bond with the cosmos in its fundamental, crucial connections, which are the foundation of the rational organization of matter, of that organization which appears to human thought in the form of laws.

Of course this is a hypothesis, but an interesting and fruitful one, sketching an ever wider entrance of spirit into the world of matter to which it first submits, which it cognizes, which it directs, and which it finally—as Christian revelation teaches—is to subject to its laws. This hypothesis would well explain the special status of the human being's "psychosomatic" make-up. For the spirit, forming the body for itself in the mother's womb with the participation of the parents, attains objective knowledge in human life of matter in an embryonic state. The same spirit, attaining to the fullness of self-consciousness in the moment of death, unites with the very heart of matter, which is rationally taking shape, in order to bestow upon it ultimately its own personal, spiritual visage.

It is true that death affects the human being, that the whole human being dies, but the act of death can, again, be understood passively or actively. Death in the passive sense is inflicted upon the whole human being, but understood in the active sense it is a personal act of completing and, by an ultimate decision, definitively actualizing the personal potential be-ing. And although it is true that the subsisting soul cannot in the strict sense be called a person, which is the subsisting "I" of a rational human nature actually embracing the whole of spirit and body, yet personal identity is not interrupted because self-cognition remains! In addition, the soul does not lose its relation to the body, but at most only loses the actualization of this same necessary relation. Hence, the essential foundations of personal being are the same. The human soul, having an actual relation to matter, is expressed through the body organized for the soul.

In losing the body the soul does not lose its inner richness, which it acquired through the body; it does not lose its relation to matter, thanks to which it is empowered in suitable conditions to organize for itself anew a body from matter, one that can continue to be regarded as the same body thanks to the identity of the relation (transcendental—necessary!) that it continues to maintain. After all, our body itself is in the constant "flux" of matter, and despite this it is identical due to the identity of the relation. Consequently, in the soul those functions that can be exercised without a body continue to be maintained, i.e., the whole acquired richness of the spiritual life.

Furthermore, we do not know what sort of other functions will be added to the separated soul in the changed conditions. In any event, however, the act of existence constituting the human being as a person is not interrupted but changed. It is true that one cannot simply call the still subsisting being a human person, due to a lack thereof of a complete "nature," but nevertheless the being of the human does not perish. That which is the source and foundation of the being of the human survives. And for this reason perhaps Norwid's verse, composed under the inspiration of Fichte (*Die Anweisung zum seligen Leben, oder auch die Religionslehre*. 6. *Vorlesung*—is close to the truth. Here is a fragment of it:

And yet she (i.e., death) wherever she touched,

The background—not the essence against the background having rent.

Except for the moment in which she took—took nothing—The human being—older than she!

CHAPTER I

Notes and References

Cf. pp. 375-78 (Unabridged Edition of *I-Man*) for additional notes and references.

1. C. Werner, Jaeger, *Die Theologie der frühen griechischen Denker* (Stuttgart, 1953), pp. 89-98, also *Religions of the World* (Warsaw, 1957), pp. 245 ff.

2. Cf. Plato, *Timaeus*: Jaeger, *Paideia* (New York: Oxford University Press, 1945).

3. Aristotle, *De Anima*, II, 1 (412a 29).

4. *Ibid.*, II, III, *passim*.

5. *Ibid.*, III, 5 (430a 13).

6. *Ibid.*

7. *De Anima*, ed. Warzink, p. 31.

8. Cf. Etienne Gilson, *History of Christian Philosophy in the Middle Ages* (New York: Random House, 1955).

9. In the author's opinion, Thomas Aquinas' treatment of the topics studied in the present work transcends the treatments of many other philosophers, contemporary as well as ancient and mediaeval. Therefore his development of these topics will be presented in this volume.

10. Descartes, *Meditations on First Philosophy*, Med. VI.

11. *Ibid.*, Med. VI.

CHAPTER II

Notes and References

Cf. pp. 379-80 (Unabridged Edition of *I-Man*) for additional notes and references.

1. These points are clearly presented in J. Bocheński, *Philosophy: An Introduction* (Dordrecht, 1962), pp. 73-82.

2. Plato's *Phaedo* provides excellent testimony to this fact.

3. Cassirer attempts to present this thesis in his work, *An Essay On Man* where, beginning with Neo-Kantian assumptions, he sees the meaning of human life in cultural creativity. E. Rothaker, *Probleme der Kulturanthropologie* (Bonn, 1948) likewise perceives the problem of cultural creativity as a factor of human nature.

CHAPTER III

Notes and References

Cf. pp. 381-85 (Unabridged Edition of *I-Man*) for additional notes and references.

1. P. Teilhard de Chardin, "My Universe, "*Science and Christ* (New York and Evanston, 1958). The other English editions used here are: "The Phenomenon of Spirituality," *Human Energy* (London, 1969); "A Mental Threshold Across Our Pacific: From Cosmos to Cosmogenesis," *Activation of Energy* (New York, 1971).

2. T. de Chardin, "The Phenomenon of Spirituality," *op. cit.*, pp. 96 ff.

3. "From Cosmos to Cosmogenesis," *op. cit.*, pp. 262-63.

4. "My Universe," *op. cit.*, pp. 65-66.

5. Cf. M. Krapiec, "Religion and Science," *Znak*, 7-8 (1967), 861-87.

6. An interesting examination of P. Teilhard de Chardin's doctrine is found in O. A. Rabat, *Dialogue avec Teilhard de Chardin* (Paris, 1958). For another presentation cf. C. Cuénot, *Science and Faith in Teilhard de Chardin* (London, 1967).

7. Cf. below, Chap. III.

8. Cf. unabridged edition of *I-Man*, pp. 274,276.

9. A. Schaff, *Marxism and the Human Individual* (New York, 1970), pp. 168 ff. On the Marxist conception of man, cf. Schoeps, *Was ist der Mensch* (Göttingen, 1960), pp. 33-57.

10. A concise and very informative presentation on the problematics of man can be found in T. Slipko, "A Conception of Man in the Light of Contemporary Marxist Anthropology in Poland," *Zeszyty Naukowe KUL*, 2 (1967) 3-16. Perhaps the most exhaustive presentation of the Marxist theory of man is to be found in Lucien Sève, *Marxisme et théorie de la Personalité* (Paris, 1972).

11. Schaff, *op. cit.*, p. 70.

12. A different presentation of this question can be found in Slipko, *op. cit.*; cf. also R. Garaudy, *Perspectives de l'homme* (Paris, 1959).

13. For Freud's works, cf. *The Standard Edition of the Complete Psychological Works of Sigmund Freud* (London, 1955); _____, "Three Essays on Sexuality," *op. cit.*, VII, p. 165.

14. C. Thompson, *Psychoanalysis: Evolution and Development* (New York, 1950), pp. 30ff.

15. *Ibid.*, pp. 34, 50 ff. Cf. J. Prokopiuk, "Epilogue" in *S. Freud, Man, Religion, Culture* (Warsaw, 1967), pp. 326 ff.

16. A. Adler, *The Neurotic Constitution* (New York, 1917).

17. *The Collected Works of C.G. Jung* (London, 1953), VII. *Two Essays on Analytical Psychology*, pp. 40-43, 64 ff.

18. Karen Horney, *New Ways in Psychoanalysis* (New York, 1939).

19. Cf. Thompson, *op. cit.*, pp. 206 ff.

20. C. Lévi-Strauss, *The Savage Mind* (Chicago, 1968), p. 252; P. Watte, "L'ideologie structuraliste," *Bilan de la theologie du xxe siècle* (Paris, 1970), pp. 339-45; P. Blanquart, "Ateismo e strutturalismo," *Ateismo contemporaneo*, vol. II, pp. 493-520.

21. Lévi-Strauss, *op. cit.*, pp. 249; 252-55.

22. C. Moeller, "Renewal of the Doctrine of Man," *Theology of Renewal*, vol. II (Montreal, 1968), pp. 420-63. The author develops here a trenchant critique from a Christian conception of man. According to him, structuralism is the most radical atheism of all time. A denial of man's subjectivity is a denial of the foundations of transcendence because it leads to a denial of the presence of a subjective spirit in the world. Paul Ricoeur (*Esprit*, II (1963) 652, note), underscored the radical agnosticism which characterizes structuralism and its dependence on the law of chance.

23. D. Hume, *A Treatise on Human Nature*, ed. A. Selby-Bigge (Oxford, 1978), I, Pt. IV, par. VI.

24. Ultimately we are dealing with a voluntaristic interpretation of fundamental metaphysical notions.

25. A. Wawrzyniak, "Metaphysics and Man," *On God and Man*, Vol. I (Warsaw, 1968), p. 266; Hegel, *Phenomenology of the Spirit*, pp. 114 ff.

26. Heidegger's seminal work is *Sein und Zeit*, which deals with an analysis of man. Part I appeared in 1927. Part II has never appeared. Heidegger changed some notions of his first period (Heidegger I), when he entered upon what is called the period of Heidegger II. Cf. Lescoe, *Existentialism: with or Without God, Dasein*, pp. 192-95; being-in-the-world, pp. 198-202; thrownness, p. 207; being-toward-death, pp. 216-18; nothingness, pp. 235-44.

27. For other critiques, cf. Lescoe, *op. cit.*, pp. 188-92 (Being of beings); pp. 203-03 (Mit-Sein); pp. 250-52 (waiting for God); pp. 253-63 (theism or atheism).

28. M. Scheler, *Die Stellung des Menschen im Kosmos* (München, 1947) pp. 45 ff.

29. J. J. Schoeps, *Was ist der Mensch?* (Göttingen, 1960), p. 206.

30. Scheler himself supports such a position in his *Philosophische Weltanschauung (München, 1955), p. 104.*

CHAPTER IV

Notes and References

Cf. pp. 386-93 (Unabridged Edition of *I-Man*) for additional notes and references.

1. St. Thomas, ST I, 76, 1.

2. On this topic, cf. Karol Wojtyla, *The Acting Person*, Chap. II.

3. *A Treatise on Human Nature*, ed. L.A. Selby-Bigge (Oxford: Oxford University Press, 1968), Bk. I, pp. 251-52.

4. For the human body to exist means to be organized and formed by the soul. The body, therefore, does not possess an individual, separate, ontic existence of some sort; it exists due to the fact that it is matter organized by the human soul. The process of the organization and disorganization of the body is continuously in motion. The disorganized matter of the human body is no longer the human body.

5. Cf. *Q. Disp. De Anima*.

6. Ontical subsistence is something different than fullness in the aspect of the so-called "species." For soul-ego is not man, but through it man exists as a being of a definite "species." Cf. Thomas Aquinas, *Q. Disp. De Anima*, a. 1.

7. Cf. the analyses in *Contra Gentiles*, II, 68-72.

8. This is shown quite clearly in Baeumker, *Das Problem der Materie in der griechischen Philosophie* (Münster, 1890).

9. Throughout scholastic philosophy, this position was in force: "immaterialitas est radix cognitionis."

10. René Le Troquer, *What Is Man?* trans. Eric Earnshaw Smith (New York: Hawthorne Books, 1961), pp. 110, 114 ff.

11. *Ibid.*

12. ST I, 75, 6.

CHAPTER V

Notes and References

Cf. pp. 394-400 (Unabridged Edition of *I-Man*) for additional notes and references.

1. E. Gilson. *Elements of Christian Philosophy* (New York, 1960), p. 220.

2. *Ibid*.

3. Usually many arguments are presented as classical proofs for the existence of reason as a different cognitive power from the senses (including the imagination). Some of the most frequently used arguments are: (1) The existence of general concepts in man which are different from representations. The fact of the real existence of such concepts testifies to their real source which is called intellect (reason).

   (2) The fact of cognizing immaterial objects testifies to a proportionate faculty likewise immaterial, which is capable of achieving such a cognition.

   (3) The fact of affirming existence in judgmental acts testifies to the existence of a power which affirms be-ing.

   (4) The manner of intellectual cognition is radically different from that of sensible cognition. We are able to cognize everything, all forms, and articulations of matter. Hence this power is immaterial because a material cognitive power can achieve a cognition of only a certain portion of matter and in a concrete way.

   (5) The fact of objectivization of the area of consciousness of self knowledge.

   Sometimes there is talk about the "thinking" of computers. Obviously we cannot identify human thinking—even if it is understood in a most primitive way as an "operation on ideas" (Cartesian conception)—with the "thinking" of electronic machines, even if there is a certain similarity directed to one of the areas of activity.

   For if we distinguish in human cognition three "strata" of signs: (a) conventional signs: speech and writing (b) natural signs: the meaning of general expressions and (c) individual signed things, then, we meet in the activity of computers only an operation dealing with conventional signs but not with meanings and even less with designations.

   In addition, an operation dealing with conventional signs is accomplished basically from a syntactical aspect. This means that the electronic machine is fully capable of translating the language-symbol, insofar as it fulfills the syntactical function.

   But a man is needed who could decipher, by means of a living intellect, the meaning of the coded verbal signs that were fully converted with respect to their assigned direction of translations. Hence computers operate on only one level of language; they deal solely with conventional signs from a syntactical aspect, which is only an external "instrumental" side of thinking. What is foreign to the machine is that which in its minimal understanding, is thinking: an activity dealing with meanings which only human reason can accomplish, i.e., understanding the meaning of conventional signs.

4. Cf. Gilson, *op. cit.*, p. 155.

5. This does not mean that I first enunciate an existential judgment which asserts contentless existence. (By means of an existential judgment), I affirm an existence in being. I affirm this existence as affecting the content which I know better with each additional act of intellectual cognition. But the reason for all further operations is the primordial affirmation of the existence of being.

6. The cognitive axis of subject-object which would seem to be the fundamental location of all cognition is fundamentally the "conscious" starting point in pursuit of philosophy. A more primordial situation where no "hiatus" of subject-object as yet exists and where the fact of the "world's" existence strikes me and immerses me in the order of real being, is the point at which a metaphysical analysis should begin.

7. E. Gilson, *L'existence et l'être*, p. 253.

8. Cf. Plato, *Phaedo*, 72E.

9. E. Gilson, *History of Christian Philosophy in the Middle Ages* (New York, 1955), pp. 76-77.

10. R. Descartes, *Meditations*, III.

11. The theory of the human person emphasizes the personal character of a human being who actualizes himself in and through matter. The body becomes not only a "place" but also a co-element constituting man. Cf. ST, I,56.

12. The theory of instrumental activity performs a very important function in the system of Thomistic thought. It explains, for example, such problems as the function of senses in the process of intellectual cognition, the theory of the operation of the sacraments, Biblical inspiration etc.

13. What is known directly through sensible cognition is known indirectly through intellectual cognition. The same material object is known both materially and intellectually in its different aspects and reasons. In sensibly grasped contents, there are also structures which are "unreadable" to the senses, but which must be grasped by the senses so that they could be "readable" to the intellect. Hence there is an uninterrupted cognitive sequence passing from "readable" sensible structures to necessary structures disclosed only to the intellect.

14. St. Thomas, ST, I, 79; SCG, II, c. 77; *De Spir. Creat.*, a. 9; *Comp. Theologiae*, c. 83; *De Anima*, a. 4; *De An.*, lect. 10.

15. To my mind, Thomas Aquinas' theory is the only one which takes into account, different undeniable facts and it gives a concrete definitive explanation of the problem.

16. Cognition is information ABOUT reality, whereas thinking is an activity on concepts acquired in cognition.

17. Thomas emphasizes that the dematerialization of an impression depends on changing it from a potential state of being an object of intellectual cognition to an *actual state*, in which appear the constitutive notes (at least non-contradictability). Cf. ST, I,79, 3 ad 2; 84, 5;SCG, II, c. 59; *Quodlib.* 7, a 3; *De Anima*, III, lect. 10.

18. The specific modification of a cognizing intellect takes place here.

19. The process of cognition can be summarized under the following five headings:
    (1) The representation of the object of potentially intellectual cognition.
    (2) The activity of the agent intellect on the potentially intellective representation. Next comes the "dematerialization." The dematerialized representation is now able to act as a stimulus on the possible intellect.
    (3)As a result of the "striking" by the dematerialized representation in the intellect, an intellectually cognitive form arises and takes shape in the intellect.
    (4) As an "impressed species," the form begins the process of intellectual cognition, which terminates in an internal "utterance" and which assumes the form of the concept as an "expressed species."
    (5) The "produced" concept becomes the intermediary between the "transparent" cognition and the contemplation of the thing itself and a further process of cognition.

20. It seems that the distinction between universalizing and trancendentalizing cognition is essential for the distinction between the individual sciences and philosophy, especially of its classical source.

21. Not only are there different philosophical directions but also different conceptions of philosophy. It is customary to speak of a philosophy which explains (chiefly classical philosophy); of a philosophy which elucidates (chiefly phenomenology); and of a philosophy which expresses (chiefly existentialism).

22. It is only after good has been seen, that a vision and obligation follow. Duty does not present itself to us a priori. Rather, it is merged, as a relation, with a concrete decision which is coupled with different elements.

23. Such a transcendental beauty also includes usefulness. In this union, every creativity would ultimately have, as a goal, a transcendentally understood beauty, even if this is not always directly discernible.

24. Cf. M. Krąpiec, "Intentional Character of Culture," in *Logos i Ethos* (1971) 203 ff.

25. The problematic of *art* in the creativity of St. Thomas has a special meaning because it becomes the notion of underlying activity not only for man but also for God.

26. Cf. R. Ingarden, *Studies in Aesthetics*, Vol. III (Warsaw, 1970).

CHAPTER VI

Notes and References

Cf. pp. 401-402 (Unabridged Edition of *I-Man*) for additional notes and references.

1. When we speak of an intellectualization of nature, we hold that such an intellectualization can be joined with other values—either good or bad. This presupposes, however, a more basic and fundamental grounding. Unfortunately, even concentration camps were works of culture but of a degraded and perverted culture with respect to an evil use of the intellect.

2. A listing of literature on the subject of Thomism and of the Thomistic conception of intentionality is contained in the work, A.M. Heimler, *Die Bedeutung der Intentionalität im Beriech des Seins nach Thomas v. Aquin (Forschungen zur neueren Philosophie und ihrer Geschichte*, Bd. XIV (Würzburg, 1962).

3. R. Ingarden, *Dispute on the Existence of the World*, Vol. II (Cracow, 1948), pp. 230-32.

4. N. Moreau, *Querrelle de la science normative* (Paris, 1969), p. 113.

5. When I assert that cultural works bear the character of a sign or symbol, (a) I do not wish to move to a Neokantian position, especially that of E. Cassirer who holds that human cognition is, of its very nature, a symbolic cognition. In order to locate myself, I assert something diametrically opposite by affirming realism.
(b) I am concerned with a very fundamental understanding of a sign, the kind that St. Augustine already knew. I am not concerned here with emphasizing some very particular function of a sign, i.e., as referring to something, expressing itself, representing something, a signal etc., because these are further particularizations of the problem.

CHAPTER VII

Notes and References

Cf. pp. 403-08 (Unabridged Edition of *I-Man*) for additional notes and references.

1. *Zur Phänomenologie und Metaphysik der Freiheit.*

2. S. Kamiński, "*The Experimental Point of Departure of Ethics*," *Studia Philosophiae Christianae*, 1968, 2, pp. 48 ff.

3. The analysis of the already existing and accomplished decision, and not the consciousness of its obligation, is the foundation and the object of the classical explanatory treatment, leading to the construction of ethics as the theory of that act. These issues will be touched upon below in Chap. VIII.

4. This inclination is precisely an act of spiritual love.

5. The following exposition is based on the classical analysis of Thomas Aquinas (ST, I-II, q. 17, 7-9; q. 23, q. 25; q. 56; *De Verit.*, q. 25, 26; 2. 20 a. 2.)

6. Thomas writes, characteristically: "The truth of the matter is to be found by considering natural movements. For if, in natural movements, we observe those of approach and withdrawal, approach is of itself directed to something suitable to nature, while withdrawal is of itself directed to something contrary to nature." ST, I-II, 36, 1.

7. Describing the experience of the feeling of fear, St. Thomas observes: "The outer parts become cold . . . thirst ensues, sometimes indeed the result is a loosening of the bowels . . . the lip, too, and the lower jaw trembles . . . chattering of the teeth." CF. ST, I-II, 44, ad 1, ad 2; q. 47, a. 4; *De Verit.*, 26, 8.

8. For this reason Thomas wrote: "Quando constituitur in propria operatione connaturali et non impedita, sequitur delectatio." ("When a thing is established in its proper connatural and unhindered operation, delight follows.") ST, I-II, q. 31, 1 ad 1.

9. Cf. Thomas Aquinas, *De Verit.*, q. 26, a. 2 ad 3.

10. For this reason also philosophers in the Middle Ages thought that there exist in us two distinct emotional powers (like two hands): appetitive, which have for an object the concrete good known by the senses, easily attained; and irascible (aggressive), having as an aim the attainment of difficult good, with the inclusion of a whole mechanism of combat, or removal of evil.

11. The question of the sublimation of feelings is extensive and has its various

198

theories, e.g., of Freud, Scheler, theories of course related to certain models of man. A theory of the sublimation of feelings against the background of the structure of human existence was also given by St. Thomas. The basic text for the study of St. Thomas on this theme is found in ST, I-II, 56, 4; q. 17, a. 7-9; *De Verit.*, q. 20, a 2. The sublimation of feelings in the understanding of St. Thomas is the constant conformability of the affective life with the exigencies of reason.

12. The existentialists, especially Jean-Paul Sartre, focus attention on the possibility of the "objectification" of a human being, already even in the unreflective knowledge of oneself. CF. *Being and Nothingness* (New York: Philosophical Library, 1956).

CHAPTER VIII

Notes and References

Cf. pp. 409-10 (Unabridged Edition of *I-Man*) for additional notes and references.

1. More extensive considerations of this subject are contained in Pope John Paul II's *The Acting Person*.

2. This is Thomas Aquinas' conception of man (ST 90, 2; 75, 2; 76, 1), along with a seminal theory of the human being as personal.

3. CF. ST, I-II, 19, 9; 94, 4 ad 3; II-II, 104, 4 ad 2.

4. *Ibid.*, I-II, 94, 1 ad 2; I, 79, 9; II-II, 47, 6 ad 3. In the last text cited, Thomas significantly says, "Synderesis movet prudentiam, sicut intellectus primorum principiorum scientiam."

5. The bases for distinguishing between a proper, a pleasant, and a useful good in human desire constitute various manners of desire-love. If one desires some good or loves it only for itself, then it is a just good. Such a good can be only a person. If we desire some good because the function itself of desiring that good is desirable, we are dealing with a pleasant good. If, however, we desire some good with respect to some other good, we realize a useful good which is fundamentally a means to an end. This does not exclude the possibility that some good, for example some loved person, could perform the functions of all three goods.

CHAPTER IX

Notes and References

Cf. pp. 411-13 (Unabridged Edition of *I-Man*) for additional notes and references.

1. Quoted in F. Copleston, "The Human Person in Contemporary Philosophy," in *Contemporary Philosophy* (Westminster, 1956), p. 106.

2. Questions concerning the structure of the personal being (cf. below, chap. XI) are fundamental for accomplishing these investigations. For such relations which can be observed in "groups": "I-world," "I-Thou," "I-we" presuppose a suitable ontic structure and hence a personal independence, intellect, will and characteristic manners of activity, on the part of these principal powers.

3. Cf. Lescoe, *Existentialism: With or Without God*, pp. 156-65 (on Buber) and pp. 98-104 (on Marcel).

4. The problem of love is the object of very interesting analyses by St. Thomas Aquinas (ST, I-II, 26-28), in which he considers the nature of love, its cause and effects.

5. G. Marcel writes, "Each one of us tends to become a prisoner of himself, not only in respect to his material interests, his passions, or simply his prejudices but, still more essentially, in the predisposition which inclines him to be centered on himself, and to view everything from his own perspective. The fraternal man, on the contrary, *is somehow enriched by everything which enriches his brother*, in that communion which exists between his brother and himself. "—*Existential Background of Human Dignity* (Cambridge, MA, 1963), p. 147.

6. G. Marcel observes, "The self-centered person . . . will be incapable of sympathizing with other people, or even of imagining their situation. *He remains shut up in his petty circle of his private experience*, which forms a kind of hard shell round him that he is incapable of breaking through."—*Being and Having*, vol. I (New York, 1965), p. 201.
   Seymour Cain (*Gabriel Marcel*, New York, 1963, p. 66), writes that such a person (indisponible) is self-preoccupied, self-encumbered, self-enclosed, incapable of giving of himself, of opening up and of giving out.

7. The question of family and state is treated by Aristotle in *Pol.* chap. I: "The family is the association established by nature. . . . The state is by nature clearly prior to the family." In chap. II, Aristotle writes, "Seeing that the state

is made up of households . . . we must speak of the management of the household. The parts of household management correspond to the persons who compose the household." Aristotle's last statement survives today in the concept of states as a family of families but it seems that such a notion is too dangerous for the individual concrete man, and it can lead to a disguised form of fascism. For the human being is not merely a function of some kind of society but he is also a being "in-itself-and-for-itself."

8. Aristotle, *Nic. Ethics*, chap. I.

9. St. Augustine, *Confess.*, Bk. I, chap. I., St. Thomas SCG, III, 47, 52-63. Cf. K. Wojtyla, *The Acting Person*, pp. 288-90—pseudo-laws not binding.

10. K.R. Popper, *The Open Societies and Its Enemies* (London, 1948).

11. A. Kasia, *Antinomies of Freedom. From the Chronicles of a Philosophy of Freedom* (Warsaw, 1966), p. 28.

12. J. Messner, *Das Naturrecht* (Wien, 1969), pp. 279 ff: (1) The authority of the social power is absolute and the aims of the authority are, at the same time, the goal of all organizations subordinated to the supreme government, so that there can be no mention of a contradiction or independence of the groups' aims and that of the government. (2) There are no associated groups which do not fulfill the will of the supreme government. (3) There is no law against the supreme government because the individual cannot assume the role of a judge against the supreme government. (4) The supreme government possesses the only official public opinion. (5) The source of power goes "from the top to the bottom" and this is the same direction which orders and decisions follow. (6) There is either no representation of the citizens or it is a decorative organ of power which performs only a propaganda role. (7) The social government is fundamentally a government of force, where the individual can be completely trampled upon by external pressure. (8) In such a government, there are no organs for the control of power. (9) In such a government there is no freedom of thought or speech. (10) Neither is there any possibility of organizing legal opposition. (11) Man's rights are not generally respected in such governments. (12) Basically, the government is the only true possessor of goods.

13. Cf. J.J. Rousseau, *Social Contract*, IV, 1-3.

13a. Cf. Wojtyla, *The Acting Person*, pp. 272-75.

14. Cf. the insightful observations on this subject in J. Maritain, *Principes d'une politique humaniste* (Paris, 1945), pp. 37 ff.

15. Cf. Wojtyla, *op. cit.*, pp. 289-90.

CHAPTER X

Notes and References

Cf. pp. 414-19 (Unabridged Edition of *I-Man*) for additional notes and references.

1. Cf. note 2, *I-Man*—unabridged edition), p. 414 for extensive bibliographical listings on the subject.

2. Although each of these writers interprets the phenomenon of religion differently, they all come to the unanimous conclusion that religion impedes the full development of the human personality.

3. We must distinguish clearly between two phenomenologies of religion: (1) Phenomenology of religion as a *humanistic science*. Religious phenomena are described as they are given in all kinds of empirically accessible areas: historical, psychological, and sociological. The resulting conception of religion is almost philosophical (van der Leeuw, M. Eliade). (2) Phenomenology of religion as an *eidetic science* and hence somewhat philosophical, since it observes phenomena in consciousness and through an "essential inspection" (*Wesenschau*), it apprehends and describes the essence of religion in a most general way. The foremost exponent of this type is M. Scheler.

4. Phenomenology of religion investigates only sensibility and not reality which corresponds to acts of a religious object. In this connection, even the factual genesis of sense does not come within the area of concern.

5. Cf. E. Fromm, *Psychoanalysis and Religion* (New York, 1972).

6. There is an enormous number of definitions of religion. R. Pauli, *Das Wesen der Religion* (München, 1947), cites approximately 150 definitions. Cf. note 17, pp. 415-16, *I-Man*, unabridged edition.

7. M. Scheler, *Vom Ewigen in Menschen* (Berlin, 1933).

8. Cf. E. Gilson, *God and Philosophy* (New Haven, 1941), for a personalistic understanding of the object of religion in the mind of the Greeks.

9. R. Otto, *The Idea of the Holy: An Inquiry into the Non-Rational Factor in the Idea of the Divine and its Relation to the Rational* (London, 1950), *passim*.

10. Scheler, *op. cit.*, p. 535.

11. St. Thomas, ST, I-II, 81, 1.

12. B. Häring, *Das Heilige und das Gute* (München, 1950), pp. 18-31; St. Thomas, ST, I-II, 83, 1-17. It is worth noting that *religio* in Latin also means

"religious order." This term which is used to indicate persons or co-religious points to the essential meaning and aim of this type of life, whose constitutive element is a conscious and freely willed "being-toward-God." Its fundamental activity is that which aims at an increasingly fuller realization of one's own union with others and with God.

13. Cf. M. Krąpiec, "Man in the Presence of Moral Good and Evil" (above).

14. S. Ossowski, *At the Basis of Aesthetics* (Warsaw, 1958), pp. 271-79; R. Ingarden, "Aesthetical Experience," in *Studies in Aesthetics*, vol. III, (Warsaw, 1970), pp. 97-102.

15. Cf. E. Smith, *Experience and God* (New York, 1968), pp. 169 ff.

16. Cf. Chap. X, note 44, p. 417. *I-Man* (unabridged edition).

17. I have in mind religious cognition as it is presented, for example, by Hessen and Guardini. Cf. M. Jaworski, *"Religious Cognition of God"* Zeszyty Naukowe (Scientific Journals) 3 (1961) 39-58; _____, *Religious Cognition of God According to Romano Guardini* (Warsaw, 1967).

18. Scheler, *Vom Ewigen in Menschen*, p. 535: "A religious act cannot, by itself or with the help of thought, construct that which presents itself as the object of an idea, of contemplation, of man's thought which realizes it. In some way, he must accept the truth toward which he aspires, which saves him and brings him happiness. This he 'seeks' precisely through the mediation of that being which he seeks."

19. Scheler establishes it as the highest class of value: "The ontic synthetic axiom for religious consciousness extols that which is completely only through itself of full value and is of a kind of value of holiness. This type of value cannot pass away or be lost in any other group of values, whether they are logical values, cognitive values, axiological, moral or aesthetic."—*op. cit.*, p. 390.

20. According to Martin Buber, the fundamental aspect of human existence is a dialogical relation of partnership which constitutes a personal "I," carrying on a dialogue with a "Thou," who is received in a free manner. The divine "Thou" constitutes the basis and the a priori of this relation. Cf. M. Buber, *Werke,*, Bd. I-II (München, 1962-64). Cf. also F. Lescoe, *Existentialism*, pp. 166-68.

21. Cf. W.A. Luijpen, *Existential Phenomenology* (Pittsburgh, 1962), pp. 344 ff.

22. Cf. G. Marcel, *Du refus a l'invocation* (Paris, 1940). "If we can believe in an Absolute Thou, a Being in whom unfaithfulness and betrayal are impossible, if I could believe in this Being's love for me and if I were permitted to love this Being, then I would be able definitively to consent to myself. This awareness of orientation is called 'hope;' it is the belief in Love."—Luijpen, *op. cit.*, p. 355.

23. Cf. Copleston's statement found in P. Ortegat, *Philosophie de la religion*, vol.

II (Louvain-Paris, 1948), p. 810.

24. In this regard, it is difficult to agree with E. Fromm that a personal God does not have to be for man "an object of reference and adoration," provided that he performs a positive role in human life. Such a position in the matter of the object of religion does not seem to take into account the ontic nature of man for whom the object of a religious reference cannot be an ontically inferior being. Cf. M. Jaworski, "Man and God. The Question of a Meaningful Relation Between a Human Person and God and the Problem of Atheism," in *Logos i Ethos*, 115-28.

25. Cf. A. Usowicz, *Psychology of Religion in Outline* (Cracow, 1951); L. Kaczmarek, "Man: A Religious Being" in *In the Wake of Post-Conciliar Questions*, vol. II (Warsaw, 1968), 171-210.

26. E. Smith proposes some interesting solutions on the subject of the relation of that which is holy (religious) and that which is worldly. He says that what is holy indicates the ultimate purpose which makes prominent and gives clarity to all individuals of worldly existence. That which is worldly, however, is the model and means by whose help that which is holy comes into full reality. Without the profane, the holy would become a sphere of a "pure spirit," which is impossible when we take into consideration the ontic state of man. Cf. *Experience and God*, p. 61; A. Levi, *Religion in Practice* (New York, 1966).

27. St. Thomas, ST, I-II, 3, 1.

28. The Christian truth about the resurrection of the bodies and about the "new land" emphasizes the necessity of some kind of material element in the life of a human person, even after death.

29. K. Rahner, *Zur Theologie des Todes* (Freiburg i Br., 1958), p. 85. "At the moment of death, man's period of actualization, his 'being-on-the-way' comes to an end. For this reason, the moment of death is the moment of the fullest actualization. Christian theology calls attention to the religious character of death . . . Man's final move which he brings to a close and, at the same time, terminates his earthly existence as a wanderer, is an act of rendering love. In this act, man accepts his appointment with death. He gives himself to God and commits himself to him, along with his fast vanishing life." J. Pieper, *Tod und Umterblichkeit* (München, 1968).

30. The problem of the ontic relation between God and the world is examined in greater detail in my work, *Participation of Being. An Attempt to Explain the Relation Between the World and God* (Lublin, 1972).

31. Ap., 17, 28.

32. Theories which explain the connection of religion with some social situation (Marx), or a psychological one (Fromm), or a biological one (Kołakowski) do not consider sufficiently the universal ontic status of the human person. A

discussion of such considerations, however, goes beyond the established limits of this outline.

CHAPTER XI

Notes and References

Cf. pp. 420-25 (Unabridged Edition of *I-Man*) for additional notes and references.

1. The problem of the "person" has its own abundant literature, both in the past as well as in the present. M. Landmann, *Der Mensch im Spiegel seines Gedankens* (München, 1962), lists some 1,458 bibliographical titles.

2. L. Strauss, *Natural Right and History* (Chicago, 1953), pp. 79-113, presents an extensive exposition on the subject of *phisis*. Almost all the philosophical works of the ancient Greeks were entitled *Peri Physeos*, indicating some element or structure, which was to make the world intelligible.

3. Cf. my work, *Aristotle's Conception of Substance* (Lublin, 1966).

4. In the history of the problematic of the person, there was a search for a constitutive element in some (ontic) traits of being. It referred to a Neoplatonic source, according to which the emanated hypostases represented determined ontic traits. Usually these traits had a positive character: some form of unity. But there also arose theories (John Duns Scotus), which pointed to negations, as moments which decide the character of personal being. This union of person with a determined ontic trait is, of course, understood against the background of essentializing sources of classical philosophy.

5. The theory of the personal being of Christ is connected in St. Thomas with an explanation of the dogma of the Incarnation. It signifies, above all, the duality of Christ's nature and the singleness of person who is the Divine Word. The person of the Logos "assumes" in itself and gives be-ing to the human nature of Christ. (*De rat. fidei Unione Verbi Incar.*, c. VIII; *De Un. Verbi Incar.*, a. 2.)
   If human nature were in some manner separated from the Person of the Word, then it would possess its own act of existence and, by this fact, it would become a human person itself. For this reason, the act of existence as the highest ontic perfection, as the element which ultimately bestows unity, as an ontically integrating element, as an innermost element which penetrates everything—this act of existence decides about the being-person.
   St. Thomas discusses this question (*Quodl.* II, a 4 ad 1) at length. He excludes the possibility that the element constituting a person might be some trait on the level of essence because, in such a case, the nature which has been "assumed" by the Person of the Word would possess deficiencies. Consequently, the existence of the person of the Word of God in Christ is one and it

207

actualizes this human nature. Hence Christ is one person, *a divine person*. He is, however, *man* because the person of the Incarnate Word possesses and actualizes, in the ontic order, Christ's human nature.

With respect to the relation of the human nature of the existing person of the Incarnate Word to the same act of existing, we can (with respect to this relation), call it an existence of a kind of "second order." A second order existence, however, is nothing else than the real relation of Christ's human nature to the existence of the Divine Person. This existence really actualizes the human nature. It constitutes only one reality, only one person. (*De Unione Verbi Incar.*, a. 4).

6. Sometimes there was an emphasis on the cognitive moment (Descartes), sometimes on the volitive (Maine de Biran), and sometimes even on moments of social consciousness (Del Valla).

7. By making the *cogito* a point of departure for philosophy, Descartes linked philosophy with consciousness as the place where activity concerning ideas takes place. For the English empiricists, impressions and ideas were the object of philosophical analysis in the point of departure, as well as in the ultimate argumentations. For Kant, the operational conditions of a conscious subject constitute the ontological situation.

8. The characteristic of a reasonable manner of cognizing appears in various cognitive structures: in simple apprehension, in acts of judgment, and in reasoning. We observe everywhere a fundamental "reckoning with" things, their structure, their manners of existence.

9. Acts of decision through which man expresses himself as a man and hence, as an autonomous, self-determining and conscious source of causation, constitute a special place for the manifestation of "reasonable" activity. This is so because a decision is for the sake of the production of a new being, whose author is the person.

The theory of the act of love presupposes a mastery of the investigations of such thinkers as, for example, Aristotle, St. Thomas and G. Marcel. The loving subject is "routed" out of his/her passivity by a loved good, which simultaneously "transforms" the subject. This internal "transformation" would explain the act of love.

St. Thomas points out that even if this conception explains much, nevertheless this "inner change" cannot be treated in the manner of cognitional changes; the act of love is dynamic and the transformation has a strictly dynamic character. It is an impulse which compels activity in the direction of a real uniting of the subject and object of love. In this process of uniting through love, there enters a process of giving oneself to the beloved.

10. The spirit which manifests itself is a function rather than a subject.

11. M Heidegger in *Sein und Zeit* denies the suitability of the Aristotelian categories of being in their reference to man. In their place, he accepts so-called

"existentials" as forms which better characterize the human being. Among these fundamental "existentials" is *Geworfenheit* (thrownness), which is an involuntary "casting" of things and people into the world.

12. The most general and most non-contradictable fact given us in philosophical explanation depends on showing the kind of reasons, whose contradiction would be either absurd or would lead to absurdity or, finally, to a denial of the very fact which was given is to be explained. Cf. S. Kaminski and M. Krą-piec, *On the Theory and Methodology of Metaphysics* (Lublin, 1962).

13. We must strongly emphasize the fact that to be a subject is fundamentally to be a being, to exist as a being. The conception of a subject rather than an object is more strongly bound with the concept of being. For the object can be a cognitive construction (as, for example, in Kant) but not a subject which can exist independently, since all existing is always the existence of some subject. Moreover, the level of subjectivation is at the same time the level of existing. This means that the more some being is subjectivated, i.e., it is in itself and for itself, it is thereby a "stronger" being. For Hume's position, cf. *A Treatise*, vol. I, IV, VI, ed. L.A. Selby-Bigge (Oxford, 1978), pp. 251-52.

14. Pope John Paul II correctly called attention to this fact and he expressed it in the entire structure of his work, *The Acting Person*.

15. St. Thomas, ST III, 19, 1 ad 4; Quodlib. II, a. 4 ad 4; cf. J. Szuba, *Thomistic Theory of the Structure of the Person* (Lublin, 1953).

16. A transcending person actualizes and fulfills himself in his acts. Ultimately, fulfillment of a person can be achieved only through an act of death, experienced from within, as an ultimate affirmation of the Absolute, toward whom a person was hastening while he/she was affirming and fulfilling analogical truth, goodness and beauty. Cf. Chap. XII of this work.

17. Cf. St. Thomas, ST, I, 76, 1 ad 5. The statement that man exists previously as a spirit does not apply. The problem of man's coming into being is always linked with the fact of the process of birth. But it is precisely in the process of being born that man's spirit is, as if, a composite ontic reason which later makes itself aware through the body as a subjective "I." This means that existence serves man through the spirit, which expresses itself only in the body and through the body.

As an ontic act, existence does not serve man in the result of the organization of embryonic life. In such a case, man would be a being as a result of the organization of matter and there could never appear in human life, an act of transcending matter—which is manifestly false.

18. A self understanding being would ultimately be, in the area of metaphysics, a subsisting, uncaused being or one whose essence is existence.

19. St. Augustine, *Confessions*, XIII, c. 9. When we direct our attention to an analysis of love conducted in the Middle Ages and especially by St. Thomas,

(ST, I-II, 26-28), it is clear that all the conditions necessary to achieve an act of love can be fulfilled *only by a person in relation to another person*, who alone is capable of a proportionate response to the act of love. And only a person as a subsisting being can be recognized fully as the kind of good which is the goal. (*QQ Disp. De Verit.*, q. 4, a 2 ad 7).

20. Personalistic philosophical theories only indicate a direction; they do not give concrete solutions.

21. It is very significant that in the thinking of the tradition of Catholic theology, the divine Persons are understood as being constituted through an independent interpersonal relation. The being of a divine person is being-for-another-person. A human person would be a participation in the divine Person.

CHAPTER XII

Notes and References

Cf. pp. 426-29 (Unabridged Edition of *I-Man*) for additional notes and references.

1. The problematic of death appears more clearly in contemporary philosophical as well as theological literature than in that of the past. The question occupies some of the most prominent contemporary authors such as, for example, Guardini, Rahner, Troisfontaines, Jankelewitch, Boros, Pieper, Cullman, Landsberg, Luyten, von Balthasar, and others.

2. Paul-Louis Landsberg, *The Experience of Death*, trans. Cynthia Rowland (New York: Philosophical Library, 1953), pp. 45-49.

3. Marcus Aurelius Antoninus, *The Meditations*, trans. R. Graves (London: Methuen and Co., 1905) pp. 107-08.

4. Cf. above, Chap. IV.

5. This is seen particularly in Plato's dialogues, especially in the *Phaedo*.

6. Diogenes Laertius, trans. R.D. Hicks (Cambridge: Harvard University Press, 1958), Vol. II, Book X, p. 665.

7. Plato, *Phaedo*.

8. Cf. above, Chap. IV. Only the conception of soul as form can be the foundation of an explanation of the psycho-physical unity of the human being. Cf. ST, I, 75.

9. ST, I, 75, 6.

10. Thomas repeatedly takes up this topic.

11. *L'Action*, Paris, 1959.

12. Paris, 1959.

13. Already as early as the year 1933, in a lecture entitled "Outlines of a Phenomenology of Having," delivered to the Lyons Philosophical Society (published in *Being and Having*, trans. Katherine Farrer (Westminster: Dacre Press, 1949), pp. 154 ff.), Marcel reflects upon the later elaborated problem. I use the expression "ego-soul" here, in order to emphasize that the soul constitutes the ontical subsisting foundation of the ego understood in the strict sense.

14. Karl Rahner, *Toward a Theology of Death*, pp. 17 ff.

15. Cf. *Summa Contra Gentiles*, II, c. 81.

211

APPENDIX I

A GLOSSARY OF TERMS*

ABSOLUTE—the Absolute is the ultimate object who actualizes man's potentialities to the fullest, 163; BB1.

AGENT INTELLECT—the power of the human intellect to dematerialize and universalize images or phantasms, by ignoring accidentals and grasping essential notes, 71-73; BB200.

ANALOGY OF BEING—while each concrete being is unique and different from every other being, nevertheless each has a common ultimate source, 115; BB11-12.

ANGST (Dread—Heidegger)—man discovers his care about his *Dasein* and this begets *Angst*, 37; L215-18; *Angst* is caused by man's homelessness which is the result of his thrownness, *ibid.*; L207, 225.

A PRIORI CATEGORY (Kant)—universal and necessary form imposed by the knowing mind on the object of knowledge, BB21.

ATHEISM—rejects the existence of God and considers man as a completely autonomous being, the most valuable of all reality, 138; BB24.

BE-ING (act of "to be" of a being, *esse, existence*—Thomas Aquinas)—that which ultimately activates a being's potentialities which belong to its nature, 128; BB126.

BORDER SITUATIONS (Jaspers)—death, suffering, guilt, war; to experience border situations is the same as "to exist"; such situations lead to the grasping of a "pure consciousness" which postulates the existence of an absolute consciousness, 38.

COGITATIO (Descartes)—"I think" (not know), 158.

COGNITION (Knowledge)—the understanding of a concrete thing under the aspect of a grasped meaning, 60ff.

COMMON GOOD—the ultimate foundation for joining together dynamized human persons in free personal societies, 129; BB62; common good as creating conditions for personal actualizations of man, *ibid.*

---

*BB—Walter Brugger—Kenneth Baker, *Philosophical Dictionary.* Spokane: Gonzaga University Press, 1972.

L—Francis J. Lescoe, *Existentialism: With or Without God.* New York: Alba House, 1974.

COMMUNITY—a society of rational free persons, who realize common good through acts of knowledge and love and creativity by being "for-another," 133; BB63; a gathering, a bond of categorical relations, binding persons so that they can develop the dynamism of their personality, for the purpose of fulfilling the common good of every human person, 124-25; BB63.

CONTINGENT BEING—one whose existence does not belong to its essence, 149; BB75.

CULTURE—as denoting everything that qualifies as human activity or production, 81; BB81; a transformation or "intellectualization" of nature, *ibid;* BB *ibid.*

CYPHERS (Jaspers)—finite symbols of infinity, the reading of which opens "the doors of faith," 38.

DASEIN (Heidegger)—synonymous with "man" but as one lacking a human essence or nature; *Dasein* as "creating" his/her essence through existential choices made during life "in the shadow of death," 36-38; BB85; L192-95.

DEATH—the most important act through which man ultimately fulfills his existence, 152; BB86.

DE FACTO—"as a matter of fact."

DIALECTICAL MATERIALISM—a theory formed by Marx and Engels which retains Hegel's dialectic (triadic movement and opposition) but which substitutes materialism for idealism 28-29; BB95; L43-44.

DIALECTICAL PROCESS (Hegel)—a triadic movement by way of thesis, antithesis, and synthesis, the latter of which, in turn, becomes a new thesis, 28-29; BB93; L43-45.

DIVINE LAW—the ultimate rule of all acts and movements so that all created things hasten to the goals assigned them (Augustine), 116.

DYNAMIZATION—the actualization of man through cognition, love, and freedom, 151ff; cf. K. Wojtyla, *The Acting Person,* pp. 60-101; A. Woznicki, *A Christian Humanism: Karol Wojtyla's Existential Personalism,* pp. 16, 55ff.

EFFICIENT CAUSE—the "doer" or agent cause.

EGO (Freud)—region of preconsciousness, representing reason and health and controlling Id's blind impulses, 52.

EGOCENTRICITY—as negating dialogue and treating the other not as a genuine "Thou" but as an "it," 124; L104, 161-165.

EMPIRICISM—only the sensibly given can be known; no universal essences possible (Locke, Hume, J.S. Mill, BB108.

EPISTEME (Aristotle)—"reasoning" in the widest sense, 77-78.

ESSENCE—that which makes a thing to be what it is; a nature, quiddity, definition; universal in the intellect but singular in a thing, BB114.

EXISTENCE—the be-ing of a thing; act of "to be," *esse*, 63; BB126; cf. above, BE-ING.

ETERNAL LAW—the ultimate basis for intelligibility of things and the highest law of moral conduct, 116.

FINAL CAUSE—the end or purpose; "that for the sake of which" an action is performed, BB142.

FINAL END OF MAN—union with the Highest Good and Highest Truth, 153-55.

FORM—dematerialized image which acts as a universal on the intellect, 75; BB145.

FORMAL CAUSE—the essence or nature of a thing; "arrangement of matter"; exemplar in the mind of the efficient cause.

GOOD (Aristotle)—the end or goal of every activity, 128; BB162.

HAPPINESS—complete actualization of man's potentiality in a dynamic way; a union of the person's intellect and will with the Person of the Absolute, 152; BB167.

HIC ET NUNC—here and now.

HOMELESSNESS (*Unheimlichkeit*—Heidegger)—man's feeling of abandonment, resulting from his thrownness into the world, 36-38; L14-15, 207.

ID (Freud)—the region of the unconscious, irrational by nature and great reservoir of *Libido* and death drive, 31.

IDEAS (Kant)—Soul, Universe, God: their existence as equally proved and disproved (Transcendental Dialectic); these Ideas as merely regulative and not constitutive, 35; BB423.

IDEAS OR FORMS (Plato)—universal essences or natures which have an extramental existence, 74; BB310.

ILLUMINATION (Augustinian)—a special divine help needed for knowledge of necessary and immutable truths, 66; BB25.

IMAGE OR PHANTASM—remnant or residue of previous sense perception (with accidental notes), 70ff; BB2.

INTELLECT (REASON)—immaterial power as a source of our universal and necessary knowledge, 71; BB200.

INTENTIONAL BEING—a being which exists through the existence of the subject, man, 86; BB204; the meaning disclosing itself in acts which represent the object (Husserl), 83; weakest kind of existence in relation to real, ideal, and absolute being (Ingarden), *ibid*.

INTENTIONAL OBJECTS—cognitive objects in consciousness which possess a psychical form of existence (Brentano), 83.

INTERSUBJECTIVITY—a mutual meeting and giving of an "I" and "Thou," 149; L13-14, 101-104.

I-THOU RELATIONSHIP—"I" treats another person as an autonomous subject, as another "I," reciprocal in character (Marcel, Buber), 123; L13-14, 98-106, 156-61.

LIBIDO—sex drive which Freud considered as the principal driving force of human life, 30-31.

LOVE (highest possible human act)—as the giving of oneself to the Absolute Person at the moment of death (active sense), 182; BB233; an offering of an "I" to a "Thou," enriching the "I," 123-24; L99-101.

MAN—as an ontic "structure" which is single and entire, an undivided and subsistent being, 109; BB236.

MAN AS BEING-TOWARD-DEATH (*Sein-zum-Tode*—Heidegger)—as *Dasein,* man makes all his existential choices "in the shadow of death"; For Heidegger, death is a passage from being to nothingness, 36-38; L216-18, 235-39.

MATERIAL CAUSE—that out of which something is made.

MORAL SUBJECTIVISM—a relativism which is antithetical to subjectivity and subjectivization.

NATURAL LAW—as appearing in the form of a practical judgment, "good is to be done," 110-11; BB269.

NATURALISTIC EVOLUTIONISM—a theory holding that man's origin, structure, and development are the necessary result of an evolutionary process, 25; BB121.

NATURE (Greeks)—a permanent structure and source of regular activity, 156.

NOUS ("mind"—Aristotle)—a "reading" of first principles of all philosophy, 77-78.

NUMINOSUM—a religious reality which is the object of religious experience, 142.

ONTIC UNITY OF MAN—man is a substance-subject of his own acts and possesses his own *esse*, 64ff.

ONTOLOGICAL "I"—as revealing the be-ing and subjectivity of a person, 159.

ONTOLOGISM—the idea is its own reality; knowledge as occurring through the immediate union of soul with its object, who is God, 67; BB290.

ONTOLOGY—science of contingent being; "ontological" as usually synonymous with "metaphysical," BB291.

PANTHEISTIC IDEALISM (Hegel)—as identifying thought with reality, i.e., Spirit or Idea; man as but one moment in the evolutionary process of the Spirit (no individual personal existence or free will), 35-36; BB297; God as the totality of reality, *ibid.*

PERSON (Boethius)—an individual substance of a rational nature; (Thomas Aquinas)—a person is his own existence and proportional to a given individual nature, 161; cf. K. Wojtyla, *The Acting Person,* esp. pp. 25ff.

PHENOMENOLOGICAL "I"—a dispositional center whereby we treat ourselves as a distinct center that uses objects which surround us, 159.

PHENOMENOLOGICAL-EXISTENTIAL METHOD—as striving to grasp acts of consciousness, their structure, and methods of constituting objective counterparts and meanings, 139; BB305; as a "bracketing" of real, factual existence, 84-85; L19, 88-89, 174-76.

PHENOMENON OF SPIRIT—a certain appearance of a cosmic quantum of consciousness (de Chardin), 26.

PHRONETIC (Polish neologism from Greek *phronesis*)—"prudential."

POIETIC KNOWLEDGE—creative, productive knowledge whose goal is beauty, understood in transcendental sense, 79.

POSSIBLE (Knowing) INTELLECT—an intellectually knowing power which is aroused and moved by a dematerialized form, 72-73; BB200.

PRACTICAL KNOWLEDGE—knowing for the sake of action (ethics and aesthetics).

PRESCIENTIFIC KNOWLEDGE—spontaneous, lacking organization and proper foundation, 76.

PRINCIPLE OF CAUSALITY—every effect has a cause, BB53.

PRINCIPLE OF EXCLUDED MIDDLE—a thing either is or is not.

PRINCIPLE OF IDENTITY—being is; a thing is what it is.

PRINCIPLE OF NON-CONTRADICTION—a thing cannot both be and not be at the same time, in the same place and under the same circumstances.

SEIN (Being)—Heidegger calls it "Being of beings," which manifests itself in particular beings (*Seiende*); the discovery of the Being of beings was the aim of his new ontology, 36-38; L184-92.

SLAVE MORALITY (Nietzsche)—as denoting qualities of weakness found in the slave class and antithetical to the aristocratic class; slave morality as basis for Christianity, 36.

SOPHIA (Aristotle)—"wisdom"; philosophy as studying being, 77-78.

SPECULATIVE OR THEORETICAL KNOWLEDGE—knowing for the sake of knowing, 76ff; BB385.

SUBJECTIVE-ONTIC PERSONALITY OF MAN—man as fully constituted in nature, having his own essence and act of existence, and master of all actions which he performs, 44-45.

STRUCTURALISM (Lévi-Strauss)—as holding that language is a structure which embraces all spiritual possibilities of man; as rejecting the transcendence, the subjectivity of man and all historical thinking, 33-34.

SUBJECTIVITY—as including the be-ing of being, autonomy, goodness and "reasonableness"; of an entity, 156; as an immediate experience of my being a subject of my existence and action, 160.

SUBSISTENT—not dependent on another being for its existence, 44-45; BB398.

SUBSTANCE—a subject of its own action, possessing its own existence (in contrast to accident which inheres in a subject and possesses only a vicarious existence) cf. Aristotle; Thomas Aquinas, BB399.

SUPEREGO (Freud)—region of consciousness representing moral and social demands; it is the source of so-called moral conscience, 31.

SUPERMAN (*Uebermensch*—Nietzsche)—representing a second transvaluation of values, i.e., a destruction of slave morality and, through power and force, a return to aristocratic values.

SYNDERESIS—human conscience; an aggregate of first moral principles, 111-12.

TABULA RASA ("clean slate"—Aristotle)—characterization of the mind's state prior to any sensible perceptions.

THEISTIC HUMANISM—as considering man to be of the highest value among created entities, whose existence is broadened because of a psychological and moral union with a Transcendent Being, 138.

THROWNNESS (*Geworfenheit*—Heidegger)—Man (*Dasein*) has been thrown or hurled into existence, not knowing whence he came nor where he is going; thrownness as disclosing man's nothingness and begetting dread, 36-38; 148; L207-10; 215-21; 235-44.

TRANSCENDENTAL REALITY—God, who is pure act of existence, 138; BB422.

TRANSCENDENT THOU—God, L58, 106.

TRANSCENDENTAL ANALYTIC (Kant)—level of understanding; categories as a priori forms (esp. substance and cause), which impose universality and necessity on sensibility, 35; BB423.

TRANSCENDENTALS—thing, good, truth, beauty, 112; BB426.

TRANSCENDENTAL PARTICIPATION—everything that exists, exists in the existence of the personal Absolute, 154.

UNIVERSAL ESSENCE—object of intellect; result of process of abstraction, 69ff.

"WE" (Marcel, Buber)—a new reality is co-created by a reciprocal I-Thou relationship, 125; L101-04, 115, 154-56; society as a "we" when it makes possible man's opening of himself to the Absolute Good, 126; cf. K. Wojtyla, *op, cit.*, 261ff.

CHAPTER I

Bibliography

Alquié, F. *La découverte métaphysique de l'homme chez Descartes*. Paris, 1955.
Anthropology and the Classics. New York, 1967.
Aristotle. *Aristotelis Opera*. Ed. Academia Regia Borussica. Vol. I–V. Berolini, 1831–70; Ed. altera quam curavit O. Gignon, Berlini, 1960–61.
————. *The Works of Aristotle*, 11 vols. W. D. Ross, ed. Oxford, 1928–31.
Augustine, St. Sancti Aurelii Augustini *opera omnia*. Paris, 1841–77. Migne Latin Patrology, vols. 32–47.
————. Sancti Augustini *opera*. Corpus Scriptorum Ecclesiasticorum Latinorum. Editio consilio et impensis Academia litterarum caesarae vindobonensis. Vindobonnae, 1866–1919.
————. *Confessionum* Libri XIII. Recensuit P. Knell. Lipsiae, 1896. Vol. 33.
————. *De Civitate Dei* Libri XXII. Recensuit R. Hoffman. Lipsiae, 1894. Vol. 26.
Avicenna. Avicenna Latinus. *Liber de Anima*. Ed. S. Van Riet, Louvain, 1968.
Bazán, B. C. "Pluralisme des formes ou dualisme des substances? La pensée préthomiste touchant la nature de l'âme." *Revue Philosophique de Louvain*, 67 (1969) 30–73.
Brentano, F. *Die Psychologie des Aristoteles insbesondere seine Lehre vom Nous poietikós*. Mainz, 1867.
Byrne, E. F., Maziarz, E. A. *Human Being and Being Human. Man's Philosophies of Man*. New York, 1969.
Cappelletti, A. J. *La teoria aristotelica de la visión*. Caracas, 1977.
Cartesian Essays. A Collection of Critical Studies. The Hague, 1969.
Changing Perspectives of Man. Chicago, 1968.
Chanteur, J. *Platon, le désir et la Cité*. Paris, 1980.
Chateau, J. *Les grandes de psychologie dans l'antiquité*. Paris, 1978.
Cicero. *Ciceronis Marci Tullii opera omnia*. C. F. Mueller ed. Leipzig, 1889–98.
Clark, S. R. L. *Aristotle's Man. Speculations upon Aristotelian Anthropology*. Oxford, 1975.
Cooper, L. *A Concordance of Boethius. The Five Theological Tractates and the Consolation of Philosophy*. Cambridge, 1928.
Cosenza, P. *Sensibilità, precezione, esperienza secondo Aristotele*. Napoli, 1968.
Courcelle, P. "Tradition platonicienne et traditions chrétiennes du corps-prison." *Revue des Etudes Latines*, 43 (1965) 406–43.
Cristofolini, P. "Sul problema cartesiano della memoria intelettuale." *Pensiero*, 7 (1962) 378–402.
Descartes, R. *Oeuvres et Correspondance*, publiés par Charles Adam et Paul Tannery. Vols. I–XIII. Paris, 1897–1913.

Dinkler, E. *Die Anthropologie Augustins.* Stuttgart, 1934.

Faggin, P. G. "L'anima nel pensiero classico antico." *L'Anima.* Brescia, 1954, 29–69.

Festugière, A. J. "La composition et l'esprit du *De Anima* de Tertullian." *Revue des sciences philosophiques et théologiques,* 33 (1949) 121–61.

Filipiak, M. *Biblia o człowieku* (The Bible about Man). Lublin, 1979.

Fortin, E. L. *Christianisme et culture philosophique au Ve siècle. La querelle de l'âme humaine en Occident.* Paris, 1958.

Francke, K. B. *Die Psychologie und Erkenntnislehre des Arnobius.* Leipzig, 1878.

Gangauf, T. *Metaphysische Psychologie des heiligen Augustinus.* Frankfurt, 1968.

Giacon, C. *I primi concetti metafisici. Platone, Aristotele, Plotino, Avicenna, Tommaso.* Bologna, 1968.

Giannini, G. "L'impostazione del problema antropologico nel presocratici." *Aquinus,* 6 (1963) 10–33.

––––––. "L'involuzione del problema antropologico nelle scuole post-aristoteliche e nel neoplatismo." *Doctor Communis,* 16 (1963) 18–40.

––––––. *Il problema antropologico. Linee di sviluppo storico speculativo dai Presocratici a S. Tommaso.* Roma, 1965.

Graeser, A. *Probleme der platonischen Seelenteilungslehre.* München, 1969.

Hare, M. M. *Microcosm and Macrocosm.* New York, 1966.

Jaeger, W. *Die theologie der frühen griechischen Denken.* Stuttgart, 1953.

––––––. *Paideia. Die Formung des griechischen Menschen.* Berlin, 1959.

Jäger, G. *"Nous" in Platons Dialogen.* Göttingen, 1967.

Klebba, E. *Die Anthropologie des h. Ireneaus.* Münster, 1894.

Krokiewicz, A. *Studia orfickie* (Orphic Studies). Warszawa, 1947.

Krüger, G. *Eros und Mythos bei Plato.* Frankfurt a.M., 1978.

Kucharski, P. "L'affinité entre les idées et l'âme d'après le *Phédon." Archivio di Filosofia,* 26 (1963) 483–515.

Kurdziałek, M. "Koncepja człowieka jako mikrokosmosu." *O Bogu i człowieku.* (Conception of Man as a Microcosm. *On God and Man,* T. II, Warszawa, 1969, 109–25.

Lefevre, C. " 'Quinta natura' et psychologie aristotélicienne." *Revue Philosophique de Louvain,* 69 (1971) 5–94.

Lloyd, G. E. R., Owen, G. E. L. *Aristotle on Mind and the Senses.* Cambridge, 1978.

Löwith, K. *Gott, Mensch und Welt in der Metaphysik von Descartes bis zu Nietzsche.* Göttingen, 1967.

Mathon, G. *L'anthropologie Chrétienne en Occident de saint Augustin à Jean Scot Erigene.* Lille, 1964.

Migne, J. P. *Patrologiae cursus completus. Series Latina.* T. 1–221. Paris, 1844–69.

Movia, G. *Anima e intelletto.* Padova, 1968.

Mueller, F. L. *Histoire de la psychologie de l'antiquité à nos jours.* Paris, 1968.

O'Connell, R. *St. Augustine's Early Theory of Man.* Cambridge, 1968.

Pastuszka, J. *Historia psychologii*. Lublin, 1971.

――――. *Niematerialność duszy ludzkiej u św. Augustyna (The Immateriality of the Human Soul in St. Augustine)*, Lublin, 1930.

Pfeil, H. *Das platonische Menschenbild*. Aschaffenburg, 1963.

Pieter, J. *Historia psychologii*. Warszawa, 1972.

Plato, *Platonis Opera*. Ed. J. Burnet in scriptorum classicorum Bibliotheca Oxoniensis. Vols. I–V. Oxford, 1955–57.

――――. *The Dialogues of Plato,* trans. B. Jowett, 5 vols. Oxford, 1871.

Robinson, T. M. *Plato's Psychology*. Toronto, 1970.

Romano, F. *Logos e mythos nella psicologia di Platons*. Padova, 1974.

Schefer, J.-L. *L'invention du corps chrétien. Saint Augustin, le dictionnaire, la memoire*. Paris, 1975.

Siclari, A. *L'antropologia di Nemesio di Emesa*. Padova, 1974.

Stachowiak, L. "Biblijna koncepcja człowieka." *W nurcie zagadnień posoborowych.* (Biblical Conception of Man. *In the Wake of Post-conciliar Questions).* T. II, Warszawa, 1968, 209–26.

Swiezawski, S. "Nauka o duszy w *Metafizyce* Arystotelesa." (A Study on the Soul in Aristotle's *Metaphysics) Przegląd Filozoficzny*, 41 (1938) no. 4, 395–421.

Thomas, St. S. Thomae Aquinatis Doctoris Angelici *Opera Omnia,* jussu impensaque Leonis XIII P.M. rfita. T. I–XVI. Romae, 1882–1953.

――――. S. Thomae Aquinatis. *Scriptum super Libros Sententiarum Magistri Petri Lombardi*. Ed. cura R. P. Mandonnet. T. I–IV. Parisiis, 1929–47.

――――. Sancti Thomae de Aquino *Summa Theologiae*. Textus editionis Leoninae cum adnotationibus fontium . . . ex editione altera Canadiensi Ottawa, 1953. Romae: Alba Editiones Paulinae, 1962.

――――. S. Thomae Aquinatis *Quaestiones disputatae et quaestiones quodlibetales* ad fidem optimarum editionum diligenter recusae. Romae, 1931.

――――. S. Thomae Aquinatis *Opuscula omnia . . .* Parisiis, 1927.

――――. Sancti Thomae Aquinatis *Quaestiones de Anima,* ed. J. Robb. Toronto, 1968.

――――. S. Thomae Aquinatis *Sermo seu Tractatus de Ente et Essentia,* ed. L. Baur, editio altera emendata. *Opuscula et Textus. Series Scholastica.* I. Münster i Westf., 1933.

――――. S. Thomae Aquinatis *Tractatus de Spiritualibus Creaturis,* editio critica, ed. L. Keeler. Roma, 1938.

――――. S. Thomae Aquinatis *Tractatus de Unitate Intellectus,* ed. L. Keeler, Roma, 1936.

Tracy, T. J. *Physiological Theory and the Doctrine of the Mean in Plato and Aristotle*. New York, 1969.

Ushida, N. *Etude comparative de la psychologie d'Aristote, d'Avicenne et de St. Thomas d'Aquin*. Tokyo, 1968.

Verbeke, G. "Le *De Anima* d'Avicenne, une conception spiritualiste de l'homme." *Liber de Anima*. Louvain, 1968, 1–73.

――――. "L'immortalité de l'âme dans le *De Anima* d'Avicenne. Une synthèse de l'aristotélisme et du neoplatonisme." *Pensamiento,* 25 (1969) 271–90.

CHAPTER II

Bibliography

Becker, E. *The Structure of Evil. An Essay on the Unification of the Science of Man.* New York, 1976.

Bocheński, I. *Philosophy.* Dordrecht, 1962.

Brennan, R. E. *Die menschliche Natur.* Bonn, 1961.

Bühler, W. *Der Mensch zwischen Uebernatur und Unternatur.* Nürnberg, 1966.

Chambliss, R. *Meaning for Man.* New York, 1966.

Comfort, A. *Natur und menschliche Natur.* Reinbek b. Hamburg, 1970.

Das Bild des Menschen in der Wissenschaft. Hildesheim, 1978.

Der Mensch und seine Symbole. Olten, 1968.

Der Mensch zwischen Natur und Technik. Stuttgart, 1967.

Durand, G. *Science de l'homme et tradition. Le nouvel esprit anthropologique.* Paris, 1980.

Etcheverry, A. *L'homme dans le monde.* Paris, 1964.

Flew, A. G. N. *A Rational Animal and Other Philosophical Essays on the Nature of Man.* Oxford, 1978.

Gehlen, A. *Antropologische Forschung.* Hamburg (1961) 1970.

————. *Der Mensch. Seine Natur und seine Stellung in der Welt.* Berlin, 1940; Frankfurt/M. 1971.

————. *Die Seele im technischen Zeitalter.* Hamburg, 1957.

————. *Urmensch und Spatkultur.* Bonn (1956), 1964.

————. "Zur Systematik der Anthropologie." *Systematische Philosophie,* ed. N. Hartmann. Berlin, 1942.

Gölz, W. *Dasein und Raum.* Tübingen, 1970.

Hoyle, F. *Man in the Universe.* New York, 1966.

Landgrebe, L. "Existenz und Autonomie des Menschen." *Philosophisches Jahrbuch,* 75 (1967–68) 239–49.

Landmann, M. *Fundamental-Anthropologie.* Bonn, 1979.

Litt, T. *Mensch und Welt.* München (1948), 1961.

Luyten, N. A. "Ordo Rerum." *Schriften zur Naturphilosophie, Philosophischen Anthropologie und Christlichen Weltanschauung.* Freiburg/Schweiz, 1969.

Marcie, R. *Mensch, Recht, Kosmos.* Wien, 1965.

Midgley, M. *Beast and Man.* Ithaca, 1978.

Mohr, H. *Wissenschaft und menschliche Existenz.* Freiburg (1967), 1970.

Nott, K. *Philosophy and Human Nature.* London, 1970.

Philosophy and the Future of Man. Washington, 1968.

Portmann, A. *Biologische Fragmente zu einer Lehre vom Menschen.* Basel (1951), 1969.

Rothaker, E. *Probleme der Kulturanthropologie.* Bonn, 1948.
———. *Zur Genealogie des menschlichen Bewusstseins.* Bonn, 1966.
Schmeisser, H. *Die Stellung des Menschen im Kosmos.* Linz, 1957.
Siegmund, G. *Tier und Mensch.* Frankfurt, 1968.
Stevenson, L. *Seven Theories of Human Nature.* London, 1974.
Szczepanski, J. *Sprawy ludzkie* (Human Affairs). Warszawa, 1978, 1980.
Thorpe, W. H. *Animal Nature and Human Nature.* New York, 1974.
  The Visage of Adam. Philosophical Readings on the Nature of Man. New York, 1970.
Vanni-Rovighi, S. *Elementi di filosofia.* Vol. III. *La natura e l'uomo.* Brescia, 1967.

CHAPTER III, PART I

Bibliography

Abélès, M. *Anthropologie et Marxisme*. Bruxelles, Paris, 1976.

Althauser, L. *Pour Marx*. Paris, 1966.

Amado, G. *L'être et la psychoanalyse*. Paris, 1978.

Anthropologie. (Cahiers de Philosophie) I, Janvier, 1966, Paris, 1966.

Antonowicz, I. *Sowriemiennaja filosofskaja antropolgoia*. Mińsk, 1968.

Baczko, B. *Weltanschauung, Metaphysik, Entfremdung*. Frankfurt, 1968.

Bartnik, C. *Problem historii uniwersalnej w teilhardyzmie (The Problem of Universal History in Teilhardism)*. Lublin, 1972.

————. *Teilhardowska wizja dziejów (The Teilhardian Vision of History)*, Lublin, 1975.

Bergeron, P. *L'action humaine dans l'oeuvre de Teilhard de Chardin*. Montréal, 1969.

Brodeur, C. *Du problème de l'inconscient à une philosophie de l'homme*. T. I. *Les théories freudiennes sur la structure de l'organisme psychique*. T. II. *La structure de la pensée humaine*. Montréal, 1969.

Brown, J. A. *Freud and the Post-Freudians*. London, 1963.

Cackowski, Z. *Człowiek jako podmiot działania praktycznego i poznawczego. (Man as the Subject of Practical and Cognitive Activity)*. Warszawa, 1979.

Czarnecki, Z. J., Dziemidok, B., ed. *Homo agens. Studia nad aktywnością i podmiotowością człowieka (Homo agens. Studies in the Activity and Subjectivity of Man)*. Lublin, 1981.

Evolution, Marxism and Christianity. Studies in Teilhardian Synthesis. London, 1966.

Folkierska, A. "Struktura mentalna—propozycja C. Lévi-Straussa dotycząca koncepcji człowieka." (Lévi-Strauss' Proposition of "Mental Structure" as It affects the Concept of Man). *Studia Filozoficzne*, 12 (1974) 75–87.

Frey-Rohn, L. *Von Freud zu Jung. Studie z. Psychologie d. Unbewussten*. Zürich, 1969.

Fritzhand, M. *Człowiek—humanizm—moralność* (Man, Humanism, Morality), Warszawa, 1961.

Fromm, E. *Marx's Concept of Man*, New York, 1961.

Garaudy, R. *Perspectives de l'homme*. Paris, 1961.

Hesnard, A. *L'oeuvre de Freud et son importance pour le monde moderne*. Paris, 1960.

Homans, P. "Transference and Transcendence: Freud and Tillich on the Nature of Personal Relatedness." *The Journal of Religion*, 46, (1966) 148–64.

Hook, S. ed., *Psychoanalysis: Scientific Method and Philosophy. A Symposium.* New York, 1960.

Huxley, J. *Evolution. The Modern Synthesis.* London, 1963.

———. *Man in the Modern World.* London, 1947.

Jacobi, J. *Psychologia Junga.* Warszawa. 1968.

Jaroszewski, T. M. *Osobowość i wspólnota (Personality and Community).* Warszawa, 1971.

Jung, C. G. *Psychologia a religia. Wybór pism (Psychology and Religion. Selected Writings).* Warszawa, 1970.

Kasia, A. "Leninowska koncepcja człowieka" (Lenin's Conception of Man). *Studia Filozoficzne,* 63 (1970) 138–50.

Kołakowski, L. *Der Mensch ohne Alternative,* München, 1967.

Koren, H. J. *Marx and the Authentic Man.* Pittsburg, 1967.

Korsch, K. *Marxismus und Philosophie.* Frankfurt, 1966.

Köhler, H. *Das Menschenbild des dialektischen Materialismus.* München, 1963.

Kuczyński, J. *Homo Creator. Wstęp do dialektyki człowieka (Homo Creator. Introduction to the Dialectic of Man).* Warszawa, 1966.

La conception marxiste de l'homme. Paris, 1965.

Landrière, J. *Anthropologie du Marxisme et le marxisme soviétique,* Paris, 1965.

Lauzan, G. *Sigmund Freud et la psychoanalyse.* Paris, 1962.

Lévi-Strauss, C. *Anthropologie structurale,* Paris, 1958.

———. *La pensée sauvage.* Paris, 1962.

———. "Philosophie et anthropologie." *Cahiers de Philosophie,* 1 (1966) 47–56.

Mader, J. *Zwischen Hegel und Marx.* Wien, 1975.

Marcuse, H. *Eros and Civilization.* New York, 1962.

———. *One-Dimensional Man.* Boston, 1964.

Mascall, E. L. *The Importance of Being Human. Some Aspects of the Christian Doctrine of Man.* London, 1959. *(Chrześcijańska koncepcja człowieka.* Warszawa, 1962.)

Milet, A. *Pour ou contre le structuralisme. Claude Lévi-Strauss et son oeuvre.* Tournai, 1968.

Moeller, C. "Renewal of the Doctrine of Man." *Theology of Renewal.* Montréal, 1968, 420–63.

Nowak, L. *U podstaw dialektyki marksistowskiej (At the Basis of Marxist Dialectic).* Warszawa, 1977.

Panasiuk, R. *Dziedzictwo heglowskie i marksizm (Hegelian Heritage and Marxism).* Warszawa, 1979.

Parinetto, L. *La nozione dei alienazione in Hegel, Feuerbach e Marx.* Milano, 1968.

Pigon, G. *Panorama mysli współczesnej (A Panorama of Contemporary Thought).* Paris (no date).

Plessner, H. *Die Stufen des Organischen und der Mensch Einleitung in die Philosophische Anthropologie.* Berlin, 1965.

———. *Macht und meschliche Natur.* Berlin, 1931.

———. *Philosophische Anthropologie.* Frankfurt/M, 1970.

Polkowski, A. *Świadectwo Teilharda* (The Witness of Teilhard). Warszawa, 1974.

Portmann, A. *Biologie und Geist.* Frankfurt/M, (1956) 1968.

———. *Vom Ursprung des Menschen.* Basel (1944) 1966.

———. *Zoologie und das neue Bild vom Menschen.* Hamburg (1956) 1960.

Rabit, O. A. *Dialogue avec Teilhard de Chardin.* Paris, 1958.

Ricoeur, P. *De l'interpretation. Essai sur Freud.* Paris, 1965.

Rothacker, E. *Mensch und Geschichte. Studien zur Anthropologie und Wissenschaftsgeschichte.* Berlin, 1944; Bonn, 1950.

———. *Philosophische Anthropologie.* Bonn (1964) 1970.

Schaff, A. *Filozofia człowieka (Philosophy of Man).* Warszawa, 1962.

———. *Marksizm a jednostka ludzka (Marxism and Human Individuality).* Warszawa, 1965

———. *Marx oder Sartre. Versuch einer Philosophie des Menschen.* Wien, 1964.

Schilling, O. *Geist und Materie in biblischer Sicht. Ein exeget. Beitr. z. Diskussion im Teilhard de Chardin.* Stuttgart, 1967.

Sève, L. *Marxisme et théorie de la personnalité.* Paris, 1969.

Stock. M. E. "Conscience and Superego." *Thomist,* 24 (1961) 544–79.

Stróżewski, W. "Na marginesi człowieka Teilharda de Chardin" *(On the Boundary of Teilhard de Chardin's Man). Znak,* 15 (1967) 1314–38.

Ślipko, T. "Pojęcie człowieka w świetle współczesnej filozoficznej antropologii marksistowskiej w Polsce" (The Conception of Man in the Light of Contemporary Marxist Philosophical Anthropology in Poland). *Zeszyty Naukowe KUL,* 10 (1967) z. 2, 3–16.

Teilhard de Chardin, P. *Oeuvres.* T. I–X. Paris, 1955–69.

(Przekłady polskie: *Człowiek,* Warszawa, 1962, 1964; *Srodowisko Boże,* Warszawa, 1964.

Thompson, C. *Psychoanaliza, narodziny i rozwój (Psychoanalysis. Its Genesis and Development).* Warszawa, 1964.

Tovar, S. A. "La vision humaine de Teilhard de Chardin." *Eidos,* 2 (1970) 86–105.

Walton, P., Gamble, A., Coulter, J. "Image of Man in Marx." *Social Theory and Practice,* 1 (1970–71) 69–84.

Watte, P. "L'ideologie structuraliste." *Bilan de la théologie du XXe siècle.* Paris, 1970, 339–45.

Wciorka, L. *Ewolucja i stworzenie. (Evolution and Creation).* Poznań, 1976.

CHAPTER III PART II

Bibliography

Alpheus, K. "Was ist der Mensch? (Nach Kant und Heidegger)." *Kantstudien,* 59 (1968) 187–98.

Antropologias del siglo XX. Salamanca, 1976.

Bańka, j. *Problemy współczesnej filozofii człowieka (Problems of the Contemporary Philosophy of Man).* Katowice, 1978.

Barraud, J. *L'homme et son angoisse.* Paris, 1969.

Condette, J. R. *Søren Kierkegaard, penseur de l'existence.* Bordeaux, 1977.

Demske, J. M. *Being, Man and Death. A Key to Heidegger.* Lexington, 1970.

Derisi, O. N. *El ulhmo Heidegger. Approximaciónes y diferencias entre la fenomenologia existencial de M. Heidegger y la ontologia de Santo Tomas.* Buenos Aires, 1968.

Die Welt des Menschen—Die Welt der Philosophie. Den Haag, 1976.

Fazio-Allmayer, B. *L'uomo nella storia in Kant.* Bologna, 1968.

Gromczyński, W. *Człowiek, świat rzeczy, Bóg w filozofii Sartre'a (Man, the World of Things and God in the Philosophy of Sartre).* Warszawa, 1969.

Guéroult, M. "Nature humaine et état de nature chez Rousseau, Kant et Fichte." *Cahiers pour l'Analyse,* 6 (1967) 1–19.

Hegel, G. W. F. *Werke,* 18 vols. Berlin, 1832–45.

Heidegger, M. *Budować, mieszkać, myśleć (To Build, To Live, To Think).* Warszawa, 1977.

―――. *Nietzsche.* Pfullingen, 196.

―――. *Sein und Zeit.* Tübingen, 1927.

―――. *Vorträge und Aufsätze.* Pfullingen, 1952.

Hopkins, J. "Theological Language and the Nature of Man in Jean-Paul Sartre's Philosophy." *The Harvard Theological Review,* 61 (1968) 27–38.

Izenberg, G. M. *The Existentialist Critique of Freud. The Crisis of Autonomy.* Princeton, 1976.

Jaspers, K. "Die Frage nach dem Menschen." *Universitas,* 20 (1965) 673–80.

―――. *Psychologie der Weltanschauungen.* Berlin, 1966.

Juszezak, J. *L'anthropologie de Hegel à travers la pensée moderne: Marx, Nietzsche, A. Kojvé, E. Weil.* Paris, 1977.

Kierkegaard, S. *Samlede Veerker,* 2nd ed. by A. B. Drachmann, J. L. Heiberg, H. O. Lange. 15 vols. Copenhagen, 1930–1936.

Konigshausen, J. H. *Kant's Theorie des Denkens.* Amsterdam, 1977.

Kuderowicz, Z. "Klasyczna filozofia niemiecka jako źródło współczesnej antropologii filozoficznej" (Classical German Philosophy as a Source of Contemporary Philosophical Anthropology). *Humanitas,* 1 (1978) 7–40.

226

Lacombe, O. *L'existence de l'homme*. Paris, 1951.

Laird, J. *Hume's Philosophy of Human Nature*. Hamden, 1967.

Lakebrink, B. *Klassische Metaphysik. Eine Auseinandersetzung mit der existentialen Anthropozentrik*. Freiburg, 1967.

Lepp, T. *L'existence authentique*. Paris, 1951.

Luijpen, W. A. *Existentiele Fenomenologie*, Utrecht, 1959. (Fenomenologia egzystencjalna. Warszawa, 1972)

Meyer, H. *Martin Heidegger und Thomas von Aquin*. München, 1964.

Michalski, K. *Heidegger i filozofia wspólczesna* (Heidegger and Contemporary Philosophy). Warszawa, 1978.

Norris, P. A. *Sartre's Concept of a Person*. Amherst, 1975.

Papone, A. *Existenza e corporeità in Sartre*. Firenze, 1969.

Pintor, Ramos A. *El humanismo de Max Scheler. Estudio de su antropologia filosofica*. Madrid, 1978.

Pflaumer, R. "Sein und Mensch in Denken Heideggers." *Philosophische Rundschau*, 13 (1966) 161–234.

Pruche, B. *L'homme de Sartre*. Paris, 1949.

Ramirez, N. *Filosofia de hombre en su realidad existencial*. Guadalajara, 1969.

Regina, U. *Heidegger. Dal nichilismo alla dignita dell'uomo*. Milano, 1970.

Rogalski, A. *Myśl i wyobraźenia (Thought and Images)*. Warszawa, 1977.

Rudziński, R. *Człowiek w obliczu nieskończoności. Metafizyka i egzystencja w filozofii Karla Jsspera. (Man in the Presence of Infinity. Metaphysics and Existence in the Philosophy of Karl Jaspers.)* Warszawa, 1980.

Salvucci, P. *L'uomo di Kant*. Urbino, 1963.

Sartre, J. P. *L'Être et le néant*. Paris, 1957.

―――. *L'existentialisme est un humanisme*. Paris (1946) 1959.

―――. *L'homme et les choses*. Paris, 1947.

Scheler, M. *Abhandlungen und Aufsätze*. Leipzig, 1915.

―――. *Die Stellung des Menschen im Kosmos*. Darmstadt, 1928.

―――. *Die Wissenformen und Gesellschaft*. Leipzig, 1926.

―――. *Zur Idee des Menschen*. Leipzig, 1955.

―――. *Zur Phänomenologie und Theorie der Sympatiegefühle*. Halle, 1913.

Schwartländer, J. *Der Mensch ist Person*. Stuttgart, 1968.

Siegmund, G. *Der Mensch in einem Dasein. Philosophische Anthropologie*. Bd. I. Freiburg, 1953.

Suchodolski, B. *Kim jest człowiek? (Who is Man?)*. Warszawa, 1974.

Trębicki, J. *Etyka Maxa Schelera. (Ethics of Max Scheler)*. Warszawa, 1973.

Wawrzyniak, A. "Filozofia Martina Heideggera w świetle nowszych opracowań." (The Philosophy of Martin Heidegger in the Light of More Recent Studies). *Roczniki Filozoficzne*, 13 (1965) 119–28.

―――. "Metafizyka a człowiek." (Metaphysics and Man) *O Bogu i o człowieku*, 1968, 257–65.

Znaniecki, F. "Antropologia filozoficzna Maxa Schelera." (Philosophical Anthropology of Max Scheler) *Studia Pelplinskie*, 1969, 143–78.

CHAPTER IV

Bibliography

Abelson, R. *Persons. A Study in Philosophical Psychology.* London, 1977.

Adamczyk, S. "Pierwastki duchowe w człowieku w świetle nauki Sw. Tomasza z Akwinu" (Spiritual Elements in Man in the Light of St. Thomas Aquinas' Teaching). *Roczniki Filozoficzne,* 2–3 (1949–50) 60–84.

Bars, H. *L'homme et son âme.* Paris, 1958.

Bernath, K. *Anima forma corporis. Eine Untersuchung über die ontologischen Grundlagen der Anthropologie des Thomas von Aquin.* Bonn, 1969.

Bier, A. *Die Seele.* München, 1966.

Bejze, B. "W poszukiwaniu współczesnego pojęcia duszy ludzkiej" (In Search of a Contemporary Concept of the Human Soul). *W nurcie zagadnień posoborowych (In the Wake of Post-Conciliar Questions).* T. II. Warszawa. 1968, 51–78.

Bodamer, J. *Der Mensch ohne Ich.* Wien, 1960.

Brenton, G. "Le problème actuel de l'anthropologie thomiste." *Revue Philosophique de Louvain,* 61 (1963) 215–40.

Brod, M. *Von der Unsterblichkeit der Seele.* Stuttgart, 1969.

Bruaire, C. *Philosophie du corps.* Paris, 1968.

Carretero, L. A. *Presencia del animal en el hombre.* Mexico, 1962.

Chauchard, P. *Dès animaux à l'homme. Psychismes et cerveaux.* Paris, 1961.

Chirpaz, F. *Le corps.* Paris, 1969.

Collingwood, F. J. *Man's Physical and Spiritual Nature.* New York, 1963.

Conrad-Martius, H. *Die Geistseele des Menschen.* München, 1960.

Davy, M. M. *La connaissance de soi.* Paris, 1966.

Delay, J. *La psycho-physiologie humaine.* Paris, 1959.

Di Napoli, G. *L'immortalità dell'anima nel Rinascimento.* Torino, 1963.

Disertori, B. *De Anima.* Milano, 1959.

Donceel, J. F. *Philosophical Psychology.* New York, 1961.

Ehrenstein, W. *Probleme des höheren Seelenlebens.* München, 1965.

Etudes d'anthropologie philosophique. Par A. Waelhens, J. Ladrière, P. Marschal, R. Pirard, M. Renaud, J. Taminiaux, A. Vergote. Bibliothèque philosophique de Louvain, 28 26, Louvain-La-Neuve, 1980.

Eymann, F. *Die geistigen Grundlagendes menschlichen Lebens.* Bern, 1966.

Fromm, E. *The Heart of Man.* New York, 1964.

Garcia Fernandez, A. *El hombre y su encrucijada existencial.* Alcante, 1976.

Geist und Leib in der menschlichen Existenz. München, 1962.

Gogacz, M. *Istnieć i poznawać* (To Exist and To Know). Warszawa, 1969.

Grzegorczyk, A. *Refleksje o psychologicznej koncepcji człowieka (Reflections on the Psychological Conception of Man).* Teksty, no. 3, 9–36.

Hartman, E. *Substance, Body and Soul.* Princeton, 1977.

Hengstenberg, H. E. "Phenomenology and Metaphysics of the Human Body." *International Philosophical Quarterly,* 3 (1963) 165–200.

Henry, M. "Le concept d'âme a-t-il un sens?" *Revue Philosophique de Louvain,* 64 (1964) 5–33.

————. *Philosophie et phénomenologie du corps.* Paris, 1965.

Hirschberger, J. *Seele und Leib in der Spatantike.* Frankfurt/M, 1969.

Hirschmann, E. E. *On Human Unity,* London, 1961.

Hörz, H. *Materie und Bewusstsein.* Berlin, 1965.

Iwanicki, J. "Psychiczne i duchowe według materializmu dialektycznego i według tomizmu" (The Psychic and the Spiritual according to Dialectical Materialism and Thomism). *Studia Philosophiae Christianae,* 1 (1965) 17–44.

Javelet, R. "Le duo *corps et âme* en question? Anthropologie moderne et trichotomie." *Revue des Sciences Religieuses,* 44 (1970) 101–27.

Kłosak, K. "Dusza ludzka w perspektywie filozofii przyrody i metafizyki" (The Human Soul in the Perspective of the Philosophy of Nature and Metaphysics). *Analecta Cracoviensis,* IO (1978) 29–47.

Kostenbaum, P. *The New Image of the Person. The Theory and Practice of Clinical Philosophy.* Westport, 1978.

Kozielecki, J. *Koncepcje psychologiczne człowieka* (Psychological Conceptions of Man). Warszawa. 1976.

Krąpiec, M. A. "Die Theorie der Materie im physikalischer und philosophischer Sicht." *Philosophisches Jahrbuch,* 69 (1961) 134–76.

————. "O realizm metafizyki." *Zeszyty Naukowe KUL,* 4 (1969).

————. "Poznawalność Boga i duszy" (The Knowability of God and the Soul). *Znak,* 11 (1959) 745–63.

————. *Realizm ludzkiego poznania (Realism of Human Cognition).* Poznań, 1959.

————. *Struktura bytu (Structure of Being).* Lublin, 1963.

————. "Theoria materii ujęcia fizykalne i filozoficzne." (Theory of Matter: Physical and Philosophical Conceptions.) *Zeszyty Naukowe KUL,* 2 (1959) 3–48.

————. "Z filozoficznej problematyki badań nad koncepcja materii jako składnika realnego bytu" (On Philosophical Problematic Investigations on the Concept of Matter as a Constitutent of Real Being). *Studia Philosophiae Christianae,* 2 (1967) 17–48.

Kuksewicz, Z. *Filozofia człowieka. Teoria duszy./Dzieje filozofii średniowiecznej w Polsce (Philosophy of Man. Theory of the Soul. History of Mediaeval Philosophy in Poland).* T. V. Wrocław, 1975.

Lakebrink, B. *Hegels dialektische Ontologie und die Thomistische Analektik.* Henn, 1968.

Langre de M. *Ame humaine et science moderne.* Paris, 1963.

Lanteri-Laura, G. *Phénoménologie de la subjectivité.* Paris, 1968.

L'Ecuyer, R. *La genèse du concept de soi.* Québec, 1975.

Lotz, J. *Der Mensch im Sein.* Wien, 1967.

Łukaszewski, W. *Osobowość: struktura i funkcje regulacyjne (Personality: Structure and Regulating Functions).* Warszawa, 1974.

Manser, G. *Das Wesen des Thomismus.* Freiburg, 1948.

Marquette de J. *La créativisme, essai sur l'immortalisation de l'âme.* Genève, 1969.

Metz, J. *L'homme. L'anthropocentrique chrétienne. Pour une interprétation ouverte de la philosophie de saint Thomas.* Tours, 1968.

Montagné, P. *Manuel du connaître philosophique. T. I. La psychologie.* Paris, 1959.

Möller, J. *Von Bewusstsein zu Sein. Grundlegung einer Metaphysik.* Mainz, 1962.

Nancy, J.-L. *"Ego Sum."* Paris, 1979.

Nuttin, J. *Psychoanalyse et conception spiritualiste de l'homme.* Louvain, 1961.

Owens, J. "The Unity in a Thomistic Philosophy of Man." *Mediaeval Studies,* 25 (1963) 54–82.

Pegis, A. C. *At the Origins of the Thomistic Notion of Man.* New York, 1963.

Poirier, R. *Réflexions sur l'immortalité de l'âme.* Paris, 1970.

Psychologie et metaphysique. T. I–II. Paris, 1961.

Pucci, R. *La fenomenologia contemporanea e il problema dell'uomo.* Napoli, 1963.

Robb, J. H. *Man as Infinite Spirit.* Milwaukee, 1974.

Rocca, O. *Argamentazione scientifica sulla spiritualità ed immortalità.* Sorento, 1976.

Rossi, G. L. *L'uomo, animalità e spiritualità.* Torino, 1967.

Rodriguez, V. "Diferencia de las almas humanas a nivel substancial en la antropologia de Santo Tomaś." *Doctor Communis,* (1971) 25–39.

Roy, J. *La métaphysique de la vie.* Paris, 1964.

Royce, J. E. *Man and his Nature. A Philosophical Psychology.* New York, 1961.

Samona, A. *I misteri della psiche.* Palermo, 1966.

Scherer, G. *Strukturem des Menschen. Grundfragen philos. Anthropologie.* Essen, 1976.

Schwentek, H. *Mensch und Automat.* Stuttgart, 1965.

Schulze-Wegener, O. *Der Leib—Seele—Zusammenhang und die Wissenschaftliche Forschung.* Meisenheim am Glan, 1967.

Seifert, J. *Das Leib—Seele—Problem in der gegenwärtigen philosophischen Diskussion.* Darmstadt, 1979.

Siwek, P. *Psychologia metaphysica.* Roma, 1962.

Sombart, W. *Vom Menschen. Versuch einer geisteswissenschaftliche Anthropologie.* Berlin (1938) 1956.

Stępien, A. B. *"Zagadnienie genezy duszy ludzkiej z materii" (The Question of the Genesis of the Human Soul from Matter).* Zeszyty Naukowe KUL, 3 (1960) 108–17.

Stybe, S. E. "Antinomies" in the Conception of Man. An Inquiry into the History of the Human Spirit. Copenhagen, 1962.

Swieźawski, S. "Albertyńsko-tomistyczna a kartezjańska koncepcja człowieka· (The Albertinian-Thomistic and Cartesian Conception of Man). *Przegląd Filozoficzny,* 43 (1947) 87–104.

Thomas Aquinas, St. *Tommaso d'Aquino nel suo VII Centenario. Congresso Internazionale. Roma, Napoli: 17–24 aprile 1974.* Roma, 1974.

Ulrich, F. "Zur Ontologie des Menschen." *Salzburger Jahrbuch für Philosophie,* 7 (1963) 25–128.

Vanni-Rovighi, S. *L'antropologia filosofica di San Tommaso d'Aquino.* Milano, 1965.

Van Peursen, C. A. *Le corps—l'âme—l'esprit. Introduction à une anthropologie phenoménologique.* La Haye, 1979.

Verbeke, G. *Avicenna Latinus. Liber de Anima.* Louvain, 1968.

Vries de, J. *Materie und Geist.* München, 1970.

Weiler, R. *Die Frage des Menschen; wer bin ich?* Köln, 1968.

Węgiełek, J. *Mam ciało* (I Have a Body). Warszawa, 1978.

White, V. *Seele und Psyche.* Salzburg, 1964.

Witkiewicz, J. S. *Zagadnienia psychofizyczne (Psycho-physical Questions).* Warszawa, 1978.

Wisser, R. "Homo vere humanus. Probleme und Aussagen der Philosophischen Anthropologie in Geistesgeschichtlicher Sicht." *Zeitschrift fur Religions und Geistesgeschichte,* 16 (1964) 223–50.

CHAPTER V

Bibliography

Adamczyk, S. *Obiektywizm poznania ludzkiego w nauce arystotelesowsko-tomas-zowej (Objectivity of Human Cognition in Aristotelian-Thomistic Teaching).* Lublin, 1967.

———. "Ontyczno-psychologiczna struktura actu poznawczego w nauce Arystotelesa i św. Tomasza z Akwinu" (The Ontico-psychological Structure of the Cognitive Act in the Teaching of St. Thomas Aquinas). *Roczniki Filozoficzne,* 8 (1960) z. 4, 5–30.

Arendt, H. *The Life of the Mind.* Vol. *I. Thinking.* New York, 1977.

Aune, B. *Knowledge, Mind and Nature.* New York. 1967.

Ayer, A. J. *The Problem of Knowledge.* London, 1961.

Ayer, S. A. J., MacDonald, G. F. *Perception and Identity.* London, 1979.

Bateson, G. *Mind and Nature: A Necessary Unity.* New York, 1978.

Bertalanffy, L. *Robots, Men and Minds.* Wien, 1970.

Boden, M. A. *Artificial Intelligence and Natural Man.* New York, 1977.

Bogliolo, A. *De Homine,* Vol. I. *Structura gnoseologica et ontologica.* Roma, 1963.

Capaldi, N. *Human Knowledge.* New York, 1960.

Consciousness and the Brain. A Scientific and Philosophical Inquiry. New York, 1976.

Crossman, R. *The Structure of the Mind.* Madison, 1965.

David, A. *La cybernétique et l'humain.* Paris, 1965.

Denis, M. *Les images mentales.* Paris, 1979.

Feigenbaum, E. A., Feldman, J. *Computers and Thought.* New York, 1966 (*Maszyny matematyczne i myślenie.* Warszawa, 1972.)

Fink, D. G. *Computers and the Human Mind.* New York, 1966.

Flahault, F. *La parole intermédiaire.* Paris, 1978.

Glover, J. *The Philosophy of Mind.* London, 1977.

Gogacz, M. "Tomaszowa teoria intelektu i jej filozoficzne konsekwencje" (Thomistic Theory of the Intellect and its Philosophical Consequences). *Roczniki Filozoficzne,* 13 (1965) z. 1, 21–32.

———. *Obrona intelektu (In Defense of the Intellect).* Warszawa, 1969.

Hoffman, P. *Language, Minds and Knowledge.* London, 1970.

Juritsch, M. *Sinn und Geist. Ein Betrag zur Deutung der Sinne in Einheit des Menschen.* Freiburg/Schw., 1961.

Kainz, H. P. "The Multiplicity and Individuality of Intellects: A Re-examination of St. Thomas' Reaction to Averroes." *Divus Thomas,* 74 (1971) 155–79.

Kalinowski, J. *Teoria poznania praktycznego (Theory of Practical Cognition).* Lublin, 1960.

Kamiński, S. *Pojęcie nauki i klasyfikacja nauki (The Concept of Science and Class-ification of the Sciences)*. Lublin, 1970.

Kamiński, S., Krąpiec. M. A. *Z teorii metodologii metafizyki (On the Theory of the Methodology of Metaphysics)*. Lublin, 1962.

Knittermeger, H. *Grundgegebenheiten des menschlichen Daseins*. München, 1963.

Krąpiec, M. A. *Realizm ludzkiego poznania (Realism of Human Cognition)*. Poznań, 1959.

―――. *Teoria analogii bytu (Theory of the Analogy of Being)*. Lublin, 1959.

―――. "The Problem of Cognition." *Modern Catholic Thinkers*. London, 1960, 548–62.

Levin. M. E. *Metaphysics and the Mind-Body Problem*. Oxford, 1979.

Margolis, J. *Persons and Minds*. Dordrecht, 1978.

May, W. E. "Knowledge of Causality in Hume and Aquinas." *The Thomist, 34* (1970) 254–88.

Moreau, J. *De la connaissance selon S. Thomas d'Aquin*. Paris, 1976.

Neue Erkenntnisprobleme in Philosophie und Theologie. Wien, 1968.

Nicholas, J. M. *Images, Perception and Knowledge*. Dordrecht/Boston, 1977.

Ong, W. ed. *Knowledge and the Future of Man. An International Symposium*. New York, 1968.

Penfield, W. *The Mystery of the Mind. A Critical Study of Consciousness and the Human Brain*. Princeton, 1975.

Perception and Personal Identity. Proceedings of the 1967 Colloquium in Philosophy. Cleveland, 1969.

Rahner, K. *Geist in Welt. Zur Metaphysik der endlichen Erkenntnis bei Thomas von Aquin*. München (1957) 1964.

Rickman, H. P. "Philosophical Anthropology and the Problem of Meaning." *The Philosophical Quarterly* 10 (1960) 12–20.

Rossi, E. *Das menschliche Begreifen und seine Grenzen*. Bonn, 1968.

Ryle, G. *The Concept of Mind*. New York, 1959.

Schmidt, H. *Die Anthropologische Bedeutung der Kybernetik*. Quckborn, 1965.

Schneider, M. "The Dependence of St. Thomas' Psychology of Sensation upon his Physics." *Franciscan Studies,* 22 (1962) 2–31.

Stępién, A. B. "W związku z teoria poznania tomizmu egzystencjalnego" *Roczniki Filozoficzne,* 1 (1960) z. 1, 173–83.

The Philosophy of Perception. London, 1967.

Thinking in Perspective. Critical Essays in the Study of Thought Processes. Andover/Hampshire, England, 1978.

Thomas, S. N. *The Formal Mechanics of the Mind*. New York, 1978.

Toinet, P. *L'homme en sa verité. Essai d'anthropologie philosophique*. Paris, 1968.

Warnock, M. *Imagination*. London, 1976.

Werkmeister, W. H. *The Basis and Structure of Knowledge*. New York, 1968.

White, A. R. *The Philosophy of the Mind*. Westpost, 1978.

CHAPTER VI

Bibliography

Aquila, R. E. *Intentionality: A Study of Mental Acts*. Pennsylvania State University, 1977.

Augé, M. *Symbole, fonction, histoire. Les interrogations de l'anthropologie*. Paris, 1979.

Benoist, L. *Signes, symboles et mythes*. Paris, 1975.

Bosio, F. *Antropologia filosofica e occultamento ideologica*. Urbino, 1968.

Bril, J. *Symbolisme et civilisation. Essai sur l'efficacité anthropologique de l'imagination*. Lille, 1977.

Brun, J. *La main et l'esprit*. Paris, 1963.

Cassirer, E. *An Essay on Man*. New York, 1944.

Chauchard, P. *L'homme normale. Eléments de biologie humaniste et de culture humaine*. Paris, 1963.

Chiari, J. *Art and Knowledge*. London, 1977.

Court, R. *Le musical. Essai sur les fondements anthropologiques de l'art*. Paris, 1976.

Di Marco, D. *Scienza, arte e morale*. Roma, 1977.

Dirks, W., Hanssler, B. *Der neue Humanismus und das Christentum*. München, 1968.

Dumont, E. *Le lieu de l'homme. La culture comme distance et mémoire*. Montréal, 1968.

Flam, L. *L'homme et la conscience tragique. Problèmes du temps présent*. Paris, 1966.

Geneslay, E. H. *Un mal connu, l'homme*. Paris, 1968.

Godel, R. *De l'humanisme à l'humain*. Paris, 1963.

Hanke, J. W. *Maritain's Ontology of the Work of Art*. The Hague, 1973.

Heidegger, M. *Der Ursprung des Kunstwerkes*. Stuttgart, 1970.

Heimler, M. *Die Bedeutung der Intentionalität im Bereich des Seins nach Thomas v. Aquin*. Würzburg, 1962.

Helbling, H. *Der Mensch im Bild der Geschichte*. Berlin, 1969.

Hessen, G. *Studia z filozofii kultury (Studies in the Philosophy of Culture)*. Warszawa, 1968.

Huizinga, J. *Homo Ludens*. Warszawa, 1967.

Ingarden, R. *Spòr o istienie świata (Debate on the Existence of the World)*. Kraków, 1948.

Joyce, R. *The Esthetic Animal*. New York, 1975.

Kmity, J. ed. *Wartość, dzieło, sens. Szkice z filozofii kultury artystycznej (Value, Work, Meaning. Outlines of a Philosophy of Artistic Culture)*. Warszawa, 1975.

Krąpiec, M. A. "O filozofii kultury" (On the Philosophy of Culture). *Znak*, 16 (1964) 813–25.

──────. "Pròba ustalenia struktury bytu intencjonalnego" (An Attempt to Determine the Structure of Intentional Being). *Collectanea Theologica*, 28 (1957) 303–81.

La fonction symbolique: Essais d'anthropologie. Textes réunis par M. Izard et P. Smith. Paris, 1979.

Landmann, M. *Der Mensch als Schöpfer und Geschöpfer der Kultur.* München, 1961.

Langer, S. K. *Philosophical Sketches. A Study of the Human Mind in Relation to Feeling, Explored Through Art, Language and Symbol.* New York, 1964.

Löwith, K. *Natur und Humanität des Menschen.* Göttingen, 1957.

Marcel, G. *Les hommes contre l'humain.* Paris (1957) 1968.

Menschliche Existenz und moderne Welt. Berlin, 1967.

Pacholski, M., Znaniecki, F. *Spoleczna dynamika kultury (The Social Dynamics of Culture).* Warszawa, 1977.

Philippe, M. D. *L'activité artistique.* T.I. *L'homme dans son dialogue avec l'univers.* T.II. *Philosophie du faire.* Paris, 1968.

Reneville, R. J. "Signification anthropologie totalisatrice et intégrative des divers sciences de l'homme." *Laval théologique et philosophique.*, 26 (1970) 25–28; 147–66.

Rodziński, A. "Kultura i chrystianizm" (Culture and Christianity). *Roczniki Filozoficzne*, 17 (1969) z. 2, 107–18.

──────. "Personalistyczna koncepsja kultury a prawo naturalne" (Personalistic Conception of Culture and Natural Law). *Roczniki Filozoficzne*, 18 (1970), z.2 (77–90).

Rotenstreich, N. *Theory and Practice. An Essay in Human Intentionalities.* The Hague, 1977.

Rösel, M. *Conditio Humana.* Meisenheim, 1975.

Rothacker, E. *Probleme der Kulturanthropologie.* Nonn (1948) 1965.

Sapir, E. *Anthropologie.* T.I. *Culture et personnalité.* T. II. *Culture.* Paris, 1967.

Stępień. A. B., *Nauki o kulturze (Studies about Culture)* Warszawa, 1971.

Stróżewski, W. *Studia z teorii poznania i filozofii wartośći (Studies in the Theory and Philosophy of Value).* Warszawa, 1978.

Tatarkiewicz, W. *Dzieje sześciu pojęć (History of Six Concepts).* Warszawa, 1975.

──────. *Parerga.* Warszawa, 1978.

Zygulski, K. *Wstęp do zagadnień kultury. (Introduction to the Question of Culture).* Warszawa, 1972.

CHAPTER VII

Bibliography

Amato, D. *Il problema della libertà*. Palermo, 1969.

Anderson, J. M. *The Truth of Freedom*. New York, 1979.

Aune, B. *Reason and Action*. Dordrecht/Boston, 1977.

Chauchard, P. *Biologie et morale*. Tours, 1959.

Choza, J. *Consciencia y afectividad/Aristoteles, Nietzsche, Freud*/Pamplona, 1978.

Cristaldi, M. *Libertà e metafisica*. Bologna, 1964.

Day, J. P. "On Liberty and the Real Will." *Philosophy*, 45 (1970) 177–92.

Dubouchet, J. *La condition de l'homme dans l'univers. Déterminismes naturels et liberté humaine*. Paris, 1977.

Edwards, R. B. *Freedom Responsibility and Obligation*. The Hague, 1969.

Foulquie, P. *La volonté*. Paris, 1968.

Frankfurt, H. G. "Freedom of the Will and the Concept of a Person." *The Journal of Philosophy*, 68 (1971) 5–20.

Freedom and Determinism. New York, 1966.

Gabaude, J. M. *Liberté et raison*. Toulouse, 1970.

Geiger, L. B. "On Freedom." *Philosophy Today*, 4 (1960) 184–95.

Gibbs, B. *Freedom and Liberation*. London, 1976.

Hartmann, O. J. *Freiheit: Wodurch? Wovon? Wozu?* Schaffhausen, 1977.

Gogacz, M. "Ontyczne wyznaczniki wolności ludzkiej według marksizmu" (Ontical Determinants of Human Freedom According to Marxism). *Studia Philosophiae Christianae*, 4 (1968) 5–20.

Guilead, R. *Etre et liberté*. Louvain, 1965.

Hampshire, S. N. *Freedom and the Individual*. London, 1965.

Jaffa, H. V. *The Conditions of Freedom*. Baltimore, 1975.

Kenny, A. J. P. *Free Will and Responsibility*. London, 1978.

Klubertanz, G. "The Root of Freedom in St. Thomas' Later Works." *Gregorianum*, 42 (1961) 701–24.

Körner, S. Experience and Conduct. Cambridge, 1976.

Krąpiec, M. A. "O wolności woli" (On the Freedom of the Will). *Znak* 16 (1964)0 597–602.

———. "Struktura aktu miłości u św. Tomasza" (Structure of the Act of Love in St. Thomas). *Roczniki Teologiczno-kanoniczne*, 6 (1950) z. 1–2, 135–54.

La liberté et l'homme du XXe siècle. Paris, 1966.

Lebacqz, J. *Libre arbitre et jugement*. Paris, 1960.

Lucas, J. R. *The Freedom of the Will*. Oxford, 1970.

Mazzantini, C. *Il problema filosofico del "libro arbitrio" in S. Tommaso e Duns Scoto*. Torino, 1966.

236

McCloskey, H. J. "Liberty of Expression. Its Grounds and Limits." *Inquiry,* 13 (1970) 219–37.

Montanari, G. *Determinazione e liberta in San Tommaso.* Roma, 1962.

Phenomenology of Will and Action. The Second Lexington Conference on Pure and Applied Phenomenology. Louvain, 1967.

Oakeshott, M. *On Human Conduct.* Oxford, 1975.

O'Sullivan, P. N. *Intentions, Motives and Human Action. An Argument for Free Will.* Brisbane, 1977.

Parsons, T. *Action Theory and the Human Condition.* New York, 1978.

Połtawski, A. "Czyn a swiadomość" (Act and Consciousness). *Logos i Ethos.* Kraków, 1971, 83–113.

Quilliot, R. *La liberté aux dimensions humaines.* Paris, 1967.

Reghaby, H. *Philosophy and Freedom.* New York, 1970.

Reitmeister, L. A. *A Philosophy of Freedom. An Attempt to Explain the Basis of Freedom.* New York, 1970.

Richardson, W. J. "Heidegger and the Quest of Freedom." *Theological Studies,* 28 (1967) 286–307.

Ricoeur, P. *Philosophie de la volonté.* Paris, 1963.

Rivier, W. *Deux exposés d'une philosophie de la liberté.* Neuchatel, 1975.

Sartre, J. P. *Of Human Freedom.* New York, 1967.

Scheler, M. "Rozważania dotyczące fenomenologii i metafizyki wolnośći." (Considerations Regarding Phenomenology and the Metaphysics of Freedom). *Znak,* 15 (1963) 1272–82.

Schrödinger, E. *Geist und Materie.* Braunschweig, 1956.

Simon, J. *Wahrheit als Freiheit.* Berlin/New York, 1978.

Siwek, P. *La conscience du libre arbitre.* Rome, 1976.

———. *La psychophysique humaine d'après Aristote.* Paris, 1930.

Splett, J. *Der Mensch in seiner Freiheit.* Mainz, 1967.

Steenberghen, F. "Connaissance divine et liberté humaine." *Revue Théologique de Louvain,* 2 (1972) 46–68.

Thalberg, I. *Perception, Emotion and Action.* New Haven, 1977.

Tischner, J. "W poszukiwaniu istoty wolnośći" (In Search of the Essence of Freedom). *Znak,* 22 (1970) 821–38.

Vergez, A. *Faute et liberté.* Paris, 1969.

Welte, B. *Determination und Freiheit.* Frankfurt/M, 1969.

Wendt, D., Vlek, O. *Utility, Probability and Decision-Making.* Dordrecht, 1975.

Werner, C. *L'âme et la liberté.* Paris, 1960.

Woroniecki, J. *Katolicka etyka wychowawcza (Catholic Educational Ethics).* Krakow, 1948.

Wright, G. H. von *Freedom and Determination.* Amsterdam, 1980.

CHAPTER VIII

Bibliography

Amado, E. Levi-Valensi *Les niveaux de l'êtr et de la connaissance dans leur relation au problème du mal*. Paris, 1962.

Beehler, R. *Moral Life*. Oxford, 1978.

Bouillard, H. "Autonomia człowieka a obecność Boga" (Man's Autonomy and God's Presence). *Znak,* 19 (1967) 1096–112.

Brandt, R. B. *A Theory of the Good and the Right*. London, 1979.

Brennan, J. M. *The Open Texture of Moral Concepts*. London, 1977.

Brunner, E. *Der Mensch in Widerspruch*. Stuttgart, 1965.

Bujo, B. *Moralautonomie und Normenfindung bei Thomas von Aquin*. Paderborn, 1979.

Cua, A. *Dimensions of Moral Creativity. Paradigms, Principles and Ideals*. Pennsylvania State University Press, 1978.

Cultrera, F. *Mutabilità e immutabilità della legge naturale*. Napoli, 1977.

Donagan, A. *The Theory of Morality*. Chicago, 1977.

Etcheverry, A. *La morale en question*. Paris, 1977.

Gewirth, A. *Reason and Morality*. Chicago, 1978.

Gillet, M. *L'homme et sa structure. Essai sur les valeurs morales*. Paris, 1978.

Grenier, J. *Absolu et choix*. Paris, 1970.

Grygiel, S. "Ludzka twarz prawa natury" (The Human Face of Natural Law). *Znak,* 21 (1969) 1–30.

Hartmann, O. J. *Der Kampf um den Menschen in Natur. Mythos und Geschichte*. Freiburg/Br. 1969.

Hałowka, J. *Relatywizm etyczny (Ethical Relativism)*. Warszawa, 1981.

Krąpiec, M. A. *Człowiek i prawo naturalne. (Man and Natural Law)*. Lublin, 1975.

———. *Dlaczego zło? (Why Evil?)*. Kraków, 1962.

Kozielecki, J. *O godnośći człowieka (On the Dignity of Man)*. Warszawa, 1977.

Lottin, O. *Psychologie et morale au XIIe et XIIIe siècles*. T. I–IV. Louvain, 1948–60.

Manaranche, A. *L'esprit de la foi. Moral fondamentale*. Paris, 1977.

Olejnik, S. "Problem ostatecznego kryterium dobra w moralnośći" (The Problem of the Ultimate Criterion of Good in Christian Morality). *O Bogu i człowieku*. T. II. Warszawa, 1969, 175–91.

Patka, F. *Value and Existence. Studies in Philosophy and Anthropology*. New York, 1964.

Pinckaers, S. *Le renouveau de la morale*. Tournai, 1964.

Plessner, H. *Lachen und Weinen. Eine Untersuchung nach den Grenzen menschlichen Verhaltens.* München (1941) 1961.

Rodziński, A. "Egzystencjalny status moralnośći" (The Existential Status of Morality). *Logos i ethos.* Kraków, 1971, 357–69.

Rosik, S. "Formowanie sumienia praktycznego w etyce sytuacyjnej" (The Formation of a Practical Conscience in Situational Ethics). *Roczniki Teologiczno-kanoniczne,* 11 (1964) z. 3, 39–57.

Ślipko, T. "Etyka intencji czy etyka przedmiotu aktu. Zagadnienie wewnętrzej moralnośći aktu ludzkiego w filozofii św. Tomasza" (Ethics of Intention or Ethics of the Object of the Act. The Problem of Inner Morality of the Human Act in the Philosophy of St. Thomas). *Logos i ethos,* 1971, 281–326.

————. *Życie i płeć człowieka (The Life and Sex of Man).* Kraków, 1978.

Styczeń, T. "Doświadczenie moralnośći (Experience of Morality). *Logos i ethos.* Kraków, 1971, 327–55.

————. *Etyka niezależna? (An Independent Ethics?)* Lublin, 1980.

Szostek, A. *Normy i wyjątki (Norms and Exceptions).* Lublin, 1980.

Szyszkowska, M. *Człowiek wobec siebie i wobec innego (Man in the Presence of Himself and in the Presence of Another).* Warszawa, 197.

Taylor, C. T. *The Values.* New York, 1977.

Thomae, H. *Der Mensch in der Entscheidung.* München, 1960.

Ullmann-Margalit, E. *The Emergence of Norms.* Oxford, 1978.

Ulrich, R. *Weg und Weisung. Eine Philosophie des menschlichen Lebens.* Heidelberg, 1958.

Value and Man. New York, 1966.

Wallace, J. D. *Virtues and Vices.* New York, 1978.

Ward, R. *The Divine Image. The Foundation of Christian Morality.* London, 1976.

Wojtyła, K. *Miłość i odpowiedzialność (Love and Responsibility).* Kraków, 1962.

————. *Osoba i czyn (Man and Act).* Kraków, 1969.

CHAPTER IX

Bibliography

Addis, L. *The Logic of Society*. Minneapolis, 1975.
Aronson, E. *Człowiek istota społeczna (Man, a Social Being)*. Warszawa, 1978.
Bauman, Z. *Zarys marksistowskiej teorii społeczeństwa (An Outline of the Marxist Theory of Society)*. Warszawa, 1964.
Calvet, L. J. *Langue, corps, societé*. Paris, 1979.
———. *Les jeux de la societé*. Paris, 1978.
Chantebout, B. *De l'Etat, une tentatative de démythification de l'univers politique*. Paris, 1975.
Fontanet, J. *Le social et le vivant*. Paris, 1977.
Fralin, R. *Rousseau and Representation. A Study of the Development of His Concept of Political Institutions*. Irvington, 1978.
Gehlen, A. *Studien zur Anthropologie und Soziologie*. Berlin, 1963.
Gilson, E. *La société de masse et sa culture*. Paris, 1967.
Harré, R., Secord, P. F. *The Explanation of Social Behavior*. Oxford, 1976.
Kampits, P. *Sartre und die Frage nach dem Anderen*. Wien, 1975.
Kaczmarek, E., ed. *W kręgu zagadnién antropologii społeczno-filozoficznej (In the Sphere of Socio-philosophical Anthropology)*. Poznań, 1978.
Kłys, J. "Powołanie do rozwoju." *W nurcie zagadnień posoborowych* (A Call for Development. *In the Wake of Post-Conciliar Questions*). T. II. Warszawa, 1968, 227–38.
Krąpiec, M. A. "Jednostka a społeczeństwo" (The Individual and Society) *Znak,* 21 (1969) 684–712.
Maccagnolo, E. *L'uomo e la società*. Brescia, 1967.
Majka, T. "Człowiek w społeczeństwie." *O Bogu i człowieku* (Man and Society. *On God and Man*). T. II. Warszawa, 227–38.
Man and Society. New York, 1966.
Maritain, J. *Principes d'une politique humaniste*. Paris, 1945.
Matson, F. W. *The Idea of Man*. New York, 1976.
Mordstein, F. "Die philosophische Anthropologie als Grundlage politischer Theorienbildung." *Philosophisches Jahrbuch,* 67 (1958) 115–29.
Morel, G. *Question d'homme*. Paris, 1976.
Northrop, S. *Philosophical Anthropology and Practical Politics*. New York, 1960.
Oraison, M. *Être avec la rélation à autrui*. Paris, 1968.
Otmann, H. *Individuum und Gesellschaft bei Hegel*. Berlin/New York, 1977.
Parsons. T. *The Evolution of Societies*. Garden City, 1977.

Plessner, H. *Diesseits der Utopie in Immer noch philosophische Anthropologie? Soziale Rolle und menschliche Natur.* Köln, 1966.

Pocock, D. F. *Social Anthropology.* New York, 1961.

Polin, C. *L'esprit totalitaire.* Paris, 1977.

Popper, K. R. *The Open Society and its Enemies.* London, 1948.

Riezler, K. *Man: Mutable and Immutable. The Fundamental Structure of Social Life.* Chicago, 1950.

Rouvier, J. *Les grandes idées politiques de J. J. Rousseau à nos jours.* Paris, 1978.

Rybicki, P. *Struktura społecznego świata (Structure of the Social World).* Warszawa, 1979.

Sarano, J. *Connaissance de soi, connaissance d'autrui.* Paris, 1967.

The Human Dialogue. Perspectives on Communication. New York, 1967.

Torowski, J. "Człowiek a społeczeństwo" (Man and Society). *Zeszyty Naukowe KUL,* 1 (1958), z.2, 3–28.

Walgrave, J. H. *Cosmos, personne et société.* Paris, 1968.

CHAPTER X

Bibliography

Abernathy, G. L., Langford, T. A., ed. *Philosophy of Religion.* London, 1968.

Berger, P. *La religion dans la conscience moderne.* Paris, 1971.

Brien, A. "L'homme religieux." *Seminarium,* 12 (1972) 203–19.

Burke, P. *The Fragile Universe.* London, 1979.

Cahn, S. M. *Philosophy of Religion.* New York, 1970.

Caracciolo, A. *Religione e eticità. Studi di filosofia della religione.* Napoli, 1971.

Collins, J. *The Emergence of Philosophy of Religion.* New Haven, 1967.

Comstock, R., Baird, R. D. *Religion and Man.* New York, 1971.

Donovan, P. *Interpreting Religious Experience.* New York, 1979.

Duméry, H. *Critique et religion. Récherches sur la méthode en philosophie de la religion.* Paris, 1957.

––––––. *La problème de Dieu en philosophie de la religion.* Paris, 1957.

––––––. *Philosophie de la religion.* Paris, 1957.

Durre, L. "Themes in Contemporary Philosophy of Religion." *New Scholasticism,* 43 (1969) 577–601.

Ferre, F. *Basic Modern Philosophy of Religion.* New York, 1967.

Filosofia e religione. Atti del XXV Convegno del Centro di Studi Filosofico fra Professori Universitari. Brescia, 1971.

Hessen, J. *Religionsphilosophie.* Bd. I–II. München, 1955.

Hick, J. H., ed. *Classical and Contemporary Readings in the Philosophy of Religion.* New York, 1970.

Hick, J. *Philosophy or Religion.* New York, 1963.

Hofmeister, H. *Wahrheit und Glaube. Interpretation und Kritik der sprachanalytischen Theorie der Religion.* Wien, 1978.

Jaworski, M. "Problem filozofii religii" (Problem of the Philosophy of Religion). *Studia Philosophiae Christianae,* 3 (1967), z. 2, 169–92.

Kaczmarek, L. "Człowiek—istota religijna." *W nurcie zagadnień posoborowych* (Man—a Religious Being. *In the Wake of Post-Conciliar Questions.* T. II, Warszawa, 1968, 171–210.

––––––. *Istota i pochodzenie religii (The Essence and Origin of Religion).* Poznań, 1958.

Kaufmann, W. *A Critique of Religion and Philosophy.* New York, 1958.

Kenny, A. *The God of the Philosophers.* Oxford, 1979.

Kowalczyk, S. *Bóg w myśli wspołczesnej (God in Contemporary Thought).* Wrocław, 1979.

Ledure, Y. S. *Dieu s'efface: la corporéité comme lieu d'une affirmation de Dieu.* Paris, 1975.

Leeuw, G. van der *Der Mensch und die Religion. Anthropologischer Versuch.* Basel, 1941.

Luypen, N. A. *Myth and Metaphysics.* The Hague, 1976.

Manzini, I. *Filosofia della religione.* Roma, 1968.

Majkowski, J. "Religia naturalnym wyposażeniem człowieka" (Religion as a Natural Endowment of Man). *Ateneum Kapłańskie,* 60 (1960) 31–44.

Mitchelle, B., ed. *The Philosophy of Religion.* New York, 1971.

Natanson, J. J. *La mort de Dieu. Essai sur l'athéisme moderne.* Paris, 1975.

Nédoncelle, M. "Les sources sensibles et axiologiques de l'affirmation religieuse." *Explorations personnalistes.* Paris, 1970.

Ortegat, P. *Philosophie de la religion.* T. I–II. Paris-Louvain, 1948.

Patterson, R. L. *A Philosophy of Religion.* Durham, 1971.

Penelhum, T. M. *Religion and Rationality.* New York, 1971.

Philippe, M. D. *De l'Être à Dieu.* Paris, 1977.

Plantinga, A. *God, Freedom and Evil.* London, 1975.

Proudoff, W. *God and the Self: Three Types of Philosophy of Religion.* Lewisburg, 1976.

Reardon, B. M. G. *Hegel's Philosophy of Religion.* London, 1977.

Rem, B. E. *Reason and Religion. An Introduction to the Philosophy of Religion.* New York, 1972.

Rideau, E. "Justification de la relation religieuse." *Nouvelle Revue Théologique,* 92 (1970) 56–75.

Roth, J. K. *Problems of the Philosophy of Religion.* Scranton, 1971.

Sarnowski, S. "*Zmierzch absolutu? Z problemów filozofii Chrzescijańskiej i egzystencjalistycznej (The Twilight of the Absolute? Problems of Christian and Existentialist Philosophy).* Warszawa, 1974.

Smart, N. *Philosophy of Religion.* New York, 1970.

Szmyd, J. *Osobowość a religia (Personality and Religion).* Warszawa, 1979.

Tinello, F., ed. *Filosofia religioni.* Roma, 1966.

Trillhaas, W. *Religionsphilosophie.* Berlin, 1972.

Van Riet, G. *Philosophie et religion.* Louvain, 1970.

Vergote, A. "La philosophie de la religion." Revue Philosophique de Louvain, 68 (1970) 385–93.

Vries, J. de *Warum Religion?* Berlin, 1958.

Zdybicka, Z. J. *Człowiek i religia (Man and Religion).* Lublin, 1977, 1978.

CHAPTER XI

Bibliography

Ariotti, A. M. *L'homo viator en Gabriel Marcel*. Torino, 1965.

Arnitz, A. "Prawo naturalne i jego dzieje" (Natural Law and Its History). *Concilium*, 1 (1968) 363–74.

Arrese, D. de *La persona humana*. Madrid, 1962.

Beiträge zum Verständnis der Person. Düsseldorf, 1967.

Beni, G. *La persona umana*. Roma, 1967.

Benjamin, R. *Notion de personne et personnalisme chrétien*. La Haye-Paris, 1971.

Binder, H. *Die menschliche Person*. Stuttgart, 1964.

Boelen, B. J. M. *Personal Maturity. The Existential Dimension*. New York, 1978.

Chisholm, R. M. *Person and Object. A Metaphysical Study*. London, 1976.

Comfort, A. *Nature and Human Nature*. London, 1966.

Congar, Y. "L'historicité de l'homme selon Thomas d'Aquin." *Doctor Communis*, 2 (1969) 297–304.

Copleston, F. *Contemporary Philosophy: Studies of Logical Positivism and Existentialism*. London, 1963.

––––––. "Osoba ludzka w filozofii współczesnej" (The Human Person in Contemporary Philosophy). *Znak*, 15 (1963) 1283–1301.

Degl'Innocenti, U. *Il problema della persona nel pensiero di S. Tommaso*. Roma, 1967.

Domenach, J.-M. *Le sauvage et l'ordinateur*. Paris, 1976.

Fagone, V. "Dialogo e persona." *La Civiltà Cattolica*, 116 (1965), 1, 129–42.

Feldstein, L. C. "Reflections on the Ontology of the Person." *International Philosophical Quarterly*, 9 (1969) 313–41.

Frame, F. D. *Philosophy of the Human Image*. New York, 1968.

Frings, M. S. *Person und Dasein. Zur Frage der Ontologie Wertseins*. Der Haag, 1969.

Gebsattel, V. F. *Imago Hominis. Beiträge zur einer Personalen Anthropologie. (Das Bild des Menschen in der Wissenschaft.)* Schweinfurt, 1964.

Girardi, G. "Ente e persona in ontologia." *Salesianum*, 29 (1967) 368–408.

Gogacz, M. "Problem teorii osoby" (Problem of the Theory of Person). *Studia Philosophiae Christianae*, 7 (1971), z. 2, 46–67.

Gollwitzer, G. *Die Menschengestalt*. Stuttgart, 1967.

Granat, W. *Osoba ludzka (The Human Person)*. Sandomierz, 1961.

Guardini, R. *Welt und Person*. Würzburg (1937) 1962. *(Świat i osoba*, Kraków, 1969).

Häring, B. *Personalismus in Philosophie und Theologie*. München, 1968.

Horizons de la personne. Paris, 1965.

Ilien, A. *Wesen und Funktion der Liebe bei Thomas von Aquin.* Freiburg, Basel, Wien, 1975.

Jerphagnon, L. *Qu'est-ce que la personne humaine?* Toulouse, 1962.

Krąpiec, M. A. "O tomistyczną koncepcje prawa naturalnego." *W nurcie zagadnień posoborowych* (On the Thomistic Conception of Natural Law. *In the Wake of Post-conciliar Questions).* T. II. Warszawa, 1968, 11–37.

Lacroix, J. *Marxisme, existentialisme, personnalisme.* Paris, 1950.

Lichtenstein, H. *The Dilemma of Human Identity.* New York, 1977.

Litwin, J. *Horyzonty nieokreślenia i "Ja" (The Horizons of Indeterminateness and "I").* Warszawa, 1980.

Lotz, J. B. *Der Mensch im Sein.* Wien, 1967.

Maaz, W. *Selbsschöpfung der Selbstintegration des Menschen.* Münster/Westf., 1967

Marcel, G. *Du refus à l'invocation.* Paris, 1940 (*Od sprzeciwu wezwania.* Warszawa, 1965.)

––––––. *Être et avoir.* Paris, 1968. *(Być i mieć.* Warszawa, 1962).

––––––. *Homo Viator.* Paris, 1944. *(Homo Viator,* Warszawa, 1959).

––––––. *Journal metaphysique.* Paris, 1927.

––––––. *La Dignité humaine.* Paris, 1964.

––––––. *L'homme problématique.* Paris, 1955.

Messner, J. *Naturrecht.* Wien, 1960.

Minkus, P. A. *Philosophy of the Person.* Oxford, 1960.

Moneta, G. C. *On Identity.* The Hague, 1976.

Montagu, A. *Anthropology and Human Nature.* New York, 1963.

Mounier, E. *Le personnalisme.* Paris, 1950.

––––––. *Qu'est-ce que le personnalisme?* Paris, 1947. (*Co to jest personalizm?* Warszawa, 1960).

Nasr, H. *The Encounter of Man and Nature. The Spiritual Crisis of Modern Man.* London, 1968.

Nédoncelle, M. *Personne humaine et nature.* Paris, 1963.

Pareyson, L. *Esistenza e persona.* Torino, 1966.

Perry, J. *A Dialogue on Personal Identity and Immortality.* Indianapolis, 1978.

Pinon, M. "The Metaphysics of Personality." *Philippiana Sacra,* 1 (1966) 396–451.

Pitteri, L. *La persona umana. Sua struttura, ontologica nella filosofia di Tommaso d'Aquino.* Pescara, 1969.

Plessner, H. *Conditio Humana.* Pfullingen, 1964.

Rothacker, E. *Die Schichten der Persönlichkeit.* Leipzig, 1938; Bonn, 1965.

Schwartländer, J. *Der Mensch ist Person.* Stuttgart, 1968.

Strauss, L. *Natural Right and History.* Chicago, 1953. *(Prawo naturalne w świetle historii.* Warszawa, 1969).

Szuba, J. *Tomistyczna teoria metafizycznej struktury osoby (Thomistic Theory of the Metaphysical Structure of Person).* Lublin, 1953.

Szyszkowska, M. *Dociekania nad prawem natury czyli o potrzebach człowieka (Investigation of Natural Law or about Man's Needs).* Warszawa, 1972.

The Nature of Man. New York, 1968.

Thomae, H. *Das Individuum und seine Welt. Eine Persönlichketistheorie.* Göttingen, 1968.

Tischner, J. *Świat ludzkiej nadziei (The World of Human Hope).Kraków, 1975.*

Vanni-Rovighi, S. *A proposito di uomo e natura nel secolo XII.* Torino, 1967.

Venable, V. *Human Nature.* Cleveland, 1966.

Verges, S. *Dimension transcendente et la persona.* Barcelona, 1977.

Vetter, A. *Personale Anthropologie.* Freiburg, 1966.

Warnach, V. "Satzereignis und personale Existenz." *Salzburger Jahrbuch für Philosophie,* 10–11 (1966–67) 81–104.

Waskiewicz, H. "Powszechność prawa naturalnego" (The Universality of Natural Law). *Studia Philosophiae Christianae,* 4 (1968), z. 2, 119–34.

Winckelmans de Cléty, C. *L'univers des personnes.* Paris, 1969.

Wojtyła, K. "Osoba: podmiot i wspólnota" (Person: Subject and Community). *Roczniki Filozoficzne,* 24 (1976), z. 2, 5–39.

Wright, von G. H. *What Is Humanism?* Lawrence, 1977.

Zdybicka, J. Z. "Osoba ludzka a filozofia jako problem współczesności." *Międzynarodowe Sympozjum Filozoficzne.* (The Human Person and Philosophy as a Contemporary Problem. International Philosophical Symposium). Kraków, 22–25 VIII, 1978 roku. *Znak,* 10 (1979) 1069–83.

CHAPTER XII

Bibliography

Alquié, F. *Le désir d'éternité*. Paris, 1968.

Boros, L. *Erlöstes Dasein*. Mainz, 1967 *(Istnienie wyzwolone*. Warszawa, 1971).

_____. *Mysterium mortis. Der Mensch in der letzten Entscheidung*. Olten, 1968.

Demsek, J. M. *Sein. Mensch und Tod. Das Todesprobleme bein Martin Heidegger*. München, 1963.

Durandeaux, J. *Wieczność w życiu codziennym (Eternity in Everyday Life)*. Warszawa, 1968.

Gargan, G. *L'amour et la mort*. Paris, 1959.

Guardini, R. *Freiheit, Gnade, Schicksal*. München, (1948) 1956. *(Wolność, łaska, los*. Krakow, 1969).

Hounder, Q. *Das Unsterblichkeitsproblem in der abendländischen Philosophie*. Stuttgart, 1970.

Huant, E. *Finalité temporalité . . . Une nouvelle analyse scientifique du problème de la survie*. Paris, 1975.

Jankélevitch, V. *La mort*. Paris, 1966.

Krąpiec, M. A. "Człowiek w perspektywie śmierći. *"O Bogu i człowieku* (Man in the Perspective of Death. *On God and Man)*. T. I. Warszawa, 1968, 124–48.

Lamont, C. *The Illusion of Immortality*. London, 1959.

Lamouche, A. *La destinée humaine*. Paris, 1959.

Landsberg, P. L. *O sprawach ostatecznych (On Ultimate Matters)* Warszawa, 1967.

Laporta, J. *La destinée de la nature humaine selon Thomas d'Aquin*. Paris, 1965.

Lavelle, L. *Le Moi et son destin*. Paris, 1936.

Marcel, G. *Présence et immortalité*. Paris, 1959.

Maritain, J. "Między czasem a wiecznośćią (Between Time and Eternity). *Więz*, 5 (1958) 8–10.

Martelet, G. *Victoire sur la mort. Eléments d'anthropologie Chrétienne*. Lyon, 1962.

Mayer, C. L. *L'homme face à son destin*. Paris, 1968.

Morin, E. *L'homme et la mort*. Paris, 1970.

Pieper, J. *Tod und Unsterblichkeit*. München, 1968. *(Smierć i nieśmiertelność*. Paris, 1970).

Rahner, K. *Zur Theologie des Todes*. Freiburg, 1938.

Scherer, G. *Das Problem des Todes in der Philosophie*. Darmstadt, 1979.

Sciacca, M. F. *Morte e immortalità*. Milano, 1968.

Sens choroby. Sens zycia. Sens śmierći. (The Meaning of Sickness. The Meaning of Life. The Meaning of Death). Kraków, 1980.

Sublon, R. *Le temps de la mort. Savoir, parole, désir*. Paris, 1980.

Thomas, L. V. *Anthropologie de la mort*. Paris, 1980.

Vanhengel, M. C. "Immortality, Experience and Symbol." *The Harvard Theological Review*, 60 (1967) 235–79.

Ziegler, J. *Les vivants et la mort*. Paris, 1975.

Zwolski, E. "U progu greckiej myśli eschatologicznej" (On the Threshold of Greek Eschatological Thought). *Zeszyty Naukowe KUL*, 11 (1968) z. 1, 44–57.

GENERAL BIBLIOGRAPHY

Ademar, G. *Zur medizinischen Psychologie und philosophischen Anthropologie.* Darmstadt, 1968.

Antonini, F. *Antropologia e filosofia.* Roma, 1966.

Atti del XII Congresso Internazionale di Filosofia (Venezia, 12–18 settembre 1958). Vol. II *L'uomo e la natura.* Firenze, 1960.

Brüning, W. *Philosophische Anthropologie.* Stuttgart, 1960.

Cantoni, R. *Scienze umane e antropologia filosofica.* Milano, 1966.

Caturelli, A. "Filosofia, metafisica, antropologia." *Eidos,* 2 (1970) 7–15.

Chabal, R. *Vers une anthropologie philosophique.* Paris, 1964.

Coreth, E. "Was ist philosophische Anthropologie?" *Zeitschrift für katolische Theologie,* 91 (1969) 252–73.

Cruz, J. "Sobre el metodo de antropologia filosofica." *Anuario Filosofico,* 1 (1969) 29–111.

Demolder, H. "Orientations de l'anthropologie nouvelle." *Revue des Sciences Religieuses,* 43 (1969) 147–73.

Diem, H. *Was ist der Mensch?* Tübingen, 1964.

Donceel, J. F. *Philosophical Anthropology.* New York, 1967.

Dufrenne, M. *Pour l'homme.* Paris, 1968.

Duroux, P. E. *La conception anthropologique.* Lyon, 1964.

Emonet, P. *Philosophie de l'homme.* Paris, 1967.

Ferrater, J. M. *The Idea of Man.* Kansas, 1961.

Giannini, G. "Rileri su alcuni aspetti dell'antropologia filosofica nella linea aristotelico-tomista." *Lateranum,* 29 (1963) 89–110.

Groethuysen, B. *Philosophische Anthropologie.* München, 1928.

Haecker, T. *Was ist der Mensch?* Frankfurt/M, 1959.

Hengstenberg, H. E. *Philosophische Anthropologie.* Stuttgart (1957) 1966.

Heschel, A. J. *Who Is Man?* London, 1966.

Ingarden, R. *Książeczka o człowieku (A Short Work on Man).* Kraków, 1972.

Jolif, J. Y. *Comprendre l'homme.* T. I. *Introduction à une anthropologie philosophique.* Paris, 1967.

Kamiński, S. "Antropologia filozoficzna a inne działy poznania." *O Bogu i człowieku* (Philosophical Anthropology and Other Divisions of Cognition. *On God and Man).* T. I. Warszawa, 1968, 149–64.

———. "O koncepcjach filozofii człowieka." (On the Conceptions of the Philosophy of Man). *Zeszyty Naukowe KUL,* 13 (1970) z.4, 9–17.

Keller, W. "Ueber philosophische Anthropologie." *Studia Philosophica,* 20 (1960) 37–57.

Kelly, W. J. Tallon, A. *Readings in the Philosophy of Man.* New York, 1967.

Knowledge and the Future of Man. An International Symposium. New York, 1968.

Krąpiec, M. A. "Idee przewodnie we współczesnej filozofii człowieka" (Principal Ideas in the Contemporary Philosophy of Man). *Zeszyty Naukowe KUL,* 13 (1970) z. 4, 21–33.

Landmann, M. *De Homine.* München, 1962.

————. *Philosophische Anthropologie.* Berlin (1955) 1969.

Landsberg, P. L. *Einführung in die philosophische Anthropologie.* Frankfurt/M (1934) 1960.

Le Trocquer, R. *Homme, qui suis-je?* Paris, 1957. *(Kim jestem ja—człowiek?* Paris, 1968).

Manners, R. A., Kaplan, D. ed. *Theory in Anthropology.* London, 1968.

Menschliche Existenz und moderne Welt. Bd. II. Ein internat. Symposion z. Selbstverständnis d. huetiger Menschen. Berlin, 1967.

Molear, G. F., ed. *Philosophy and Contemporary Man.* Washington, 1968.

Möller, J. *Zum Thema Menschsein.* Mainz, 1967. *(Człowiek w świecie.* Paris, 1969).

Pannenberg, W. *Was ist der Mensch?* Göttingen, 1962.

Peursen, C. A. van Lichaam—Ziel—Geest. Utrecht, 1956. *(Antropologia filozoficzna.* Warszawa, 1971).

Plessner, H. *Die Aufgabe der philosophischen Anthropologie.* Bern, 1953.

Readings in the Philosophy of Man. New York, 1967.

Ricoeur, P. "L'antinomie de la réalité humaine et le problème de l'anthropologie philosophique." *Pensiero,* 5 (1960) 273–90.

Ristrutturazione antropologica dell'insegnamento filosofico. Atti del II Convegno Nazionale dei Docenti nelle Facoltà, Seminari e Studentati d'Italia. Napoli, 1969.

Schoeps, H. J. *Was ist der Mensch?* Göttingen, 1960.

Tempo ed eternita nella condizione umana. Atti del XX Convegno del Centro di Studi Filosofici Universitari. Gallarte 1965. Brescia, 1966.

Was ist das, der Mensch? München, 1968.

Zimmerli, W. *Was ist der Mensch?* Göttingen, 1964.

INDEX

Abbreviations, xxi
Abélès, M., 223
Abelson, R., 228
Abernathy, G., 242
ABSOLUTE, 107, 126, 138, 180ff;
as source of all contingent and
analogical beings, 115; as most
intelligible, *ibid*; as cause of
derived beings, 153; as ultimate
object who actualizes man's
potentialities to the fullest, 165;
Absolute Goodness as ultimate
goal of human will and bringing
about complete actualization,
164; Absolute Spirit (Hegel), 35.
Cf. GOD.
Abstract ideas: ideas of
immaterial things as proving
immateriality of the ego, 56; as
having nothing temporal-spatial
or quantifiably measurable in
their structure, *ibid*. Cf. PLATO
ABSTRACTION, as absolutely
necessary to draw cognitive
content from sense impressions,
71-72; spirit of abst. as
substituting definition for the
defined, 64; Platonism as
example of above, *ibid*. Cf.
ARISTOTLE, ST. THOMAS,
COGNITION, KNOWLEDGE.
ACT AND POTENCY, 51-52; as
the only concept for expressing
ontical state of human being; act
as form and potency as matter,
50-52.

Adamczyk, S., 228, 232
Addis, L., 240
Ademar, G., 249
Adler, 29; as denying Freud's
foundations for neuroses, 32; as
holding that a threatening feeling
of uncertainty and inferiority is
starting point of neurosis, *ibid*.
Aesthetic experience, 145
Aesthetics, 79-80
Affective life, as comprising eleven
fundamental acts, 97ff.
AGENT INTELLECT, 71-74;
intellectual power enabling man
to grasp universal and necessary
contents given in sensible
representations, 72; as itself
uncovering immaterial structures
in matter, *ibid*.; as constituting
intellectually cognitive forms in
sensibly cognitional data, 72-73;
as a power making knowing
possible; a power actually
constituting object of intellectual
knowledge, *ibid*.; function of ag.
int. as production of intellectually
knowing forms which can
become objects of intellectual
knowledge, *ibid*.; St. Thomas as
advancing moderate position
concerning agent and possible
intellect, 74
Alexandrian School, 7
Alienation of man (Marx), 28-29
Alpheus, K., 226
Alquié, F., 247

251

for *Libido* and *Thanatos*); Ego: representing reason and health; Superego: source of moral conscience, *ibid.*
CRITIQUE: mistaking cultural phenomena for biological-instinctual phenomena; placing all emphasis on erotization of a situation when case may have been purely developmental, 31; F's psychoanalytical model of man wrong, since denies the one, subsistent, substantially-personal subject of activity, who is man; man considered as only something secondary, arisen from the dialectical (and sometimes mechanical), 31-32; man a mere combination of forces, called instinct, and his consciousness only something historical, *ibid.*; F's explanation of consciousness as contrary to acknowledged ontic unity of man, *ibid.*; F's use of consciousness in reality, the old Hegelian concept of dialectical evolution, 32; man merely a "moment" or "reflection" of the whole (cf. Hegel), *ibid.*; F's denial of subjective-ontic personality as making his model unacceptable for universal understanding of man, *ibid.*
Frey-Rohn, L., 223
Frings, M., 244
Fritzhand, M., 223
FROMM, E., 223, 228; that God does not have to be an object of reference and adoration, 205;

religion and psychological situation, *ibid.*; neuroses arising from needs that society has created in man, 33
Functionalization of man (Marcel), man presented exclusively as an agglomeration of functions, 122

Gangauf, T., 219
Garaudy, R., 223
Garcia Fernandez, A., 228
Gargan, G., 247
Gebsattel, V., 244
Gehlen, A., 221, 240
Geneslay, E., 234
Gewirth, A., 238
Giacon, C., 219
Gibbs, B., 236
Gillet, M., 238
Gilson, E., 52, 61, 64, 194, 203, 240
Giannini, G., 219, 249
Gioberti, 66
Girardi, G., 244
Glossary of terms, 212
Glover, J., 232
GOD: existence of, 66; Absolute and highest Being 59; Absolute Person, 59, 164; the only self-intelligible being, possessing his own reason for his existence (Thomas), 82; first and final cause of all existence and being, 116; creating freely and according to a plan or idea, 153; source of world's existence; planner of world and as loving the world, 154; not able to create a contradiction, since only being can be object of his activity, 55;

philosophy of nature and
philosophy of spirit, *ibid.*;
ultimate triad: art (thesis),
religion (antithesis), philosophy
(synthesis), *ibid.*
CRITIQUE: community not a
dialectical unfolding of Absolute,
of which persons are only
fleeting moments; man's be-ing
not from society but vice versa;
a social structure subordinating
man as fundamentally wrong and
evil, 134; H's community a
servile one which deforms
personhood of its members,
ibid.; persons viewed as only
means to the end of preserving
power of society, *ibid.*; H's
anthropology only an application
of dialectic to psychology; the
"self" only a spirit passing
through dialectical differentiation
which is very heart of totality;
since a pantheism, denies the
reality of a subsistent subject of
existence, 36
HEIDEGGER, M., 36-38, 122,
148, 226, 234: influenced by
Nietzsche and Dilthey, 37; task
of metaphysics: attainment of
Being *(Sein)* by
phenomenological analysis of
beings *(Seiende)*; Being of beings
and *Dasein*, *ibid.*; "time aspect"
of man's existence *ibid.*; man as
discovering world not by
cognition but by use; *Sorge*
(care): concern for one's *Dasein*
resulting in *Angst* (dread); man's
homelessness begetting dread,
which is result of man's

thrownness into the world, *ibid.*;
93; "being-toward-death," *ibid.*,
166; thrownness of man
disclosing nothingness; death:
passage from being to
nothingness; man's death linked
with temporality of human
existence, 37-38
CRITIQUE: "existentials" like
thrownness as characterizing
human being better than
Aristotelian categories, 37, 208;
man, as a concrete conscious
being, who is in the world and in
history, *ibid.*; man preoccupied
with meaning of his being, *ibid.*
Heimler, M., 234
Helbling, H., 234
Hengstenberg, H., 229, 249
Henological concept of being, 27-28
Henry, M., 229
Heraclitus, 3, 89
Heschel, A., 249
Hesnard, A., 223
Hessen, G., 234
Hessen, J., 242
Hic et nunc (here and now), 113
Hick, J., 242
Hierarchy of being, (Thomas):
    entire universe constituting a
    hierarchy of lower and higher
    forms, 52
Hindu yoga, 143
Hirschberger, J., 229
Hirschmann, E., 229
Hoffman, P., 232
Hofmeister, H., 242
Homans, P., 223
Homer, 2
Hook, S., 224

referring to a psychic as a
"medium," 43
PSYCHOLOGY: contemporary, 19;
depth, 23; experimental 69;
psych. approach differing from
psychology of consciousness in
six ways, 30
PSYCHOANALYTICAL
interpretation of man: already
presupposing theoretical interp.
of man, understood as neurotic
"I," 30; its danger in conceiving
man as a set of relations of
certain powers or drives (chiefly
biological), 31. cf. FREUD
Ptaszynski, S., xix
Pucci, R., 230
Pyramid of value, 42
Pythagoras, 3

Quilliot, R., 237

Rabat, O., 189
Rahner, K., moment of death as
that of fullest actualization of
man, 185, 233
Ramirez, N., 227
Reardon, B., 243
REASON, a power different from
senses and imagination;
arguments for its existence, 71;
cf. INTELLECT
"REASONABLENESS," man's
ability of "going outside himself"
in order to attain essential
structures of things, 158
Rectitudo voluntatis ("right
desire"), 111; rectitude of will
and synderesis, as attitude of

person toward an actual, suitable
good revealed by the intellect,
111ff.
Referendum (Rousseau), 132
Re-Harachte, 141
Reitmeister, L., 237
RELIGION, 137-55; def. of:
reference to a superhuman reality,
140; cultural happening
(objective sense) which includes
human knowledge and activity
directed to a Transcendence,
145; an intersubjective relation
(I-Thou), 147; containing a set
of truths, 145-46
RELIGIOUS ACT, every kind of
conscious and free actualization
bringing man, a potential being,
closer to Personal God, 153; as
completely disposed to man's
fullest actualization, 150;
involving volitional-emotional
moments (love), 144; aimed at
"spiritualizing" man, 150
RELIGIOUS DOCTRINE, dealing
with living practical truth,
looking to revelation as its
source, 146
RELIGIOUS EXPERIENCE:
contact with a religious reality,
the "taking-over" by the activity
of subject and actualization of a
conscious bond with God, 141
RELIGIOUS FACT: man's reference
and direction to transcendent
reality, 140; interpersonal union
between man and person of
Absolute, 154; linked with man's
awareness of his contingency,
148

ALSO AVAILABLE

Andrew N. Woznicki, A CHRISTIAN HUMANISM: KAROL WOJTYLA'S EXIS-
TENTIAL PERSONALISM
"There is no more useful introduction to the meaning and profundity of Pope John
Paul II's thought."—James V. Schall, S. J., Georgetown University.
. . . . . $2.95
Francis J. Lescoe, PHILOSOPHY SERVING CONTEMPORARY NEEDS OF THE
CHURCH: THE EXPERIENCE OF POLAND
. . . . . $1.50
Patricia J. Brewer, RAW JUDICIAL POWER: A CASE HISTORY
. . . . . $1.95
Francis J. Lescoe, David Q. Liptak, eds. POPE JOHN PAUL II LECTURE SERIES
IN BIOETHICS
Vol. I PERSPECTIVES IN BIOETHICS
I. Critical Reflections on Current Bioethical Thinking by Ronald D. Lawler
II. *"Begotten Not Made": Reflections on Laboratory Production of Human Life* by
William E. May
. . . . . $3.75
Francis J. Lescoe, SANCTI THOMAE AQUINATIS TRACTATUS DE SUBSTAN-
TIIS SEPARATIS
"Unquestionably the best critical text available."—AUGUSTINIANUM (Rome)
. . . . . $8.95
Francis J. Lescoe, ST. THOMAS AQUINAS, TREATISE ON SEPARATE SUB-
STANCES
"The author has performed a valuable service for serious students of St.
Thomas."—PHILOSOPHICAL STUDIES (Maynooth)
. . . . . $9.95
Francis, J. Lescoe, GOD AS FIRST PRINCIPLE IN ULRICH OF STRASBOURG
"An excellent work, indispensable for every philosophical library."—REVUE
PHILOSOPHIQUE (Louvain)
. . . . . $11.95
Cardinal Paul-Emile Léger, SECOND CAREER VOCATIONS
. . . . . $1.50

M.A. Krąpiec, I-MAN: AN OUTLINE OF PHILOSOPHICAL ANTHROPOLOGY.
"A gem of philosophical literature."—R. Dennehy, *Pastoral and Homiletic Review.*
. . . . . $14.95

Francis J. Lescoe, EXISTENTIALISM: WITH OR WITHOUT GOD: Kierkegaard,
Marcel, Buber, Heidegger, Sartre, Camus. Pp. 475 FOURTH PRINTING
. . . . . $8.95

MARIEL PUBLICATIONS 196 Eddy Glover Boulevard New Britain, CT 06053